THE
JEWISH HERITAGE
COOKBOOK

THE
JEWISH HERITAGE
COOKBOOK

Marlena Spieler

HH
HERMES
HOUSE

This edition is published by Hermes House, an imprint of Anness Publishing Ltd,
Blaby Road, Wigston, Leicestershire LE18 4SE; info@anness.com

www.hermeshouse.com; www.annesspublishing.com

If you like the images in this book and would like to investigate using them for publishing, promotions
or advertising, please visit our website www.practicalpictures.com for more information.

Publisher: Joanna Lorenz
Managing Editor: Linda Fraser
Editor: Susannah Blake
Copy-editors: Jennie Fleetwood and Susanna Tee
Editorial Reader: Richard McGinlay
Photographer: William Lingwood
Home Economist: Justine Kiggin (reference) and Sunil Vijayakar (recipes)
Assistant Home Economists: Joss Herd, Kate Lewis and Christine Rodrigues
Stylist: Helen Trent
Designer: Nigel Partridge
Jacket Designer: Chloë Steers
Production Controller: Wanda Burrows

© Anness Publishing Ltd 2012

PUBLISHER'S NOTE
Although the advice and information in this book are believed to be accurate and true at the time of
going to press, neither the authors nor the publisher can accept any legal responsibility or liability for
any errors or omissions that may have been made nor for any inaccuracies nor for any loss, harm or
injury that comes about from following instructions or advice in this book.

NOTES
Bracketed terms are intended for American readers.
For all recipes, quantities are given in both metric and imperial measures and, where appropriate, in standard
cups and spoons. Follow one set of measures, but not a mixture, because they are not interchangeable.
Standard spoon and cup measures are level. 1 tsp = 5ml, 1 tbsp = 15ml, 1 cup = 250ml/8fl oz.
Australian standard tablespoons are 20ml. Australian readers should use 3 tsp
in place of 1 tbsp for measuring small quantities.
American pints are 16fl oz/2 cups. American readers should use 20fl oz/
2.5 cups in place of 1 pint when measuring liquids.
Electric oven temperatures in this book are for conventional ovens. When using a fan oven, the temperature
will probably need to be reduced by about 10–20°C/20–40°F. Since ovens vary, you should check with
your manufacturer's instruction book for guidance.
Medium (US large) eggs are used unless otherwise stated.

CONTENTS

There is no festive celebration without eating and drinking

THE TALMUD

Jewish food. The phrase conjures up images of borscht, chicken soup with matzo balls, salt beef and chopped liver. These certainly are Jewish foods, relished by generations of Eastern European Jews, but the Jewish cuisine is much, much more varied than that.

I grew up in California. The foods we ate were those of West Coast America – artichokes and oranges and avocados – but our culinary souls were also nourished by the foods of the Old Country of our grandparents' era: kasha, gedempte flaiche and knaidlach, matzo brei and kishke from Ashkenazi Russia, Poland, the Ukraine and Lithuania, all served with a delicious overlay of Old New York.

Jewish food is a combination of richly varied cuisines from all over the globe, reflecting the multi-ethnicity of the Jewish people, and the many places where they have settled. For years I thought the little savoury pastries called empanadas were typically Jewish, because that's what my cousin used to make when we visited her. It was only years later that I discovered they were native to Uruguay, where she was raised. One of my friends, whose family fled Germany to South America because of World War II, and who grew up eating her grandmother's food, told me she thought that Jewish food was *mole*, that typically Mexican dish. And so it is, at least for Mexican Jews.

In the past, the Ashkenazim and Sephardim were often far removed from each other; the spicy food of the Sephardim was seldom served on traditional Ashkenazi tables and vice versa. The establishment of the State of Israel, migration and modern travel have changed this considerably, and brought Jews together again, starting at the table where they can share their own flavours and dishes.

Regardless of where history has taken them, the food Jews eat is governed by the laws of Kashrut – the code of fitness that applies to what may be eaten, how food must be prepared and which foods can be combined with other foods. There are variations in how different ethnic groups adhere to Kashrut, and degrees of observance, but the basics are the same. Certain types of meat, fish and fowl are allowed, while others are forbidden. Rules govern the slaughter and inspection of animals, as well as which parts may be used, and there is an injunction against combining meat foods with dairy foods. This set of rules has kept the Jewish people culturally distinct, as well as giving an underlying flavour to their food.

The preparation, eating and rituals involved with Kashrut have always played an important part in the lives of the Jewish people. In the Torah, the Patriarch Abraham is noted for the hospitable table he sets. It is recorded that Isaac asked his son for a nice dish of savoury meat, and also that Esau sold his birthright for a big, soupy lentil stew. In Chapter 11 of the book of Numbers, the story is told of how the Israelites fleeing Egypt wept with longing for the garlic and leeks they had eaten during their captivity – even freedom lacked flavour without delicious seasonings.

The noted Andalucian-Egyptian philosopher and physician Moses Maimonides (Moses ben Maimon) emphasized the importance of serenity of spirit, both for cook and diner. He also stressed the value of eating healthy food, prepared appealingly. Sharing sociable meals, he suggested, not only made for a happier, less anxious individual; it also bridged the differences between ethnic groups.

When Jews gather together, we eat, and what we eat are often the traditional foods, because each food has its own story. The flavour of remembrance seasons all our meals as we recall where we have wandered and who we met along the way, the meals we shared and the ingredients that filled our pots along each mile, in every place.

Even in terrible times of deprivation and despair, we like to prepare special foods. I was very touched when a Holocaust survivor told me how she and her companions had once made pancakes using greens that grew wild on a tiny patch of earth. Under cover of darkness, they had picked the greens, patted them into little cakes and fried them in a drop or two of oil. "Ach", her eyes lit up, "they were so good."

For Jews, eating is a celebration of survival. A meal enjoyed with family, friends and community means "we are alive", and we are grateful. A basic tenet of the Jewish table is that good food is a gift from God. Jews take every opportunity of offering thanks and appreciation, with blessings for the food and also for the good health that allows them to enjoy it. However different, culturally, Jews might be, we are united by beliefs and laws, as well as an interwoven history – in the way we pray, speak, eat, drink and celebrate life; the laws of Kashrut that guide what we eat and how we prepare it; and the prayers that sanctify it all. Our food is more than just a cuisine represented by recipes; it is a part of the glue that holds us together.

In this book I would like to share with you my favourite recipes from various Jewish communities throughout the world, and from my own life and traditions as well. In the words of the Hebrew expression that translates as *bon appetit*, I wish you all *B'tay avon*. MARLENA SPIELER

HISTORY
AND TRADITION

*The food of the Jewish table is inextricably linked to the history of its
people. From the time of their first exile in 70CE (AD), Jews have adopted
the flavours of the lands they dwelt in. Each time they were forced to flee they
re-established their community in a new country, taking on the new foods found
there, always in keeping with the basic laws of the Kashrut. Even the religious
table is tightly bound up with history. Holidays commemorate the events of the
past and demand traditional and ritual foods — from the matzos of Pesach to
the fried dishes of Chanukkah and the sweet foods of Rosh Hashanah.*

THE JEWISH DIASPORA

Exile has been a common thread throughout the history of the Jewish people. It is this, linked with intrinsic religious and cultural considerations, that has been a major factor in developing a cuisine that is as diverse as it is delicious. As communities fled from one country to another, they took with them their culinary traditions but also adopted new ones along the way.

With the destruction by the Romans of the Second Temple in Jerusalem in 70CE (AD), the Jews were banished from their holy city. Since that date, they have travelled the world, establishing communities, many of which lasted for centuries, before being forced to flee once more.

Jews spread to nearly every corner of the globe and this dispersal or diaspora has helped to create the cultural and liturgical differences that exist within a single people. Following the dispersal, two important Jewish communities were established, which still define the two main Jewish groups that exist today: the Sephardim and the Ashkenazim who each have their own individual culture, cuisine and liturgy.

The first of these communites was in Iberia and was called Sepharad after a city in Asia Minor mentioned in Obadiah 20. The second was in the Rhine River Valley and was called Ashkenaz, after a kingdom on the upper Euphrates, which is referred to in Jeremiah 51:27.

Iberia, which was ruled by Muslims, was a relatively tolerant society. The Jews had a revered place in it, living undisturbed and in harmony with their Islamic neighbours for long periods of time. Jews also often held influential positions as doctors, scholars or advisers to the kings.

In contrast, the Christian lands of Europe were restrictive, feudal, and often hostile. The Ashkenazim tended to live apart in ghettos or shtetlach, away from the non-Jewish population with whom they had settled. They also spoke a different language from their neighbours and became very strict regarding their dietary laws as they were surrounded by people who ate pork, rabbit, shellfish and other non-kosher foods that were forbidden to Jews.

Over the centuries both communities blossomed in their new environments, but each developed very differently, creating their own cultures. Ashkenazi Jews developed different customs, laws,

Below: A painting by Francesco Hayez depicting the destruction of the Jewish Temple in Jerusalem by the Romans under Titus in 70CE (AD) (1867).

liturgy, Hebrew pronunciations and cooking styles from their Sephardi cousins, despite having the same roots in the Babylonian Talmud.

Yemenite Jews, known as Tienamim, are the third largest Jewish ethnic group today. Although, historically, they do not belong to the Sephardim, they are often grouped with them, possibly because of their Eastern culture and traditional spicy cuisine. Other ethnic groups that are not either Ashkenazi nor Sephardi include Jewish communities from Iran, Azarbaijan, Bukhara (Uzbekistan), Georgia (Russia), Kurdistan, India, Ethiopia and K'ai-feng (Canton).

THE SEPHARDIM

Jews who settled in Iberia spoke *Ladino*, a dialect of Castilian Spanish written in Hebrew script. In many respects, their lifestyle was not so very different from that of their Arab neighbours, who had a similar outlook of generous hospitality. The Arabs also prepared their food ritually: meat was ridded of blood and pork was forbidden.

Jews lived in Jewish Quarters, which were known as mellahs, generally by choice. This helped to strengthen their culture and community and allowed them to be near the centres of Jewish life such as the synagogue, kosher butcher and ritual baths.

As the Iberian Jews settled and moved, four main groups emerged. Judeo-Spanish Jews settled in the Ottoman lands of Turkey and Greece. Maghrebi or North African Jews settled in Morocco, Tunisia, Algeria and Libya. Arab Jews lived in Babylon and Persia and, for over ten centuries, Iraqi and Babylonian Jews were the leaders of world Jewry. Syria, Iraq, Lebanon and Iran all produced Jewish communities of greatness – centres of excellence for culture, learning and commerce.

The communities could have grown in different directions but the caravan trade allowed communication and mobility between the different groups. Matters of Rabbinical law, politics and business exchanged hands easily. Migration in search of new opportunities also became common.

This interaction between the different communities allowed a mingling and unification of flavours in the Sephardi cuisine. The food the Sephardi Jews ate, and the way they cooked it, was a blend of their own heritage and dietary laws, with distinct influences from the Iberian and Arabic culinary tradition. What emerged was a cuisine rich with the flavours of the region.

At its heart, Sephardi cooking still has the warm undertones of Spain: it is olive oil-based, rich with fish from the sea and the vegetables of a warm climate, fragrant with garlic, herbs and spices. When meat is used, it is usually lamb.

The Sephardim also introduced their own influences on the Iberian and Arab cuisines. Even today, if you enquire in

Above: An illumination from a Hebrew manuscript showing a synagogue in northern Spain (c.1350).

Andalucia in Spain as to what have been the major influences on their cuisine, the Jewish contribution will always be acknowledged alongside that of the Moors.

Sephardi cooking reflected Sephardi life: sensual and embued with life's pleasures. This attitude went further than just the food. It is reflected in the celebrations for life's happy occasions too. For instance, in Sephardi tradition, a wedding celebration lasted for two weeks, and a Brit Milah or Bar Mitzvah celebration lasted for a week. These traditions live still on today.

Morocco, Egypt and Romania, they acquired a love of new and often exotic flavourings, and when they moved on, whether by choice or because they were forced to do so, they took their recipes with them. For instance, when Iraqi Sephardi Jews migrated to India in the 19th century, they introduced Middle Eastern flavours to the Bene Israel and Cochinese Jews already there. They used spices in ways unknown before, and these methods were embraced enthusiastically by the Indian Jews.

Left: North African Sephardi Jews wear traditional prayer shawls in a synagogue on the island of Djerba off the coast of Tunisia (1952).

Below: A Jewish grocer in a Moroccan souk (market) sells the specialities of his community.

Into Exile Again

The Sephardim, who had flourished in Spain for centuries, now found the tide beginning to turn against them. Shortly before the end of the 14th century, antagonism erupted into violent riots and thousands of Jews were massacred.

Many of those who survived were forced, on pain of death, to convert. These Jews were known as conversos or – less politely – marranos, which means pork eater. They and their families often continued their religious practices in secret. At times such as these, food was a great comfort, not only because eating familiar, traditional dishes reminded conversos of their history, but also because, in their own kitchens, they could observe the rituals bound up with preparation and serving.

For a few decades these clandestine Jews flourished but they were a thorn in the flesh of the Spanish rulers and led to the Spanish Inquisition at the end of the 15th century. In 1492 all the remaining Jews in Spain were expelled. They scattered to North Africa, Europe, the Middle East and the New World.

With each migration, Sephardi Jews encountered new flavours, which they introduced into their own cooking. From countries such as Iraq, Turkey, Greece,

THE ASHKENAZIM

The Jews who fled to the Rhine Valley were, over the centuries, to spread across Europe. Ashkenazi Jewish communities of France, Italy and Germany, which were so numerous in the early Middle Ages, were pushed further and further eastwards due to persecutions from the time of the Crusades, which began early in the 11th century. Many Jews fled to Eastern Europe, especially Poland. They spoke Yiddish, which is a combination of Middle High German and Hebrew, written in Hebrew script.

Their non-Jewish neighbours ate abundant shellfish and pork, cooked with lard, and mixed milk with meat freely, none of which was permitted for Jews, so the only answer for them was to keep themselves apart. In Czarist Russia, they were only allowed to live in the Pale of Settlement, a portion of land that stretched from the Baltic Sea to the Black Sea. The Ashkenazi Jews lived – often uneasily – in shtetlach (villages) and never knew when they would be forced to flee again.

For the Jews who settled in Germany and Austria, the age of enlightenment was the Haskalah (18th–19th century), when the reform movement freed them from the more restrictive bonds of religious adherence and allowed them to enter the secular world of arts, philosophy, science and music. German Jews amassed great knowledge and created a culture of depth and finesse. They became so intertwined with the culture of Germany that when the Holocaust was upon them they could not fathom how it could have happened, because they considered themselves German first and foremost.

Ashkenazi food was the food of a cold climate. Vegetables were pickled in salt and fermented, for instance cabbage became sauerkraut, which was stored to last the winter. Cucumbers were transformed into pickles, piquant treats to enliven the bland fare of winter. Fermented beetroot (beets) became

Right: A group of Ashkenazi Jews sit outside their home in Jerusalem (1885).

russel, the basis for a traditional borscht. Fish – freshwater, rather than the sea fish enjoyed by the Sephardi Jews – were smoked and salted, as were meats. Because there was often insufficient kosher meat to go round, very small amounts would be bulked out with other ingredients and served as dumplings and pastries, or in casseroles and stews.

Grains and beans were eaten in abundance: healthy, hearty and filling, they were also pareve, so they could be mixed with either meat or milk. Often, but most usually for Shabbat or a festival, beans were cooked slowly with meats in a dish known as cholent, which could be eaten when the family returned home from the synagogue.

Horseradish was shredded into an eye-watering condiment, and fresh herbs and other aromatics such as spring onions (scallions), dill and parsley were delighted in.

Ashkenazi food was often cooked in chicken or goose fat, enriched with golden onions. It was sometimes flavoured with honey, or a mixture of honey and piquant vinegar, to make a tangy sweet and sour sauce.

When potatoes were introduced from the New World, the Ashkenazi Jews adored them and incorporated them into their cuisine with great enthusiasm. Latkes and kugels, soups and dumplings were all prepared from this new and filling vegetable.

JEWS IN BRITAIN

The history of the Jews in Britain is long and complex. They first arrived in 1066 and were expelled by Edward I in 1290, a hundred years after the massacre at Clifford Tower of York's entire Jewish community. In 1655, after negotiations had been held between Manashe ben Israel and Oliver Cromwell, Jews were allowed to return and live in England.

Sephardi Jews then came to settle in England. They came via Holland, bringing with them the flavours and specialities of their native Portugal, which included their favourite dish, battered or crumbed fried fish. This was very likely the origin of Britain's traditional fish and chips, as the fish was subsequently combined with fried potatoes and eaten by the hungry masses – mostly Jews, often young women who worked in sweat shops in London's East End.

Today, most of Britain's Jewish communities live in London, specifically north London, with smaller communities scattered around the rest of the country, including Brighton, Essex, Manchester, Liverpool, Glasgow and Edinburgh. Stamford Hill in north London is home to one of the largest communities of Chassidic Jews in the world. Most of the Jewish communities in Britain are Ashkenazi, though there are a few Sephardi groups.

INFLUENCING THE FRENCH CUISINE

The French cuisine shows a strong influence from the Jewish community that settled there. Foie gras, often considered to be typically French, originated in ancient Egypt and was undoubtedly introduced to France by Jewish immigrants – Ashkenazim in Alsace, and possibly by Sephardim in the south-west.

Some say the cassoulet of south-west France was originally cholent, the bean and meat stew baked slowly in a low oven and served still warm on Shabbat; and that the spices that are so well loved in eastern France – cumin, ginger and cinnamon – are testament to the Jewish community that flourished there. Chocolate, like aubergines (eggplant), came to France with the Sephardi Jews expelled from Spain.

Chassidic Jews

This group of very observant Jews, recognizable by their traditional Eastern European dress – black coats for the men, large hats of either black cloth or fur, and often scarves covering the women's hair – originated in Central Poland, Galicia and the Ukraine. The movement was founded by Israel ben Eliezer, also known as the Ba'al Shem Tov (master of the good name), in the 17th century.

A JEWISH HERITAGE IN ITALY

The Italian Jewish community (Italkim), which is now very small as a result of the Holocaust and post-World War II emigration, was once grand, influential and active. It is said that the true Roman is the Jewish Roman, for there has been a Jewish community in Rome for longer than any other. The Italian cuisine has been influenced very strongly by these long-established settlers. To this day, carciofi alla Giudia (artichokes in the Jewish manner) is a speciality of the ghetto of Rome, *ghetto* being a word that originated in Italy to describe an area set aside for Jews.

The little town of Pitigliano in Tuscany was once such an important centre of Jewish life, religious study and culture that it was known as Little Jerusalem. The Jewish community built the aqueduct, and the matzo ovens they used are still there. During World War II, the Jews of Pitigliano were saved by local people, who smuggled them out of the city and hid them in the countryside. Although there are no Jews there now, all of them having emigrated to either America or Israel, the citizens of Pitigliano rejoice in the fact that Jews from Israel often come to their town to be married in the synagogue there.

Left: Jews struggling to make a living in London's East End (1900s).

Opposite: A bakery selling matzos in the Jewish area in the 4th arrondissement of Paris (1923).

THE UNITED STATES AND THE DELI

In the early part of the 20th century there was a great wave of immigration to the United States, which influenced the American table a great deal. The most obvious influence was the emergence of the delicatessen – or deli as it is more commonly known. In places that were home to Jewish communities from Eastern Europe, such as Chicago and Old New York, delis were places where hungry men with no homes of their own could go for a good meal. These men had usually travelled ahead – often years ahead – of their wives and children to establish a new life. Lodging in rented rooms and working hard to save enough money to pay for their families to join them, they needed somewhere to eat that was kosher, and that gave them a taste of the land they left behind.

Other ethnic groups discovered delis and began to enjoy the hearty foods they served, which became the flavour of America: bagels, soups, pastrami and other robust meats, huge sandwiches, dill pickles, salads and juicy sausages.

MODERN TIMES

The 20th century saw the end of many of the great Jewish communities of the world – some as old as 2,500 years – and the start of others. Ashkenazim emigrating from Germany, Central Europe and Russia towards the end of the 19th century and the start of the 20th century often packed little by way of possessions, but they did take the traditions of the cuisine that we typically think of as Jewish: chicken soup and matzo balls, Viennese pastries, rye bread and bagels, delicate noodles and robust chopped liver. The same dishes – familiarly called the food of the Old Country – travelled to Great Britain, Israel, Latin America and the United States with the refugees before, during and after World War II.

Left: Jewish immigrants stand on Ellis Island, awaiting entry into New York.

Right: The Jewish deli is a wonderful legacy from the Ashkenazi Jews who settled in the United States.

The Holocaust destroyed much of European Jewish culture, and the Communist control of Eastern Europe and Russia swept away most of the remainder, although here and there communities continued to keep the faith, albeit in secret, allowing their traditions to survive.

In many places, communities have regrouped. In Los Angeles you will find the Jewish community of Iran, reborn after the Islamic revolution. This community had been in Persia since 600BCE (BC) and held tight to their customs and cuisine. In Brooklyn, a suburb of New York, there is a thriving Cochinese synagogue, where Indian Jews cook their spicy delicacies for feast celebrations. In Cochin itself there are barely a handful of Jews left. In the Israeli port of Jaffa, you can eat wonderfully spicy, zesty Libyan food

thanks to Libyan Jews who have relocated and settled there. In Beijing in China, a fledgling synagogue and Jewish community have recently emerged, consisting primarily of international workers and their families.

Traditionally, when Sephardi and Ashkenazi Jews settled in the same country, they tended to keep apart, maintaining their distinctive cultures, but that too has changed in recent times. When Askenazim from Eastern Europe and Germany emigrated to South America, they frequently found themselves living alongside Sephardi Jews from Spain. Conversely, Sephardim from North Africa moved to France after World War II and helped to breathe new life into the Ashkenazi communities destroyed by Hitler.

A NEW HOME IN ISRAEL

With the establishment of the State of Israel in 1948, hundreds of thousands of Jews who had been both isolated and stateless for generations made their way back. Each group brought with them the ways of cooking and the flavours of the countries in which they had been living.

At first, this diversity wasn't always appreciated. The halutzim (settlers) were eager to be integrated and to divorce themselves from a past that included what they saw as the foods of bondage. There was great pressure to abandon individual traditions and other cultures, to throw all into one melting pot labelled Israeli food.

Luckily, at last, all this is changing. Moroccan Jews in Israel are beginning to celebrate their traditional flavours, recognizing that they are delicious in their difference, and not something to be ashamed of. Yemeni restaurants are terribly chic, as are other ethnic eating

houses. The waves of recent Russian and Ethiopian immigrations (the last of Ethiopia's ancient tribe of Jews were flown to Israel in 1992) have added their own ingredients to a cuisine that includes flavours from almost every corner of the globe, set against a background of the Middle East and a belief that what grows easily tastes best.

In an almost complete circle, Ashkenazi food has found a certain cachet in Israel in recent years, with classic dishes such as cholent, chicken soup with matzo balls and pickled vegetables reaching almost cult status. However, in the marvellous fusion of foods that has arisen with the bringing together of the various different Jewish communities, Israeli Ashkenazim have been influenced by other cuisines. For example, classic chicken soup might come with a spoonful of hot and spicy zchug, the Yemenite sauce made of garlic and fiery chillies.

Above: Yemenite Jews look at their new homeland, Lydda in Israel (1950).

Below: Jewish refugees crowd on the top deck of the Haviva Reik *as they arrive in Palestine (1946).*

JEWS TODAY

It is at times of both celebration and commemoration that Jewish cooking really comes into its own, whether the occasion be the weekly sabbath meal, an annual festival such as Chanukkah or Pesach or one of the events that mark the cycle of Jewish life – such as Brit Milah (ritual circumcision), Bar or Bat Mitzvah (the coming of age), a wedding or a funeral.

Many Jewish families celebrate the traditional religious holidays, but do not necessarily keep kosher or are Shomer Shabbat (those who strictly observe the sabbath). Thus all over the world, but especially in the USA, where Reform (Progressive) Judaism has become mainstream, there are many different ways of being Jewish other than being strictly Observant.

In the modern world, many Jews are beginning to adapt their traditions, and they are also making changes in terms of their cuisine. For example, Ashkenazi Jews often use olive oil for cooking, as in the ancient Sephardi tradition. The dishes of the Middle East are also enjoying a resurgence of popularity, and convenience foods are used when time is short.

The laws of Kashrut continue to be a focus of daily life for Observant Jews. In recent years, in addition to traditional Jewish homes, there has been a strong emergence of modern Orthodox Jews,

Above: Yemenite Jews in Jerusalem enjoy a traditional Pesach Seder meal. (Photograph by David Harris.)

those who are returning to a strict adherence to Kashrut, especially in the USA and Israel.

Whether the traditional Jewish table is Sephardi, Ashkenazi, Conservative, Reform (Progressive), Orthodox or Chassidic is not what matters most. The most important factor is that the food it holds reflects both a people's lives and its culture. It is food for enjoying and for bringing families closer together, for giving reassurance in an ever-changing world and for sharing with old and new friends alike.

HOLIDAYS, FESTIVALS AND OBSERVANCES

The Jewish calendar is punctuated by holidays, festivals and observances, which are shared by the entire community. Personal milestones in the lives of individuals such as Bar or Bat Mitzvahs, weddings and celebrations attending the birth of a baby are also celebrated. Each festival has a special significance, and is accompanied by its own songs, stories, admonitions, activities, prayers and, of course, foods.

The Jewish year follows the 354–5 day lunar calendar, as opposed to the 365–6 day solar year, so while each Jewish festival falls on precisely the same date in each year of the Jewish calendar, the dates will differ on a Gregorian calendar. For synchronicity, and also to keep the months in their appropriate season, a thirteenth month is added to the Jewish calendar every two or three years. In the northern hemisphere, therefore, Rosh Hashanah will always be celebrated between summer and autumn, while Chanukkah always heralds winter and Pesach

ushers in the spring, regardless of how different the actual dates will be on Christian calendars.

Jewish holidays always begin at sundown on the day before. The year of celebrations starts around September, with Rosh Hashanah, the Jewish New Year, and progresses through Yom Kippur, the Day of Atonement, which is marked nine days later. Sukkot, the harvest festival of thanksgiving, follows, ending with Simchat Torah, the festival of the Torah. Around December comes Chanukkah, the festival of lights, when gifts are traditionally exchanged. Tu b'Shevat, the Holiday of the Trees, comes next, around February, and this in turn is followed by Purim, a flamboyant festival that involves dressing up in colourful costumes, and that could be considered a kind of Jewish Mardi Gras or carnival.

Pesach commemorates Israel's deliverance from Egypt. During this eight-day festival, Jews consume particular foods and drinks, eschewing

those that contain leaven. Shavuot celebrates the Giving of the Torah, while Tish b'Av is a day of fasting, when the Destruction of the Temple is mourned.

Many communities also observe Yom Hatsmaut, Israeli Independence Day, which is celebrated on 14 May with festivities, including outdoor gatherings where falafel is traditionally eaten. Yom Ha Shoah, the Holocaust Remembrance Day, is observed shortly after Pesach, honouring the millions who died.

The most important festival and observance of them all is the Sabbath or Shabbat. This is celebrated every week, and forms a model for all the other holidays. It is a day for refraining from work, escaping the chaos of the ordinary working week, focusing on the spiritual, appreciating nature and enjoying family life.

Below: This Mizrah scroll, hung on the west wall of the house to indicate the direction of Jerusalem, illustrates the major Jewish festivals.

SHABBAT

This is the sabbath, the day of rest. It is said to be the most important Jewish holiday, and it comes not once a year, but once a week. It is the weekly oasis of peace in the sea of hectic life. Even those who are not Observant in other ways will often enjoy keeping Shabbat. The word *shabbat* means cessation of labour and it is a treasured time to relax with the family, perhaps taking walks through the countryside or visiting friends for lunch.

The origins of Shabbat are related in Genesis, the first book of the Bible, which describes how God created the world in six days and rested on the seventh. In the fourth commandment of the Ten Commandments, it is decreed that Shabbat is a day of rest that must be kept holy (Exodus 31:17).

A set of rules has been laid down, encompassing what it means to keep Shabbat. Observant Jews do not do any work, handle money, carry loads, light fires, tear paper, watch television or listen to the radio. They also may not cook, which has led to ingenious ways of providing warm, freshly cooked food without infringing the rule.

Below: An illumination depicting God's creation of the world (c.1530).

Above: Shabbat begins with the blessings being said over a loaf of challah and a cup of wine.

The Festive Meal

On the eve of Shabbat a festive meal is served. It begins with the lighting and blessing of the candles before sundown. Further blessings are then said over the challah, and the Kiddush (sanctifying blessing) is said over the wine.

The lighting of the candles marks the dividing line between the rest of the week and the start of Shabbat. When the candles are lit, traditionally by the woman of the household, she passes her hands lightly over the flame in a movement that seems to gather up the light, then she covers her eyes.

The greeting on Shabbat is "Shabbat Shalom", often accompanied with a kiss – or two – on the cheek, as participants wish each other a Shabbat filled with peace.

Different families have different customs regarding the blessing of the challah. It is traditional in a number of households for everyone to gather around the table, with their hands on the challah during the blessings, after which they pull it apart, making sure that each person has at least a tiny bite of the blessed bread.

A welcoming song might be sung, for example Sholem Aleichem, and/or Shabbat Shalom, a light and evocative melody that welcomes the holiday and puts everyone in a mellow mood.

The meal on Friday night usually includes chicken soup, and a chicken or braised meat. Guests will often be invited, and the table set with white linen, flowers and the finest china and cutlery. Meanwhile, the next day's meal will be simmered slowly in a low oven, as no cooking is allowed on the Sabbath itself. This is usually a dish of beans and meat taken from the Sephardi or Ashkenazi tradition.

Morning Services

Services are held on Saturday mornings in the synagogue; this is a popular time for Bar and Bat Mitzvahs. If one of these is taking place, a light celebration meal will be served at the synagogue for the whole congregation. This includes herring, salads, cookies and perhaps cakes, in addition to the Kiddush wine, challah, coffee and tea.

The main meal is served at midday or in the early afternoon as the family observes Shabbat. The steamy warm

Below: Polish Jews celebrate Shabbat in a traditional synagogue (1956).

SHABBAT BLESSINGS

Candle Lighting

As soon as the candles are lit, signifying the start of Shabbat, this blessing is recited:

Baruch Ata Adonai Elohaynu Melech Haolam, asher kedashanu b'mitzvotav, v'tzivanu l'hadleek neer shel Shabbat.

Blessed are You, Lord our God, Eternal One, who enables us to welcome Shabbat by kindling these lights.

If there are children present, then a blessing is said over them. The head of the household places his or her hands on the children and asks that they strive to carry on the traditions of the Jewish people, the boys like Ephraim and Menasshe, the girls like Sarah and Rebeccah, Rachel and Leah.

A plea is always offered for God's blessing, safety, warmth and protection, and peace.

Friday Night Kiddush

The blessing that follows is said over the goblet of Kiddush wine.

Baruch Ata Adonai Elohaynu Melech Haolam, boray p'ree hagafen.

Blessed are You, Lord God, Eternal One, who creates the fruit of the vine.

Baruch Ata Adonai Elohaynu Melech Haolam, asher kedashanu b'meetzvatov, v'rahzah banu, v'Shabbat Kodsho b'ahavah oov'rahzon heen'heelanu, zeekahron l'maasay b'raysheet. Kee hoo yom t'heela l'meekrah-ay kodesh, zaycher l'tzeeat meetzraheem. Kee vanu vacharta ohtanu keedashta meekol ha'ahmeem v'Shabbat kodshecha b'ahavah oov'ratzon heenaltanu. Baruch Ata Adonai M'kadest HaShabbat. Amen.

Blessed are You, Lord God, Eternal One, Who sanctifies us with holy acts and gives us special times and seasons to rejoice. Shabbat reminds us of the times for celebration, recalls the days of Creation of the world and how God rested from that work. Shabbat reminds us of the Exodus from Egyptian slavery. God has distinguished us from all people and given us the Shabbat full of joy. Blessed are You, Lord God, Eternal One, who sanctifies the Shabbat.

Saturday Midday Kiddush

This blessing is said over the wine to begin the Shabbat meal.

Al ken bayrah Adonai et Yom Hashabbat v'kodsho. Baruch Ata Adonai Elohaynu Melech Haolam, boray p'ree hagafen.

Behold the Eternal blessed the seventh day and called it a holy time. Blessed are You, Lord God, Eternal One, who created fruit from the vine.

Blessing over the Challah

This blessing is said over bread: challah, rye bread, matzo etc.

Baruch Ata Adonai Elohaynu Melech Haolam, hamotzi lechem meen ha'aretz.

Blessed are You, Lord God, Eternal One, who creates bread from the earth.

The Birkat Hamazon is the grace said after the meal. It is only said after meals in which bread or matzo has been eaten.

cholent or other fragrant dish that has been keeping warm in the oven will be taken to the table, where the whole family will share it.

Both Friday night's and Saturday's meal, and indeed any meal that includes a loaf challah, should end with the saying of grace over finishing the meal, the Birkat Hamazon, or the blessing of thanksgiving.

Shabbat is over when the first three stars are visible in the night sky. At this time Havdalah will be observed. The Havdalah ceremony comes from the word *hevdal*, which means different, to signify the difference or separation between Shabbat and the other days of the week.

The ceremony consists of the blessing over the wine (the Kiddush), inhaling the fragrance of sweet spices and lighting a braided candle, which is then extinguished by a few drops of wine – and so, the new week begins.

Below: A braided candle and spice box used for the Havdalah ceremony.

ROSH HASHANAH

The Jewish year begins in September or October with Rosh Hashanah, which means the head of the year. This is the start of the Ten Days of Penitence, also called the Days of Awe, which end with Yom Kippur. Jews are encouraged to spend these days in retrospection,

Left: The New Year is ushered in with the saying of prayers.

considering their behaviour and how to make amends, improving their own lives and the lives of those around them.

The holidays of Rosh Hashanah and Yom Kippur are often referred to as the High Holy Days, and many Jews consider them so important that even if they observe no other festivals in the year, at this time they will go to synagogue, partake of a festive meal, and recite the prayers and blessings.

The Ram's Horn

A ceremonial shofar (ram's horn) is blown on Rosh Hashanah, as it is on Yom Kippur. The haunting sounds of the shofar reminds Jews of their long history and of the ancient convenant between the people of Israel and God.

One tradition (tashlicht) calls for penitents to throw all their sins of the previous year into a body of running water. The gesture symbolizes a fresh start for the new year.

Above: The ceremonial shofar (ram's horn) is blown at Rosh Hashanah to welcome in the New Year.

Rosh Hashanah begins, as usual, at sundown on the evening before. Candles are lit, the bread is blessed, and the Kiddush is recited over the wine. A festive meal is prepared. This includes sweet foods such as apples dipped in honey, bringing the promise of sweetness in the year ahead. The challah, which is shaped into a round, rather than the more familiar oval plait, is studded with raisins or small sweets (candies). Honey replaces salt for the blessing of the challah.

Different Customs

Various ethnic groups have different customs for the holiday. Sephardim eat a whole fish with the head left intact, representing their hopes for a year rich with wisdom, with Israel as the head of the nations rather than the tail – the leader rather than the oppressed.

No sour or bitter foods are eaten at Rosh Hashanah – some communities will not even eat pickles or olives – as no sharp flavours may interfere with the sweetness of the festival. All the new season's fruits are enjoyed. In some communities, on the second night of the holiday a pomegranate is blessed and eaten. The numerous seeds of the fruit represent hoped-for fertility.

BLESSINGS FOR ROSH HASHANAH

Several blessings and benedictions attend this festival, which marks the beginning of the Jewish year. In addition to the blessings printed below, parents give thanks for their children, the challah is blessed as for Shabbat, and a slightly longer Kiddush (sanctifying blessing) is recited over the wine before it is drunk.

Candle Lighting

If Rosh Hashanah falls on the same day as Shabbat, then the blessing is modified and added to accordingly.

Baruch Ata Adonai Elohaynu Melech Haolam, asher Kiddshanu b'mitzvotav, v'tzivanu l'hadleek neer shel Yom Tov.

Blessed are You, Lord God, Eternal One, who enables us to welcome Rosh Hashanah, by kindling these lights.

Benediction

Versions of the prayer that follows – Shehehayanu – are recited on other important occasions or festivals, as well as Rosh Hashanah.

Baruch Ata Adonai Elohaynu Melech Haolam, shehehayanu, v'keeyomany v'higeeyanu laz man hazeh.

Blessed are You, Lord God, Eternal One, who has kept us alive and sustained us, enabling us to celebrate this New Year.

Honeyed Apples

When sliced apples are dipped in honey to symbolize sweetness for the year ahead, this blessing is recited.

Baruch Ata Adonai Elohaynu Melech Haolam, boray p'ree ha aytz.

Blessed are You, Lord God, Eternal One, who creates the fruit from the earth.

YOM KIPPUR

The 10th day of Tishri, the first month in the Jewish calendar, is Yom Kippur – the Day of Atonement. It is the most solemn day of the year and marks God's forgiveness of the early Israelites after they worshipped the golden calf while Moses received the tablets of the law from God on Mount Sinai.

It is a day devoted to spiritual life, when the physical is set aside. Sex is forbidden, as is wearing leather shoes, brushing the teeth, spending money, using perfumes or soap and wearing make-up. Everyone, other than children, pregnant women, and the ill or infirm, is expected to fast.

Making Amends

Jews are urged to take stock of their sins, to make amends for any wrongdoing, and to repent. The ancient Kapparot (expiations) ceremony is still observed in some circles. This involves passing a live chicken over the head of an individual, so that his or her sins may be symbolically transferred to the bird. Many prefer to use a coin instead. The coin symbolises giving to charity.

On the day of Yom Kippur, Jews go to synagogue, greeting each other with "Have an easy fast". Much time is then spent in quiet retrospection as individuals examine their consciences with honesty, aiming to make amends for past misdeeds, and promising to do much better in the year ahead. The Yom Kippur devotions include chanting the Kol Nidre, and the Yizkor, the memorial service at which the dead are remembered and respected. Kaddish, the prayer for the dead, is recited for the deceased family members and friends of participants, and for the Jewish martyrs. Candles are also lit for the deceased.

Below: A coloured wood engraving by Julius Schnorr von Carolsfeld depicting Moses bringing the people of Israel the new Tablets of the Law after the first set was broken (1860).

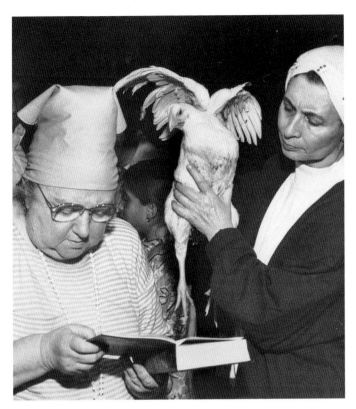

Above: During the traditional Kapparot ceremony, a live chicken is passed over the head to symbolically absorb and absolve the person's sins. (Photograph by Melvine H. Levine.)

The meal on the eve of Yom Kippur is eaten in the afternoon, before sunset. Chicken soup is the preferred food, as it is for almost every festive occasion. It is probably favoured at Yom Kippur because of the traditional Kapparot ceremony involving a chicken.

For Ashkenazi Jews it is traditional to eat the soup with knaidlach (matzo balls) or kreplach filled with chicken, while for Sephardi Jews there are many different variations. In Egypt, Jews traditionally eat a simple egg and lemon soup before the fast. Sephardi Jews often follow the soup with a simple dish

such as boiled chicken with rice or couscous. The festive challah, which is enjoyed by Ashkenazi Jews on the eve of Yom Kippur, is often shaped into raised arms or wings or a ladder, rather than the traditional braided shape. The shape represents prayers being made towards heaven on this day of praying and retrospection.

All foods eaten at this time must be light and simple and not too salty or spicy as it is terribly difficult to fast with a raging thirst. It is intended that penitents should feel a few hunger pangs while they are fasting, but they should not get into any difficulty during this period.

Right: Sephardi Jews traditionally break the fast of Yom Kippur by serving eggs, which are a symbol of life.

A Day of Purity

At Yom Kippur the synagogue is decorated in white, the Torah is draped in white and the rabbi wears a kitl (a white robe), as a symbol of purity. Observant Jews also wear white in the synagogue, and shoes made from cloth rather than leather.

Unlike other festivals and holidays when candles are lit before the meal, the candles are lit after the meal – before the start of Yom Kippur and the festival observances. A pure white tablecloth is draped on the dinner table, and instead of the challah and feasting foods that are usually enjoyed for other holidays and festivals, a Bible, prayer book and other sacred religious texts are placed on the table until the observance has been completed.

Families and friends gather together for celebrations to break the fast after Yom Kippur. It is a happy occasion after the solemnity of the day's observance. Sephardim serve eggs, the symbol of life, and almost all Jews, Sephardim and Ashkenazim alike, enjoy sweet foods with mild flavours, such as honey cake and fresh fruit.

Dishes are prepared the day before Yom Kippur so that they are ready for the end of the fast and the celebrations. For Ashkenazi Jews, it is a good time to eat bagels, cream cheese, lox (smoked salmon), kugels and marinated fish such as herring.

A break-the-fast party is much like a brunch, but with a feeling of lightness of soul and a spirit of looking forward to the new year.

SUKKOT

This festival is observed by building a sukkah, which is a little three-sided hut or booth. The Mishnah (the first code of Jewish Law) lays down how this must be done. There must only be three sides, and the roof must be covered with schach, or branches of trimmed greens or palm leaves, with enough open space to permit those inside to see the stars. A sukkah must be a temporary building, so you cannot use any other permanent structure that stays up for the rest of the year. Sometimes a few families get together to share the task of building, starting at one house and then moving to the next until all the structures are complete.

If the weather permits, meals during the seven-day festival are eaten in the sukkah. The mood of Sukkot is festive; it is a wonderful outdoor celebration. Friends and family drop by, and if the weather is mild enough, families sleep in the sukkah, too. It is wonderful to catch sight of these sukkahs in big cities where you can see their greenery perched on terraces and in courtyards and gardens.

Celebrating the Holiday

The proper greeting for Sukkot is "Chag Sameach", which translates as happy holiday. Celebrants give thanks for the previous year, and express hopes for the year to come. At the end of the festival, prayers are offered for the first rains and the Hebrew dance Mayim may be performed.

Four plants – Arba Minim – decorate the sukkah, and are held in the hands during the blessings each evening. They are: the etrog (a lemon-like citron); the lulav (palm branch); the arava (willow branch); and the myrtle. Each of these has a deep significance. The etrog is shaped like a heart and symbolizes the hope of divine forgiveness for the desires of our heart; this is held in the left hand. The right hand holds the lulav, which symbolizes Israel's loyalty to God, while the myrtle is shaped like an eye, and represents the hope that greed and envy will be forgiven. Finally, the arava is considered to be shaped like a mouth and represents forgiveness for idle talk and lies. Drawings and bright cut-outs are pinned up and fresh and dried fruits are hung from the roof.

Above: Myrtle and willow branches are placed in the sukkah along with the etrog (citron) and lulav (palm branch) as directed in Leviticus 23:40.

Observing the Festival

Since it is a harvest festival, fruits and vegetables are eaten. Cabbage is stuffed in the Eastern European tradition to make holishkes, and strudel is made from apple. Pomegranates and persimmons are considered a Sukkot treat.

The eighth day of Sukkot is Shemeni Atzeret, when memorial prayers are said. The next day, Simchat Torah, is the festival of rejoicing in the Torah, when the weekly readings of the Torah in the synagogue finish and the cycle begins again. The Torah comprises B'raisheet (Genesis), Sh'mot (Exodus), Va'yikra (Leviticus), Bmidbar (Numbers) and Dvarim (Deuteronomy). It is central to Jewish life, as it contains the laws and traditions, customs and festivals, and their history.

Children are often brought to the synagogue to celebrate Simchat Torah. They are given apples and chocolate, and little Torahs and flags, to symbolize the learning of the Torah is a happy, sweet, experience.

Left: A devout member of the ultra-orthodox Mea Shearim community in Jerusalem prepares for Sukkot.

CHANUKKAH

Throughout the world, beginning on the eve of the 25th of Kislev, which falls in November or December, Jews celebrate Chanukkah, the festival of lights, by lighting an oil lamp or menorah filled with candles, lighting one every night for eight nights until all are lit. A shamash (helper candle), is used to light each candle.

The festival commemorates the Maccabean victory over Antiochus IV, who was known as Epiphanes of Greece, in the year 165BCE (BC). When the Jewish Maccabees returned to the Temple, after defeating the Syrians who had attempted to annihilate Judaism, they found it pillaged, and the eternal light extinguished. They immediately lit the lamp, but there was only enough sacred oil to keep it burning for one day. A messenger was sent to get oil, but the supply was four days away, each way. However, a miracle occurred, and the holy lamp did not go out but continued to burn, until eight days had passed and the messenger returned with a new supply of oil. The miracle of Chanukkah is also that a small band of fighters could triumph over a powerful, well-equipped army.

At Chanukkah, Jews eat foods cooked in oil, to remind them of the lamp that burned and burned. On the first night, the Shehehayanu (the benediction of thanks) is recited, and each evening a blessing is said over the candles.

Right: Children spin the dreidel as part of the Chanukkah celebrations.

Above: Lighting candles, one for each night of Chanukkah, symbolizes the lamp that burned for eight days.

Customs and Traditions

Jewish children often make ceramic or papier-mâché menorahs (candelabras) or dreidels (spinning tops) with which to celebrate the holiday. All Jews gather together socially throughout the festival of Chanukkah, greeting each other with "Chag Sameach" meaning happy holiday, drinking spirits, exchanging gifts or giving money (Chanukkah gelt) and singing songs such as Ma-oh Tzur (Rock of Ages) or the Dreidel Song. This last will often accompany a game of dreidel, when small coins or nuts are gambled away on the outcome of the spinning of the four-sided top that plays such an important part in the festivities. Hebrew letters marked on the top signify "A Great Miracle Happened There", or, if one lives in Israel, "A Great Miracle Happened Here".

Potato latkes, crisp pancakes, are an Eastern European treat enjoyed by the Ashkenazim. They are relatively recent, as potatoes were not brought back from the New World until the 16th century. Few snacks are as evocative as these crisp brown potato pancakes, especially if you grew up eating them.

The Sephardim have different Chanukkah traditions: Persians eat snail-shaped syrupy treats called zelebis; Israelis enjoy soufganiot, which are a kind of jam-filled doughnut; and Greek Jews eat loukomades, delectable airy dough balls that are fried until golden and drizzled with honey. It is said that these sweet fritters are very similar to what the Maccabees themselves would have eaten.

Chanukkah is a happy and joyous celebration. Indeed, the Shulhkan Arukh – the code of law – forbids mourning and fasting during this time, and instead encourages great merry-making and enjoying the feast.

PURIM

This festival is one of celebration and joy, feasting and drinking. It falls on the 14th Adar, around February or March, and reminds Jews of the triumph of freedom and goodness over evil.

The story that Purim celebrates took place in Shushan, which later became Persia and then Iran. The principal characters are Queen Esther, her cousin Mordecai and the evil First Minister of King Ahasuerus, Haman. The tale is told in the Megillah, the Scroll of Esther, which is read in the synagogue on the night of Purim.

The tale relates how Haman, irate that the Jew Mordecai did not show him proper respect, plotted to kill the Jews. Mordecai's cousin, the beautiful Queen Esther, went to her husband pleading for the lives of her people. And so, at a banquet that was designed to honour Haman, the tables were turned. The king hanged Haman on the very gallows intended for Mordecai, and the Jews were saved.

Below: A painting by Filippino Lippi (1457–1504) telling the story of Esther: Mordecai's lament about Israel's lot; Esther before King Ahasuerus; and the fate of Haman.

Celebrating the Story of Esther

During Purim, children come to the synagogue dressed in costume, often as Haman, Mordecai or Esther. The Megillah is read aloud and, when Haman's name is uttered, all make as much noise as they can, either by twirling the grogger (noisemaker), or just banging things together.

Wine is a sign of happiness and inaugurates all Jewish religious ceremonies, but at Purim it is essential. Indeed, the Talmud exhorts Jews to "drink so much that you can't tell the difference between Mordecai and Haman". This is because Esther served huge quantities of wine at the banquet she gave at the palace, when Haman was exposed as a villain.

Special foods are eaten for Purim. In Ashkenazi cultures, triangular pastries filled with nuts, seeds or dried fruit are served. The filling is meant to commemorate Esther, who ate only fruits and nuts in the palace, as the kitchen was not kosher. For North African Sephardim, fried pastries drenched in honey and sprinkled with nuts, called oznei Haman (the ears of Haman), are a favourite Purim treat.

Above: Masks are often worn as part of the Purim festivities.

Gifts to Share

The giving of sweet pastries and fruit, known as shaloch manot, is a Purim observance. Charitable donation is also decreed, usually money, which is given to at least two individuals or two causes.

Some Jews observe the fast of Esther, in honour of the queen's fast before she pleaded with the king for her people's lives. Fasting, prayers and charity are all required for repentance, and the Jewish community of Shushan was saved by Esther's repentance.

to wander for an entire generation until Moses led them to the Promised Land. The festival of Pesach takes Jews on that journey via the Haggadah; the story is relived as the ritual meal is eaten.

For eight days special foods are eaten, and many very ordinary foods permitted at other times of the year are taboo. No leavened foods are permitted, which rules out any cakes or cookies prepared with flour (because when flour comes into contact with water for a certain period of time, it naturally produces leaven).

Left: A coloured wood engraving by Julius Schnorr von Carolsfeld showing the angel of death passing over the homes of the Israelites whose doorways were splashed with blood (1860).

Below: An illustration of a father placing the passover basket on his son's head during the ritual Seder meal (from Barcelona Haggadah c.1340).

PESACH

The Passover festival, Pesach, is one of the biggest in the Jewish year. It commemorates the story of the exodus of the Hebrew slaves from bondage in Egypt, a flight that turned a tribe of slaves into a cohesive people. During this festival, Jews celebrate the flight for freedom of all humanity – the freedom of spirit as well as personal, religious and physical freedom.

"Why is tonight different from all other nights?" asks a small child, quoting from the Haggadah, the narrative read at the Pesach feast. And so the story unfolds ...

Pesach falls sometime around March or April, following the Jewish calendar. The word *pesach* means passing over, and represents the passing over of the houses whose doorways the Israelites had splashed with lamb's blood, so that those inside remained unharmed when the angel of death ravaged Egypt, slaying the first-born sons. This was Egypt's final agony, the last straw that convinced Pharaoh to, in the much-quoted words of Moses, "Let my people go!" And go they did, into the desert

Special Foods for Pesach

Crisp flat breads called matzos are served at Pesach. They are a reminder of the Israelites who, in their escape to the desert, only had time to make flat breads, baked on hot stones. Instead of the two loaves of bread traditionally placed on the table during a festival, on Pesach, three matzos are served.

Because of the separation over the years of Ashkenazim and Sephardim, each group has evolved its own rules for what may or may not be eaten at Pesach. Ashkenazim forbid the consumption of corn, rice and beans (which are known collectively as kitniyot) for these can ferment and become yeasty. Sephardim, however, still eat these foods.

Above: Passover Haggadahs are often noted for their embellishments.

Matzos

The flour from which matzos are made may be exposed to water for no more than 18 minutes if they are to be kosher for Passover. Biblical teachings dictate that the dough must be allowed to rise for no longer than the time it took to walk a Roman mile, which has been timed as taking between 18 and 24 minutes. The number 18 is portentous, as it represents *chai*, the Hebrew for life.

Shmura matzo is a hand-made matzo that some very Observant Jews insist upon eating at Pesach. Bakers gather around the table while the oven is readied. A stopwatch is pressed and any matzo that is not ready in time is rejected and thrown away. Automated, assembly line baking produces matzos much more quickly, usually in about 7 minutes.

There is more to Passover matzos than the simple baking. Before the process can even begin, the flour must be inspected by the rabbi to ensure it has not come into contact with damp, and that no grains have sprouted. The inspecting rabbi turns off the water at the mill before the Passover flour arrives, and the delivery truck itself is inspected before and after loading up, then it is sealed with the rabbi's sign of inspection.

Below: Matzos are made in a Jewish factory in the Holy Land (c.1950).

In the weeks prior to the Pesach feast the house is cleaned from top to bottom, especially the kitchen. The day before the Seder or Pesach feast, the head of the household searches for anything that might contain leaven – usually there are napkins filled with crumbs left here and there for symbolic removal. Then he or she recites a blessing on the hametz (leavening) that has been gathered which is then burned. The search for hametz continues. Sometimes the searcher uses a feather, a symbolic gesture to signify that no crumbs whatsoever remain.

In addition to bread, all flour or leavened products are forbidden, as are beer and other alcoholic drinks made with yeast. Observant Jews are very careful about the dairy products they eat during Pesach. Milk should come from animals that have only eaten grass, not grain, and there must be no risk of contamination with leaven.

Sephardim eat all vegetables and some eat rice, though Ashkenazim eschew many vegetables on the grounds that they could be considered grains or ingredients to make breads or cakes. The list includes corn, green beans, peas, lentils, chickpeas, and other dried beans.

Instead of cakes based on a leavening agent such as baking powder, Pesach boasts a wealth of cakes risen with the aid of beaten eggs.

The Seder

On the first night of the festival (and the second night too, unless the participants are Reform or living in Israel) a ritual meal called the Seder is served. The word *seder* simply means order, referring to the fact that the meal has a specific order of events. The meal revolves around the reading of the Haggadah, the story of the exodus from Egypt and from slavery. The foods eaten often have symbolic significance and represent various elements of the story.

Many families use the Pesach Seder as an opportunity to highlight some facet of modern life or struggle that needs to be addressed. Some place an empty chair at the table to symbolize those who are still in slavery.

Wine, candles for the holiday, a plate of matzos, and the Seder plate are placed on the Pesach table. The Seder plate holds a selection of foods that have special meaning for the festival; the role of each is highlighted as the reading of the Haggadah progresses.

Above: A ritual Seder plate.

The Seder Plate

Maror (bitter herbs) are placed on the Seder plate to remind Jews of the bitterness of slavery. Horseradish is usually used as maror, but any sharp, bitter herb can be eaten. Charoset takes the next place. Also known as charosses, harosses and halek, this is a distinctive blend of sweet fruit and nuts. When mixed with wine, it becomes a tasty sludge, symbolizing the mortar used in the Hebrews' forced labour. Sometimes, in Morocco and other Sephardi communities, charoset is rolled into sticky balls and eaten as a sweetmeat throughout the holiday.

The cycle of life is represented by a roasted egg. It is also a symbol of the sacrifice brought to the Temple in ancient days, a symbol of mourning for the destroyed Temple. A bowl of boiled eggs is usually served with salt water as the first course of the Seder meal. The salt water represents the sad tears of the Hebrews.

Also to be dipped in the salt water are springtime greens such as parsley, lettuce and celery, which recall the oppression of the Israelites, as well as renewal represented by spring.

A roasted shank bone of lamb is placed on the plate as a reminder of the paschal sacrifice at the Temple. Some Sephardi communities put a big shoulder of roast lamb on to the Seder plate and eat it as the main course, but some individuals refuse to eat lamb at the Seder until the Temple is rebuilt. Vegetarian Jews often substitute a roasted beetroot (beet) for the lamb bone.

There are no specific rules about what must be on the Seder menu, apart from the restrictions of Pesach itself. Each community has developed its own traditions. A Persian custom, for instance, commemorating the beating of the slaves by their cruel masters, involves beating each other with spring onions (scallions). This helps to break the ice, relaxes all who are at the Seder table, and makes the whole room smell exceedingly delicious and oniony. It is great fun, too, for the children, who start getting fidgety after a while if there are too many prayers and not enough playing and eating and singing.

Four cups of wine (or grape juice) must be poured during the Seder. A fifth is left for Eliahu, the harbinger of the Messiah, who is said to visit every Jewish house on the night of the Seder, drinking from every cup.

Below: Four cups of wine are poured for the Seder, plus an extra cup for Eliahu.

Below: Hard-boiled eggs dipped in salt water, representing the tears of the Israelites, are eaten at Pesach.

SEFIRAH

Between Pesach and the next major festival, Shavuot, is a period called Sefirah. It is a solemn time of observance rather than a festival. Beginning at the end of Pesach, it commemorates the day when a sheaf of young barley – the Omer – was traditionally brought into the Temple in Jerusalem. Observing this period is called Counting the Omer. The solemnity of this period is thought to have stemmed from an ancient superstition. Partial mourning was observed in the hope that it would ensure a good harvest of grain.

During this time, the Observant do not celebrate weddings, have other celebrations or even cut their hair.

Lag b'Omer

This happy day falls on the 33rd day of counting and is the one break in the solemn time of Sefirah. Lag b'Omer is a day made for celebrating out of doors and picnicking. For Observant Jews, Lag b'Omer is the day in spring when you could schedule a wedding or have a haircut.

TU B'SHEVAT

This festival is known as the Holiday of the Trees. It is one of the four holidays that celebrate nature, as mentioned in the Mishnah (part of the Talmud). Tu b'Shevat occurs in early February, when the sap begins to rise in the fruit trees of Israel. To celebrate, it is customary to eat different kinds of fruits and nuts.

The image of trees is very important in Jewish life, for instance Etz Chaim, the Tree of Life. The Torah, too, is sometimes likened to a tree, for it protects and nourishes. Even the wooden poles around which the Torah is wrapped are called atzeem, or trees.

Tu b'Shevat is often celebrated by planting trees and collecting funds for reforestation. An old custom of holding Tu b'Shevat Seders has recently been revived. The meal progresses from fruits and nuts, through various juices, all symbolizing the awakening of nature after its slumber during winter.

Below: Lag b'Omer is a popular day for receiving a first haircut. Chassidic Jews wait until a boy is three years old. (Photograph by Ed. Toben.)

Above: Traditionally, when the Omer (a sheaf of young barley) was brought into the Temple in Jerusalem, the period of Sefirah began.

The Tu b'Shevat Seder contains three different categories of fruits and nuts: hard, medium and soft, which are said to represent the different characteristics of the Jews. The first category includes those fruits and nuts that have a hard or inedible skin or shell such as kiwi fruits, bananas, oranges, pineapples, pistachio nuts and almonds. The second category includes those fruits with a hard stone (pit) that cannot be eaten such as prunes, plums, peaches, apricots, cherries and olives. The third category includes those fruits that can be eaten in their entirety such as strawberries, raspberries, grapes, figs, pears and apples.

Certain fruits also have specific meanings. For example, pomegranates represent fertility, apples represent the splendour of God, almonds represent divine retribution (because the almond tree blossoms before other trees) and carob represents humility and penitence.

Enjoying a meal made up entirely of fruits and nuts, or simply adding fruits and nuts to a loaf of challah are all traditional ways of celebrating the festival of Tu b'Shevat.

SHAVUOT

The word *shavuot* means weeks in Hebrew, as this festival comes seven weeks after Pesach. In English it is known as Pentecost, which comes from the Greek, meaning 50 days.

It is also sometimes referred to as the Festival of the Torah, because it tells the story of the Israelites wandering through the desert and commemorates the giving of the Jewish scriptures, the Torah, and the Ten Commandments to Moses on Mount Sinai. It is also the Feast of the First Fruits, one of the ancient pilgrimages to Jerusalem, when the first fruits and grains of the season were brought as offerings.

Shavuot is celebrated for one day in Israel and among Reform Jews and for two days in other Jewish communities throughout the world. As with Shabbat, the holiday begins at sundown the night before. The table is set with a fine, festive cloth, wine and challah, as well as fresh flowers and spring greenery.

Shavuot is also a time to enjoy meals based on dairy products, although there are no rules that say this must be done. Ashkenazim enjoy blintzes, sour cream kugels, cheese pancakes and cheese dumplings, while Sephardim enjoy cheese pastries such as borekas.

Some may say the tradition of eating dairy foods is based on the abundance of milk during spring, but Jewish

Below: Prayers for Shavuot.

scholars have added other reasonings, too. To eat milk and dairy products reminds Jews of the milk and honey in the Song of Songs, say some scholars. Another explanation is that the Israelites were away so long receiving the Ten Commandments that their milk had soured and begun to turn to cheese. Still others suggest that when the Israelites finally returned to their camp they were too hungry to wait to prepare and cook a meat meal and so just drank lots of milk for sustenance.

Above: An illuminated 13th-century manuscript from the Book of Ruth, which is read at the holiday of Shavuot.

The Book of Ruth is read on Shavuot and provides a dramatic story of a woman devoted to her adopted faith, choosing it over her own family upon the death of her husband.

Shavuot is one of the four times of the year that Yizkor, the memorial prayers in which the dead are respected, are recited.

LIFE EVENTS

From birth to death, Judaism offers ceremonies and observances to mark the rites of passage and key events in the lives of individuals. Each event, observance or celebration is always accompanied by an abundance of festive food and drink.

Brit Milah

Male children are ritually circumcised on the eighth day after birth unless they have been small at birth, ill or premature; if any of these occur, the circumcision will be delayed until the child is healthy and has achieved a specific weight so as not to endanger his health.

The ritual circumcision is called *Brit Milah* in Hebrew, *Bris* in Yiddish. It is done in the home by a community specialist called a mohel, though some Reform (Progressive) Jews have the baby circumcised in hospital by a doctor. In a traditional ceremony, the baby is given no more than a few drops of wine as a painkiller and the operation is swift. The baby scarcely gives more than a little cry, but the adults often need a bit more wine or something stronger, to fortify themselves after the baby's ordeal.

After the ceremony, which includes blessings and prayers, there is a party, because this is a very happy occasion; when the newborn baby becomes part of the world's Jewish community. And, like any happy occasion, a Brit Milah is celebrated with plenty of food and drink. There is every reason to rejoice. Not only is there a new, healthy child, but the mother has come through the rigours of pregnancy and childbirth. As the baby is passed from one adoring relative to the next, and all remark on how he has his father's nose and his grandmother's eyes, the table groans with lavish offerings such as traditional salads, delicatessen specialities, breads and cakes and sweetmeats.

At the Brit Milah, the male child is given a Hebrew name. He is often named after a favourite relative; in Sephardi tradition it is a favourite living relative, in Ashkenazi tradition it is a revered deceased relative. A girl child will usually be given her Hebrew name at the synagogue, at the age of about a month. This too is an occasion for celebration and eating, with the parents hosting a reception at the synogogue after the service. In Observant families, there is a ceremony for the first-born child – Pidyon ha Ben for a boy and Pidyon ha Bat for a girl. This means redemption of the first born and marks the start of the new family.

Bar or Bat Mitzvah

The next milestone in the circle of life is a child's Bar or Bat Mitzvah. This coming-of-age ceremony marks the time when the child takes on the religious obligations of an adult.

Bar Mitzvah – the ceremony for a boy – means the son of the commandment; Bat Mitzvah, the equivalent ceremony for girls, means daughter of the commandment. After Bar or Bat Mitzvah the child may be counted as part of a minyan (quorum of ten people required to hold a religious service). In some sectors such as Orthodoxy, ten men are still required to make up a minyan, while in others such as Reform (Progressive), it is simply ten people – either male or female.

A Bar Mitzvah ceremony takes place any time after the boy's 13th birthday, while a Bat Mitzvah takes place after the girl's 12th birthday. However, many adults who have not had a Bar or Bat Mitzvah as a child decide later that they would like to study for it as adults. It is a good excuse to return to the community, and to embrace studying once again.

Left: An infant boy is presented in the synagogue for the ritual Brit Milah.

Each night during the period of mourning there is a gathering for the purpose of prayer, a minyan. Members of the community bring prepared foods with them when they come to offer support and comfort. Usually this will be traditional, homely foods that warm the soul and are easily digested, for grief is very hard on the body. The food, and the act of giving food, sustains the mourners through their ordeal, for even when there is no strength for the task it is still necessary to eat to survive. The preparing, bringing and eating of food is all about survival.

Sharing Food

The heart of Jewish celebration is the home. The taste of Judaism is in its kitchen, and the traditions of Jewish cooking are in the home table – the everyday eating with the family, and the celebrations with extended family and friends. In Jewish celebrations, food is central to the festivities and, for Jews sharing that food, it is as wonderful an experience as eating it themselves.

There is joy in the Jewish tradition of generosity at the table. As the Haggadah says: "Let all who are hungry come and eat."

Left: A young couple stand under a traditional chuppah at a wedding ceremony in London's East End (1969).

Below: A man from a Jewish community in Morocco reads psalms at the grave of a deceased family member.

A Bar or Bat Mitzvah is an occasion for rejoicing. A large party is often given, with a festive meal. There will be dancing and general merrymaking. A boy or girl can expect to be the centre of attention and everything possible will be done to make the day a special one.

Marriage

Weddings have a special role in Jewish life. They are grand, festive and full of hope. They represent the joining of two families to create a new family and new members of the community.

They are also a great excuse for a huge party and seeing family and friends. Even older people who have been married before might have a big wedding party, for it is such a happy time.

From the moment that the glass is stamped on by the groom (the moment when the couple are officially married), the merriment begins. There will be a lavish table with foods such as smoked salmon, chopped liver, herring and rye breads, and lots of dancing of the *hora*.

Bereavement

Even at the end of life food plays an important role for Jews. The period of mourning is known as Shiva, and there could be nothing more comforting than food brought by friends and relations to sustain the family through this time, when the practicalities of cooking and eating can be too much to bear alongside the great demands of bereavement.

JEWISH FOODS

The foods of the Jewish table are global by nature, reflecting the flavours of
the countries where Jews have settled. They also have their roots in ritual
and tradition. Ashkenazi and Sephardi foods are very different but
cross-cultural marriages and the intermingling of people from
different backgrounds have blurred the boundaries. With
the myriad Jewish communities coming together again,
this is a time in which Jews can feel as well as say
"Am Yisrael Chil" –
We are One People.

The Laws of Kashrut

Kashrut is the set of ritual dietary laws that are set out in the Talmud. Food that conforms to those standards is described as kosher. Whether a Jew comes from a land where onions, garlic and chicken fat are freely eaten, or one whose cuisine includes hot peppers, spices and olive oil, the meals eaten in the Observant Jewish household will not taste the same as food prepared from similar ingredients by non-Jewish neighbours, because the former will conform to the rules of Kashrut.

Though the basic principles of Kashrut are outlined in the Bible, they have been ruled upon and commented upon by rabbis in the Shulhan Aruckh, the code of Jewish law. There is no reason given for the laws of Kashrut, though many have suggested that hygiene, food safety and health might be contributory factors. The rabbis state, however, that no reason or rationale is needed; obeying the laws of Kashrut is a commandment from God.

Below (clockwise from top): Beef, goat and lamb, when prepared appropriately, are all permitted by the laws of Kashrut.

PERMITTED MEATS

Only certain types of meat are allowed, based on the text in Leviticus 11:3, which states: "Whatsoever parteth the hoof, and is clovenfooted, and cheweth the cud...that shall ye eat". These two conditions mean that ox, sheep, goat, hart, gazelle, roebuck, antelope and mountain sheep may be eaten, while pork, horse, camel, rabbit, hare and whale are forbidden. No birds or animals of prey are allowed, nor are scavengers, creeping insects or reptiles.

PERMITTED BIRDS

The Torah is not quite so clear when it comes to identifying which birds may be eaten. Instead, it lists 24 species of forbidden fowl, which are mainly birds of prey or scavengers. Permitted fowl have in common with each other a protruding claw, a crop and a stomach that can be peeled readily of its inner lining. In general, chickens, ducks, turkeys and geese are allowed, but this can vary. Goose is popular among Ashkenazim, while Yemenite Jews consider it to be of both the land and sea and therefore forbidden by Kashrut.

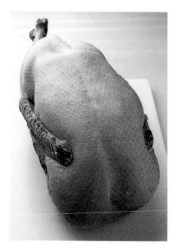

Above: Goose is very popular among Eastern European Jews who, in the past, often raised them for their fat livers and to serve at holiday meals.

RITUAL SLAUGHTER

For kosher animals to become kosher meat, they must be slaughtered ritually by shechita. An animal that dies of natural causes, or is killed by another animal, is forbidden. The knife for slaughter must be twice as long as the animal's throat and extremely sharp and smooth; even the tiniest nick in the blade renders the knife invalid for kosher butchering. The shochet (ritual slaughterer) must sever the animal's trachea and oesophagus without grazing its spine, and the knife must be wielded with care and speed; the smallest delay would bring terror and pain to the animal and render the meat unkosher.

The shochet inspects the incision to make sure the cut is smooth, and the lungs must be examined for symptoms of disease. If there is any doubt, the shochet blows air into the lungs; if they fail to hold the air, the animal is not kosher. Certain types of injury also render the animal unkosher. Some cuts of meat are considered unkosher, unless specially treated, for example the hind legs of the cow and sheep must have the sciatic nerve removed.

Kashering Meat

This is the term used to describe the removal of blood from an animal immediately after slaughter, which is essential if the meat is to be labelled kosher. To Jews, blood is a symbol of life, and the prohibition against consuming it comes from the scriptures: "Therefore I said unto the children of Israel, No soul of you shall eat blood..." (Leviticus 17:12).

Because blood is categorically forbidden by the laws of Kashrut, all meat must be kashered by soaking, salting or grilling (broiling) so that no blood remains. Hearts must be cut open, all veins removed and drained of blood. This is usually done by the butcher. It is then salted and prepared as desired. A spot of blood in an egg renders it unkosher.

How to Kasher Meat

Most kosher butchers kasher meat before offering it for sale. If your butcher does not do this, consult a rabbinical authority or follow the simple instructions below.

1 Place the meat or poultry in a large bowl or bucket as soon as possible after purchase, pour over cold water to cover and leave to stand for 30 minutes.

2 Remove the meat or poultry from the water and place on a plastic drainer, tilted to allow the juices to drain away. Leave to stand for about 5 minutes, then sprinkle with coarse kosher salt. Leave to stand for 1 hour.

3 Rinse the meat three times to rid it of all blood and salt. Pat dry with kitchen paper, then chill until ready to cook.

To kasher liver, rinse it well under cold water, then sprinkle with salt and grill (broil) on a rack or over an open fire, on each side until the flesh is cooked through.

PERMITTED FISH

To be considered kosher, all fish must have detachable scales and fins. Fish with scales that do not come away from the skin are not kosher: "These shall ye eat of all that are in the waters: whatsoever hath fins and scales in the waters, in the seas, and in the rivers, them shall ye eat" (Leviticus 11:9).

The London Bet Din lists the following as being non-kosher fish: abbot, allmouth, angelfish, angler, beluga, blonde, catfish, caviar, cockles, conger eel, crabs, dogfish, eelpout, eels, fiddlefish, fishing frog, frog-fish, glake, goosefish, guffer eel, huss, lumpfish, monkfish, mussels, ray, rigg, rock salmon, rockfish, roker, sea devil, sea pout, skate, sturgeon, swordfish, thornback ray and turbot. Other sea creatures that are forbidden by the laws of Kashrut include all shellfish and crustaceans, sea urchin, octopus and squid.

Below (from left): Red mullet, trout and salmon all have detachable scales so are considered kosher.

Kashrut Certification

To be sure that any packaged food is kosher, look for a symbol of recognized certification every time you buy, as additives and methods can change. There are numerous certifying boards, and many Jews will eat only packaged foods certified by specific boards. If a food is certified as Glatt Kosher it conforms to a particularly stringent Kashrut, which requires, among other things, that the lungs be more thoroughly examined.

Some Observant Jews will eat foods such as canned tomatoes, for the only ingredients are tomatoes and salt. Others avoid such foods, as they could have been contaminated on the production line. Very strict Jews extend their watchfulness even to the basics, and will eat only sugar with the rabbinical supervision marking, to be sure it has not been tainted by other unkosher food products or insects.

DAIRY PRODUCTS

Deuteronomy states "Thou shalt not seethe a kid in his mother's milk". This is the basis for the rule that dairy foods and meat must not be cooked together. After eating a meat meal, a certain amount of time must elapse before dairy food can be consumed. Some communities wait six hours, while others wait only two. There is no requirement to wait after eating a dairy meal before having a meat one.

There are many non-dairy products, including non-dairy margarine, that approximate the taste and texture of dairy products. These make it possible to eat meat with creamy sauces and creamy desserts after a meat meal.

To ensure the complete separation of meat and milk, kosher kitchens have separate dishes, pans and washing-up utensils for each. These must be stored separately in the kitchen.

Cheese and Rennet

Natural rennet, the ingredient used to curdle milk for cheese-making, comes from the lining of an animal's stomach. Therefore, the cheese made from it is not kosher. Much modern cheese is made with vegetable rennet and not necessarily labelled as such, but to be sure, one should eat only cheeses that are marked "Suitable for Vegetarians", or that have the appropriate kosher certification marking.

Gelatine in Dairy Products

Because gelatine is made from animal bones, it is not kosher. Kosher gelatine made from seaweed (carrageen), is vegetarian, and must be used instead. Care should be taken with products such as yogurt, as they can often contain gelatine. For this reason, many Jews will eat only milk products that are marked as kosher.

Above: The quality of kosher wines has improved tremendously over the last few years and an excellent selection is now available.

ALCOHOL

Spirits and grain alcohol are permitted by Kashrut, as is wine, although wine (and wine products such as brandy) carry a few provisos.

Since wine has been drunk by Jews since biblical times and it is an intrinsic part of observances carried out for festivals and Shabbat, wine must be labelled kosher. This means that the grapes have been harvested and the wine prepared, processed and bottled under rabbinical supervision.

In the not-too-distant past kosher wines were barely drinkable; now, however, there are some wonderful dry and deliciously drinkable wines coming out of Israel, California and France. Traditional sweet Kiddush wines are also available.

Left (clockwise from top): milk, Cheddar cheese, goat's cheese, fatmet cheese and yogurt are just a few of the dairy products that can be enjoyed in the kosher kitchen.

KOSHER FOR SHABBAT

"Ye shall kindle no fire throughout your habitations upon the sabbath day" (Exodus 35:3). No fire for domestic use can be lit in religious homes on Shabbat. No stove should be turned on, even if it is electric. A stove may be left on to keep food warm or to cook food very slowly, but it may not be used for actual cooking on Shabbat.

Many rules surround the definition of what precisely constitutes cooking if a warmer or low-heat gadget is used – some say that food must be partially cooked before Shabbat begins. Water must be previously boiled, then kept warm for Shabbat in an urn which must not be turned on or off.

This injunction applies to all holidays and celebrations, in addition to the weekly Shabbat, and has given rise to the many long-cooked dishes featured in Jewish cooking throughout the world such as dafina, cholent, and other bean and meat dishes that require long, slow cooking to make them succulent.

KASHRUT FOR PESACH

In addition to the requirements for the rest of the year, there are a special set of rules that apply to foods during the Passover festival.

During Pesach no leavened foods may be eaten. This means that no bread, breadcrumbs, flour, yeast, baking powder or bicarbonate of soda (baking soda) may be eaten. Cakes must also be eschewed unless they are prepared using special meal made from ground matzo. (Eggs can be used as a rising agent in cakes, as it is not the fermentation of grains that causes the cake to rise, but rather the air trapped in the beaten egg.)

Ashkenazim eschew many vegetables that could be considered grains or ingredients that could be made into breads or cakes. These include green beans, corn, peas, chickpeas, lentils and other dried beans. Sephardi Jews, however, eat all vegetables and some eat rice.

Before Pesach begins, the house must be cleared entirely of all leavened foods and ingredients. Many religious Jews simply seal cupboards that contain hametz (leaven) with tape, unsealing them again when the festivities are over.

Beer and other alcoholic drinks made with yeast are forbidden during Pesach, although kosher wine is permitted to carry out the observances and traditions of the festival.

Many Sephardim are careful about the milk and dairy products that they consume during Pesach, and will drink only milk that is marked kosher for Pesach to be sure that it is permissable under the laws of Kashrut.

Both Ashkenazi and Sephardi Observant families have separate sets of dishes, cutlery and pans for exclusive use during Pesach. These are stored away for the rest of the year. To make ordinary kitchenware kosher for Pesach, it must be scalded in boiling water. Even the stove must be koshered – the fire and grill (broiler) heated until red hot – before the stove is considered fit to be cooked on for the holiday.

PAREVE FOODS

In Yiddish, these foods are known as *pareve* and in Hebrew they are *parva*. These are the neutral foods that are neither meat nor dairy. They do not, therefore, have the same restrictions imposed upon them and can be eaten with either meat or dairy foods.

All plant foods such as vegetables, grains and fruit are pareve, as are eggs and permitted fish. However, if a pareve food is cooked with a fat that is derived from meat (such as chicken fat) or dairy (such as butter or cream), the food is no longer pareve.

Jews who keep kosher will not usually eat pareve foods that have been prepared outside the home as they could have been prepared using non-kosher fats.

Below (clockwise from top left): Pareve foods such as barley, onions, aubergines (eggplant), tomatoes and eggs can be eaten with either meat or dairy foods.

DAIRY FOODS

In both the Ashkenazi and Sephardi kitchen, all dairy foods are held in very high esteem, a tribute to the biblical description of the land of Israel as a "land of milk and honey". There are strict rules concerning the consumption of dairy foods, but they do not have great religious significance except during the festival of Shavuot. This is sometimes known as the dairy festival and is a time when dairy products are enjoyed for main meals, in preference to meat, which is normally enjoyed at festivals and celebrations.

MILK AND DAIRY PRODUCTS

The milk taken from any kosher animal is considered kosher. Cows, goats and sheep are all milked and the milk is then drunk or made into various dairy products such as butter, yogurt and sour cream. The influences of the past can be seen in the dairy products that are enjoyed by Jews today.

Left (clockwise from top left): Cottage cheese, cream cheese, feta and kashkaval are among the many kosher Jewish cheeses.

In the past, in Northern Europe, milk from cows was readily available and, because the weather was cool, spoilage was not a great problem. Many towns and villages had small dairies that produced sour cream, butter, buttermilk, cottage cheese and cream cheese, and families often owned a cow or two of their own. In Lithuania, however, goats tended to be kept more often than cows and were referred to as Jewish cattle. In warmer countries, especially those situated around the Mediterranean, goats and sheep were much easier to raise, and their milk was more suitable for making fermented dairy products such as yogurt, feta cheese and halloumi. Today, Israel is a great producer of yogurts and sour creams.

Left (clockwise from top): Sour cream products such as shoumenet, sour cream and smetana are very popular in the Jewish kitchen.

Cheeses

A wide variety of kosher cheeses are produced in modern-day Israel, including kashkaval, which resembles a mild Cheddar; halloumi; Bin-Gedi, which is similar to Camembert, and Galil, which is modelled on Roquefort. Fresh goat's cheeses are particularly popular in Israel and are of a very good quality.

Cream cheese has been very popular with Ashkenazim since the days of shtetlach, where it was made in small, Jewish-owned dairies, and sold in earthenware pots or wrapped in leaves. Soft cheeses such as cream cheese and cottage cheese were also made in the home. Cream cheese is the classic spread for bagels, when it is known as a schmear. It can be flavoured with other ingredients such as chopped spring onions (scallions) and smoked salmon.

Dairy Delis

These were a great legacy of New York's Lower East Side Jewish community. Among the most famous restaurants was Ratners, known for its elderly waiters who were invariably grumpy, nosy, bossy and ultimately endearing. Dairy shops and restaurants sold specialities such as cheese-filled blintzes, cheesecake, cream cheese shmears and knishes. Among other treats were boiled potatoes with sour cream, hot or cold borscht, cheese kugels and noodles with cottage cheese.

EGGS

These represent the mysteries of life and death and are very important in Jewish cuisine. They are brought to a family on the birth of a child, and served after a funeral to remind the mourners that, in the midst of death, we are still embraced by life. They also represent fertility. In some Sephardi communities, an egg will be included as part of a bride's costume, or the young couple will be advised to step over fish roe or eat double-yolked eggs to help increase their fertility.

Eggs are pareve so may be eaten with either meat or dairy foods. They are nutritious and filling and provide a good source of protein when other sources may be lacking or forbidden due to the laws of Kashrut.

EGGS FOR PESACH

These feature prominently in the Pesach Seder – both symbolically and as a food. It is said that a whole egg represents the strength of being a whole people (unbroken, the shell is strong; broken, it is weak).

Eggs are also an important ingredient during Pesach, as raising agents may not be used for baking and eggs, when beaten into a cake mixture, can help the cake to rise.

Making Roasted Eggs

A roasted egg is traditionally placed on the Seder plate to represent the cycle of life. It is not usually eaten.

Place a hard-boiled egg over a gas flame, turning occasionally, until it is lightly browned all over. Alternatively, the egg can be roasted in the oven.

Right: Eggs from any kosher bird are considered kosher, as long as they do not contain any trace of blood.

Making Eggs in Salt Water

This simple dish is the first thing eaten when the Pesach service is over. It is only eaten at this time. Allow about 1½ eggs per person.

1 Hard-boil the eggs. Meanwhile, in a small bowl, dissolve 2.5ml/½ tsp salt in 120ml/4fl oz/½ cup warm water. Cool, then chill.

2 Shell the eggs and serve with the salt water for dipping, or place them in the bowl of salt water.

HAMINADOS EGGS

These are a Sephardi speciality. Whole eggs are cooked very slowly with onion skins or coffee grounds, to colour the shells. Alternatively, they may be added to the slow-cooked stew, dafina. They are delicious mashed with leftover cholent, in savoury pastries or chopped and added to simmered brown broad (fava) beans with a little garlic, onion, olive oil and hot chilli sauce.

Making Haminados Eggs

Cooking the eggs with onion skins colours the egg shells but does not impart any flavour to the egg inside.

1 Place 12 whole eggs in a pan and add 5ml/1 tsp each of salt and pepper. Drop in the brown outer skins from 8–10 onions, pour over water to cover and 90ml/6 tbsp olive oil.

2 Bring to the boil, then lower the heat to very low and cook for 6 hours, adding more water as needed. Shell and serve.

> **Classic Deli Dishes**
> Hard-boiled egg, chopped with onion and mixed with a little chicken fat or mayonnaise is one of the oldest Jewish dishes. In modern-day Israel, an avocado is often mashed with the eggs. Scrambled eggs with browned onion and shredded smoked chicken on rye toast or bagels make a perfect brunch.

MEAT

For Observant Jews, meat must be kosher. Originally, any Jew versed in the ritual could slaughter meat, but this changed in the 13th century, with the appointment of shochets (ritual slaughterers). To qualify for this post, a man needed to be very learned, pious and upstanding.

Meat has always been an expensive but highly prized item on the Jewish table. For Ashkenazim, it was made even more costly with the levying of a hefty government tax (korobka). This, together with a community tax for Jewish charities, brought the price to twice that for non-kosher meat. None of this deterred Jews from eating meat, however; they simply saved it for Shabbat and other special occasions.

LAMB AND MUTTON

These were favoured by the Sephardim from North Africa and other Arabic lands until the early 20th century, when the strong French influence introduced beef and veal to their table. Due to the time-consuming removal of the sciatic nerve required by the laws of Kashrut, the Ashkenazim avoided eating the hindquarters of lamb and mutton until the 15th century when a meat shortage made the lengthy procedure worthwhile.

BEEF

This is very popular, especially among European Jews. Brisket is grainy and rough textured, but yields a wonderful flavour when cooked for a long time. The same applies to the short ribs and the chuck or bola. Many of these cuts are not only excellent for pot-roasting and soups; they also make good salt or corned beef and pastrami. Beef shin makes a marvellous soup.

Sausages and Salami

Both Ashkenazim and Sephardim use beef to make a wide array of sausages and salamis. The Ashkenazim tend to favour tasty cured sausages such as frankfurters, knockwurst, knobblewurst and spicy dried sausages while the Sephardim favour fresh sausages, such as the spicy merguez from North Africa and France.

VEAL

This is a favourite meat for all Jewish communities, because it is so delicate and light: shoulder roast, breast of veal, shank and rib chops are all popular cuts along with minced (ground) veal. The breast was often stuffed, then braised with vegetables; minced veal was made into cutlets and meatballs; and, in Vienna, slices of shoulder were pounded until very thin, then lightly coated in breadcrumbs and fried to make crisp, golden schnitzel.

OTHER MEATS

These include goat and deer (venison). Goat is popular in Sephardi cooking and is often used in dishes where lamb could be used such as spicy stews, curries and meatballs. Venison is cooked in similar ways to beef.

OFFAL

Historically, poorer families tended to eat cheaper cuts of meat such as feet, spleen, lungs, intestines, liver, tongue and brains. These were popular with both Ashkenazim and Sephardim, especially Yemenite Jews who are still famed for their spicy offal soups.

COOKING KOSHER MEAT

Kosher meat is usually tough because the cuts eaten tend to contain a high proportion of muscle, the meat is not tenderized by being hung but must be butchered within 72 hours of slaughter, and because the salting of meat to remove blood produces a dry result.

Because of this, meat is generally cooked slowly by stewing, braising, pot-roasting and simmering until the meat is tender. These long, slow methods are also ideal for the Shabbat meal, which can be prepared and cooked ahead of time, then left in the oven to grow beautifully tender.

Above: Veal escalopes (US scallops) are often pounded to make the classic Viennese schnitzel.

When meat is cooked quickly, for instance kebabs, the meat is marinated first to tenderize it. Chopping or mincing (grinding) meat has a similar effect, which is why so many Jewish meat recipes are for meatballs, patties and meat loaves. These dishes also allow a modest amount of meat to be stretched.

Meatballs in Many Guises

Spiced or seasoned meatballs are popular throughout the Jewish world and come in many forms.

• Russian bitkis are made from minced (ground) beef, often with chopped onion, and may be fried, grilled (broiled) or simmered, often alongside a chicken for a Shabbat or other festive meal.

• Kotleta are flattened meatballs that are fried.

• Cylindrical Romanian mitetetlai are flavoured with garlic, often with parsley, and are fried or grilled (broiled) until brown.

• The Sephardi world has myriad meatballs: albondigas, boulettes, kefta or kofta, and yullikas. They are highly spiced and can be grilled (broiled), cooked over an open fire or simmered in sauces.

Traditional Flavourings

Each region favours certain flavourings. The Polish choose sweet-and-sour flavours; the Germans sweet and fruity; the Russians savoury, with onions; the Lithuanians peppery. Sephardim favour spices and vegetables. Moroccans add sweet, fruity flavours; Tunisians prefer sharp spices; Turkish Jews add tomatoes and fresh herbs such as dill; Persians prefer delicate flavours, with herbs, fruits and vegetables and beans.

Making Meatloaf

A traditional Ashkenazi dish, meatloaf is called klops. Serve hot or cold.

1 Preheat the oven to 180°C/350°F/Gas 4. In a bowl, combine 800g/1¾lb minced (ground) meat, 2 grated onions, 5 chopped garlic cloves, 1 shredded carrot, chopped parsley, 60ml/4 tbsp dried breadcrumbs, 45–60ml/3–4 tbsp tomato ketchup and 1 beaten egg.

2 Form the mixture into a loaf and place in a roasting pan. Spread 60ml/4 tbsp tomato ketchup over the surface, arrange 2 sliced tomatoes on top, then sprinkle over 2–3 sliced onions.

3 Cover the pan with foil and bake for 1 hour. Remove the foil, increase the temperature to 200°C/400°F/Gas 6 and remove some of the onions. Bake for a further 15 minutes, or until the meat is cooked and the onions are browned.

Making Calf's Foot Jelly

This light, richly flavoured aspic, known as petcha, is a traditional Ashkenazi dish. Serve as an appetizer with slices of hard-boiled egg.

1 Cut 4 cleaned calf's feet into pieces, and place in a large pan. Pour over cold water to cover. Bring to the boil, then simmer for 5 minutes. Drain and rinse the feet well in cold water.

2 Place the feet in a clean pan and add 500g/1¼lb veal shin, 1–2 halved onions, 1 halved carrot, 1 chopped celery stick, several sprigs of parsley, thyme and rosemary, 2 bay leaves, 8–10 garlic cloves, and 7.5ml/1½ tsp salt and 30ml/2 tbsp whole black peppercorns. Pour over enough cold water to cover.

3 Bring the mixture to the boil, then simmer for about 5 minutes, skimming off any scum that rises to the surface. Simmer for a further 4 hours, skimming the surface occasionally.

4 Remove the calf's feet from the pan with a slotted spoon and set aside. Strain the stock into a large bowl and stir in 30ml/2 tbsp lemon juice.

5 Remove the meat from the bones, cut into bitesize pieces and add to the stock. Chill until set, then serve.

Meats from the Deli Counter

Traditionally, Jewish delis sold either meat or dairy foods, never both. Meat delis always have a wonderful choice of cured meats and sausages – salt beef on rye, thin slices of salami, smoky pastrami or frankfurters and knockwurst with a generous helping of sauerkraut. There are cooked meats too, such as boiled brisket with a rich, brown gravy and boiled flanken, ready to eat with a little dab of hot mustard.

Right: Beef salami, salt beef and spicy pastrami are classic deli fare.

POULTRY

This is considered meat in the laws of Kashrut, and is therefore subject to all the same rules as regards slaughter and preparation. Any part of a permitted bird can be eaten.

CHICKEN

This is probably the most popular fowl for both Sephardim and Ashkenazim. Like beef and lamb, chicken was once reserved for the Shabbat or other festive meal. However, chicken was usually served more frequently as people often raised a few chickens of their own and could take them to the shochet when the time came.

Chicken is often first simmered in water or stock to make soup, then roasted for a main course. There is no more potent an image of Jewish cooking than a bowl of steaming hot chicken soup with noodles or dumplings. It has always been considered very nourishing. Moses Maimonides, the Jewish philosopher and doctor, touted its benefits in the 12th century, and in recent years, scientific studies have confirmed its value, proving the aptness of its nickname – Jewish penicillin. Chicken backs are rich with morsels of meat and are excellent for soup; as are the feet and wings.

Meatballs made from minced (ground) chicken were a favourite food of Persian and Turkish Jews, especially when simmered along with aubergine (eggplant). Iraqis were famous for their spiced chicken croquettes, which they introduced to India and Burma. Indian Jews cook marvellous chicken curries, substituting coconut milk for yogurt, which is not permitted with chicken. A favourite Sephardi dish, eaten on the streets of Jerusalem, consists of chicken giblets and livers, grilled (broiled) until brown and crisp, and eaten with pitta bread and a hot, spicy pepper sauce.

OTHER BIRDS

Turkey, duck, goose and farmed pigeon (US squab), quail and poussin are also eaten. In Morocco, it is traditional for bridal couples to be served pigeons cooked with sweet fruits on their wedding night, to grant them a sweet life together.

In the Sephardi tradition, birds were often stuffed with couscous, spicy meat, rice and dried fruit, or with herbs and milder spices such as cinnamon. The Sephardim also liked stewed poultry with quinces or pomegranates, or flavoured with tomatoes, (bell) peppers, chickpeas or olives.

The art of raising geese for foie gras was acquired by Jews in Ancient Egypt, and it is believed that it was they who introduced the delicacy to France. In the Ashkenazi tradition, poultry necks are often stuffed with a mixture of chopped liver or kishke (stuffed derma) stuffing to make a sausage known as a helzel.

Left: Chicken is used in an array of classic Jewish dishes from chicken soup to schnitzel.

SCHMALTZ AND GREBENES

Rendered chicken fat (schmaltz), and the crisp morsels of skin left over after the rendering (grebenes), are widely used in Jewish cooking. Schmaltz was long considered a symbol of abundance and there is a traditional Yiddish saying: "He's so lucky that even when he falls, he falls right into a schmaltz bucket!" Spread schmaltz on bread with onions or use it to flavour cholent or to make chopped liver.

Making Schmaltz and Grebenes

One chicken won't make very much schmaltz, so save the fat and skin from several chickens and chill or freeze until you have 450g/1lb.

1 Using a sharp knife, cut the fat and skin into small pieces. Place in a large, heavy pan and pour over water to cover. Bring to the boil and cook over a high heat until the water has evaporated.

2 Reduce the heat and add about 2½ chopped onions and 1–2 whole garlic cloves. Cook over a medium heat, removing the garlic when golden.

3 When all the fat has been rendered and the grebenes are crunchy, remove the grebenes with a slotted spoon.

FISH

Permitted fish are classified as pareve, so have no restrictions with regard to combining with other foods. Its versatility makes fish very important on the Jewish table. It may hold centre stage, as when a whole fish is served at Rosh Hashanah, but more often it is served as an appetizer or one of several dishes on a buffet table.

From the fresh fish counter, there is a wide choice. Sea bass, cod, sole and flounder, haddock, hake and mackerel are all popular sea fish, with perch, pike and trout among the best-loved of the freshwater varieties.

Some fish are thought of as being more Jewish than others. However, this apparent preference for certain fish has simply come about because of geography and traditional availability. Carp is a particular favourite among Ashkenazi Jews, as is pike. Carp was brought to Europe by Jews who encountered it in China when involved in the silk trade in the 15th century, while pike was introduced into the USA from Germany in the 19th century and grew in popularity as waves of Jewish immigrants arrived in the country.

Making Jellied Carp

This traditional, and delicious, dish of poached carp in jelly is a legacy of the Jews of Eastern Europe.

1 Cut 1kg/2¼lb prepared fresh carp into 8–10 slices. Heat 15ml/1 tbsp vegetable oil in a large pan. Add about 2½ chopped onions and sauté until golden brown.

2 Add 2–3 bay leaves, 1–2 parsley and thyme sprigs, 1–2 lemon slices and the carp to the pan and season well with salt and black pepper.

Above: Carp is one of the fish traditionally enjoyed by Ashkenazi Jews. It is used to make such classic dishes as gefilte fish and jellied carp.

3 Pour 450ml/¾ pint/scant 2 cups hot fish stock and 250ml/8fl oz/1 cup dry white wine into the pan. Bring to the boil, then simmer for 1 hour until the fish is tender. Cool slightly, then remove the carp and pack it into a mould.

4 Strain the stock into a large bowl. Dissolve 2 sachets kosher gelatine in 150ml/¼ pint/⅔ cup of the stock, then stir into the remaining stock. Pour over the fish and chill until firm. Serve with lemon wedges and horseradish.

Fish from the Deli Counter

No Ashkenazi celebration is complete without some kind of fish from the deli counter. A good deli will smell deliciously of smoked and cured fish. The art of preserving fish is very much a speciality of the Ashkenazi Jews. They perfected the technique so that stocks of fish could be laid down to last all year. Methods used included salting, brining, smoking and marinating.

In a good deli you will find silky smoked salmon (lox), its natural orange colour providing a contrast to the smoked whitefish in its shimmering gold skin. In addition there will be salt herring, smoked herring, pickled herring, herring in sour cream, herring in brine and herring salad. Carp, smoked and seasoned with paprika, is known as sable and is a rare treat. It is sold only in the most traditional delis. You will find also gefilte fish in the deli, either freshly made or in jars, the liquid jellied and flavoured sweetly in the Polish manner, or peppery, in the Russian or Lithuanian tradition.

Below: Spicy, piquant pickled herring rollmops and thinly sliced smoked salmon are perfect for a Shabbat brunch.

GRAINS, BEANS AND LENTILS

For Jews, grains, beans, peas and lentils have long been the staff of life and have fuelled generations. In many places, a certain type of grain or pulse (legume) actually helped to define the cuisine of the community. In Romania it was mamaliga, a corn meal porridge that resembles polenta; in North Africa it was couscous; and for many places in the East, the staple food was rice. In Russia, Poland and the Ukraine, kasha (buckwheat) was widely eaten. Pulses are added to cholent, hamim and dafina, the slow-cooked stews that are traditionally served for Shabbat.

KASHA

This nutty, earthy grain is the partially milled grain or groat of buckwheat. It is traditionally used in Ashkenazi cooking and is very evocative for Ashkenazim who grew up eating it.

Kasha is traditionally served with roasts and pot-roasts, bathed in gravy and meat juices, or may be used as a filling for knishes and dumplings. It can also be combined with onions, wild mushrooms and noodles. Kasha varnishkes, a classic Ashkenazi dish of kasha, butterfly-shaped noodles and onions, is traditionally eaten at the festival of Purim.

Making Kasha

The grains may be fine, medium or coarse. Kasha should be toasted before being cooked, to keep it from going mushy and give it a nutty flavour. It is often toasted with egg before being simmered, to keep the grains separate.

To toast kasha, heat in a heavy pan over a medium heat for a few minutes until the grains start to give off their aroma. Add stock, bring to the boil, reduce the heat and cover. Simmer gently for 10–20 minutes until tender.

To toast kasha with egg, combine about 250g/9oz/1¼ cups kasha in a bowl with 1 beaten egg. Add the mixture to a cold heavy pan. Stir well, then turn on the heat to medium-high. Stir constantly while the grains toast and the egg sets. When the grains look dry, add stock or water and cook the kasha as above.

MAMALIGA

This golden corn meal is widely used in Eastern Europe and is Romania's national dish. It resembles polenta and can be eaten either soft and porridge-like, or spread out on a tray and left to chill until firm, then sliced and fried or grilled (broiled). It is good hot or cold.

Mamaliga is eaten by everyone in Romania, whether Jewish or not. For breakfast, it is drizzled with honey or jam and served with sour cream; for lunch it is topped with cottage cheese or Brinza, a cheese similar to feta, and butter. It tastes great with roasted (bell) peppers and tomatoes, or for a meat meal, with a pot-roast and gravy, or grilled beef patties or sausages.

Making Mamaliga

The corn meal used for mamaliga, like that for polenta, may have small or large grains, so the cooking time will need to be adjusted accordingly. To make mamaliga for a dairy meal, stir in a few tablespoons of butter and about 450g/1lb/2 cups cottage cheese or Brinza and serve hot.

1 Put 300g/11oz/2¾ cups golden corn meal or polenta in a bowl with 15ml/1 tsp salt. Pour in about 250ml/8fl oz/1 cup cold water, stir well and leave to stand for a few minutes. Meanwhile, bring 900ml/1½ pints/3¾ cups water to the boil.

Left (clockwise from top left): Pareve grains such as barley, kasha (buckwheat) and bulgur wheat are important staples in both the Ashkenazi and Sephardi kitchens.

2 Gradually add the corn meal to the boiling water, stirring constantly. Cook over a low heat for 20–35 minutes, stirring, until all the water has been absorbed. If it sticks to the pan, add more water and stir vigorously.

Grilling Mamaliga

Pour the hot, freshly cooked corn meal on to a buttered or oiled sheet or platter and spread it out to a thickness of about 2.5–4cm/1–1½in. Leave to cool, then cut the mamaliga into fingers, brush with oil and grill (broil). Top with grated cheese, tomatoes or mushrooms.

BARLEY

This high-protein food is a good source of B vitamins. It is an indispensable ingredient in Eastern European dishes such as mushroom and barley soup, or barley with vegetables and butter (lima) beans. A small amount of meat is sometimes added.

BULGUR WHEAT

This is the partially milled grain of the whole wheat and is widely used in the Middle East. It comes in different sizes, from small and fine through to large. Bulgur wheat is sometimes eaten in place of couscous or rice, with savoury stews or soups.

COUSCOUS

This grain-like staple actually consists of tiny pellets of pasta, though it is usually categorized as a grain. It has always been very popular with the Jews of North Africa and, when they came to Israel, they brought it with them, in various different sizes. It is easy to

Right: Israeli couscous has much larger grains than regular couscous.

Right (clockwise from top right): Beans, split peas and lentils are rich in protein and can be added to stews to eke out a small amount of meat.

prepare and is usually steamed over a light and savoury spicy stew of vegetables, meats, fish or fruit. Many different types of couscous are available and they are cooked in different ways. Ordinary couscous is first moistened with cold water and left to plump up. It is then steamed over a stew. Fast-cooking couscous usually only needs to be combined with boiling water, then heated through or left to soak.

Israeli couscous, a pea-sized toasted pasta that has become a fashionable ingredient in Europe and America, is cooked in the same way as pasta. It gives a succulent result and is very good in soups and fish dishes.

RICE

This is widely eaten by Jews throughout the world. Chelou is a classic dish of the Persian Jews. As it cooks, the rice at the base of the pan is allowed to form a crisp crust (*tahdeeg*), which is then stirred into the tender rice, providing a tasty contrast of textures. Sometimes, thinly sliced potatoes are also added. Many Iranian Jewish specialities use chelou as their base, topping it with herby vegetable or meat stews. At Rosh Hashanah, Iranian Jews particularly favour rice. The many tiny grains of rice represent the many grains of happiness that are hoped for during the coming year.

CHICKPEAS

These are eaten in great quantities by Sephardi Jews, and Eastern European Jews serve them to celebrate a Brit Milah. They are milled into flour and used as a thickener by Indian and Middle Eastern Jews, and are soaked and ground to make falafel, which is considered by many to be Israel's national dish.

DRIED BEANS AND PEAS

Broad (fava) beans and black-eyed beans (peas) are very popular with the Sephardim. Broad beans are very ancient and have been found at pre-pottery Neolithic B levels in Jericho. Black-eyed beans originated in Ethiopia about four thousand years ago and were recorded in Judea about 1500. Both are eaten in soups and stews. Dried broad beans are cooked and eaten with garlic, olive oil, hard-boiled eggs and a little tahini.

LENTILS

All types of lentil are made into soup, from split red lentils, which cook quickly, to the superior tasting brown variety. Yellow and green split peas are also popular. In Genesis, the story is told of how Esau sold his birthright for a pottage of lentils.

VEGETABLES

Many vegetables have particular significance in celebrations to mark religious festivals. At Rosh Hashanah, pumpkin may be served; its golden colour signifying prosperity. Green vegetables will be on the table too, symbolizing renewal and happiness, while dried beans and peas signify abundance. Carrots for Rosh Hashanah are cooked in honey to signify a sweet new year. In contrast, at the Pesach Seder, bitter herbs are eaten as a reminder of the bitterness of slavery. At the same time, Ashkenazim eat broad (fava) beans, since this was what the Israelite slaves were fed during their captivity in Egypt. When Ashkenazim celebrate Chanukkah, they do so with potato latkes.

Seven different types of vegetable are used by North African Jews to make one of their specialities, a soup, which represents the seven days of Creation, with Shabbat being the seventh day.

Every year, the new season's produce is eagerly anticipated, and as each vegetable is tasted for the first time, it is customary to recite the Shehehayanu, a prayer of thanksgiving.

Below: Root vegetables such as carrots, turnips and beetroot (beets) are Ashkenazi staples.

THE ASHKENAZI TRADITION

Years of struggle and poverty, when Eastern European Jews were hounded from place to place, and taxed to the limit, made them increasingly inventive as to how they prepared vegetables. Carrots, cabbages, beetroot (beets), onions and turnips may have been dull and heavy but the Jews favoured their strong flavours. They frequently pickled vegetables to improve their taste, and to preserve them through the long winters. Sauerkraut, pickled cucumbers and borscht all date from this era.

When Ashkenazi Jews from Poland and Russia migrated south, they discovered a wealth of new vegetables. Peppers soon became popular, partly because they pickled well, and could be dried to make paprika. Potatoes were eaten with great gusto because they were so tasty and filling, and aubergines (eggplant), which had made their way to Romania from Spain and Italy, became widely used. Tomatoes were not widely accepted for some time, as their red colour was the same hue as blood and there was some question as to whether or not they were kosher – which may account for the Ashkenazi speciality, pickled green tomatoes.

Making Vegetable Eingemachts

Ashkenazim often made sweetmeats from vegetables. Eingemachts is a sweet preserve made from beetroot (beets), which is traditionally eaten at Pesach. It is usually eaten with a spoon along with a hot cup of tea.

1 Put 300g/11oz/scant 1½ cups granulated sugar and 250ml/8fl oz/ 1 cup honey in a large non-reactive pan and stir to combine. Stir in 20ml/4 tsp ground ginger and 120ml/4fl oz/½ cup water. Bring the mixture to the boil, then simmer, stirring occasionally, until the sugar has dissolved.

2 Peel 1.3kg/3lb boiled fresh beetroot, then grate or cut into very thin strips. Thinly slice 3 whole lemons and remove the seeds. Add the beetroot and lemons to the pan and bring to the boil, then lower the heat slightly and cook for 30–40 minutes, or until the mixture is very thick, shaking the pan occasionally.

3 Stir 90g/3½oz/scant 1 cup chopped blanched almonds into the beetroot mixture, then spoon into hot sterilized jars. Cool, then seal. Store in the refrigerator for 2–3 weeks.

Salad Vegetables

In the early days, raw vegetables and salads were not greatly appreciated by Ashkenazim raised in cold climates, where warming, filling stews were a necessity. However, radishes of several kinds were still enjoyed, along with raw turnips, cucumbers, raw onions and garlic. The young spring shoots of garlic were much prized, and were often eaten with dense black bread. Sometimes raw carrots were grated and eaten in salads, as were the young leaves of wild greens and herbs, although these were often cooked and eaten hot as well.

THE SEPHARDI TRADITION

The Jews of the Iberian Peninsula had a much greater variety of fresh vegetables available to them than their northern neighbours. They were among the first Europeans to encounter corn, (bell) peppers, tomatoes and green beans, which were introduced from the New World, and they embraced them with enthusiasm. Jewish merchants helped to popularize these new vegetables by introducing them to the more remote parts of Spain and then, after their expulsion in 1492, to the wider world.

Right: Colourful warm weather vegetables such as (bell) peppers, globe artichokes and aubergines (eggplant) form the basis of many Sephardi dishes.

Globe artichokes and pumpkins were reputedly brought to Italy by the Jews. So too were aubergines (eggplant), which were much valued for their meaty texture, particularly when meat itself was not available, or had to be omitted because of the presence of dairy foods.

Sephardi Jews have always been known for their love of vegetables. They add vegetables to stews, pilaffs and soups. Because they cook with olive oil, vegetable dishes are pareve so they may be served with meat or dairy.

They are cooked simply, then dressed with olive oil and lemon juice. Vegetables are also perfect partners for eggs. Sephardi specialities range from the North African turmeric-tinted potato omelette, a variation on tortilla, to the Sicilian spinach tortino and a Spanish-Syrian dish of aubergine with eggs and cheese. The repertoire also includes chakshouka, a delicious Arabian dish consisting of (bell) peppers, tomatoes and eggs.

From the Deli Counter

Potato salad, coleslaw, cucumber and onions, Russian salad, roasted peppers, Romanian aubergine (eggplant) salad and marinated mixed vegetables are just some of the tasty vegetable offerings that can be found in the deli. Sauerkraut is another deli staple, while dill pickles are the star attraction. American deli kosher dill pickles are not made with added sweetening or vinegar, just brine with spices and so much garlic that you can smell them down the street. More recently, specialities from Israel such as baba ghanoush have become popular.

Left: Tubs of coleslaw, dill pickles and potato salad are just a few of the delectable offerings found in the deli.

FRUITS, NUTS AND SEEDS

Since the Garden of Eden when Eve ate the proverbial apple, fruit has always been very important to the Jewish table. The first fruits of every season are the subject of specific blessings, with special affection being reserved for melons, figs, dates and grapes, because of their prominent place in the Bible. Nuts and seeds are also widely eaten, providing valuable protein and variety to many dishes.

FRUITS

All fresh fruits are considered kosher and, for some very strict Jews, it is the only food they will eat if they are not sure of the Kashrut of a kitchen. Fresh fruit can be eaten whole, uncut by treyf (not kosher) knives. There is no need for a plate or cooking pan, which might be treyf.

Israel is one of the world's leading fruit growers. Jaffa oranges, juicy grapefruit, kumquats and tiny lime- and lemonquats are grown for local consumption and export, alongside persimmons (Sharon fruit) from the Sharon valley and delicious avocados.

Below: Quinces, dates and figs are among the warm weather fruits of the Sephardi table.

Below: Apples, plums and cherries are fruits of the Ashkenazi table.

Traditions

At Sukkot a lulav (citron) is used for making the blessings over the Sukkah. At Rosh Hashanah, apples are dipped in honey, pomegranates are eaten to celebrate fertility and abundance, quinces are baked and preserved and challah often contains dried fruit.

Ashkenazim make charoset, the fruit and nut paste enjoyed at Pesach, from apples and walnuts, while Sephardim favour tropical fruits and dried fruits.

At Tu b'Shevat, Jews taste their way through a variety of orchard fruit, and at Chanukkah, apple sauce is served with potato latkes.

Regional Specialities

Sephardim, living in lush, warm climates, have always enjoyed a wide variety of fruits including figs, dates, melons and citrus fruits. Quinces are traditionally made into sweet preserves for Rosh Hashanah, stuffed for Sukkot, candied for Pesach, and added to meat stews at other times. Another speciality of the Sephardi Jews, particularly those from North Africa, are preserved lemons that have been pickled in brine. They are often added to savoury dishes such as spicy meat stews.

Fruit was not as easily available to the Ashkenazim and soft and deciduous fruits were a seasonal delight for them. Raspberries, gooseberries, currants, cherries, plums, pears and apples were enjoyed in many dishes from pancakes and pastries to fruit soups, cakes and compotes. Baked apples filled with brown sugar and cinnamon are one of the classics of the Ashkenazi kitchen.

Surplus harvest was often dried or preserved and enjoyed during the rest of the year when the fruits were out of season. Compotes made of dried fruit are still very popular in the Ashkenazi kitchen. Dried fruit is used in cakes and strudels and is often added to meat dishes. Raisins are often added to meatballs and pie fillings, and the classic tzimmes (a savoury meat or vegetable stew) is enriched with dried apricots and prunes.

Making Fruit Soup

Classic Ashkenazi fruit soup makes a refreshing start or end to a meal. Plums, cherries or red berries give a good result, but any fruit can be used.

1 Chop 1.3kg/3lb fruit and place in a large non-reactive pan. Add 1 litre/1¾ pints/4 cups water, 475ml/16fl oz/2 cups dry white or red wine and the juice of 1 lemon. Stir in a little sugar, honey and cinnamon. Bring to the boil, then simmer until the fruit is tender.

2 Mix 10ml/2 tsp arrowroot with 15ml/1 tbsp cold water. Stir into the soup; bring to the boil and cook, stirring constantly, until thickened.

3 Remove the pan from the heat, stir in a little more water or wine if the soup seems too thick, then stir in a dash of vanilla essence (extract). If using peaches, cherries or apricots, add almond essence instead. Cool, then chill. Serve with sour cream or yogurt.

VARIATION

To make kissel, purée the soup mixture, then press through a strainer into a bowl. Serve chilled, with a drizzle of cream.

NUTS AND SEEDS

These are pareve and enjoyed by both Ashkenazim and Sephardim. They may be added to sweet or savoury dishes as an ingredient or eaten on their own as a snack. Street stalls in Israeli cities sell toasted nuts and seeds, known as garinim, for nibbling.

Almonds are used in sweet and savoury dishes. Mandelbrot (hard almond cookies) are among the classic sweets of the Askenazi kitchen, whereas almond paste is a favourite filling used in the delicate filo pastries of North Africa and Mediterranean countries.

Coconut is used for making macaroons to serve at Pesach. In India, coconut milk is used to give meat curries a creamy quality without the need for yogurt or other dairy foods.

Pistachio nuts are enjoyed throughout the Middle East. Toasted and salted, they are a favourite snack. Unsalted pistachio nuts are crushed and layered into sweet desserts such as baklava, cake fillings and cookies.

Poppy seeds are particularly popular in the Ashkenazi kitchen. They are eaten in cakes such as the classic Russian mohn torte and sprinkled on top of breads such as bagels. Their flavour is intensified when they are roasted and ground to a paste, to be used as a filling for cakes and pastries.

Below: Almonds, sesame seeds and poppy seeds are widely used in Jewish cooking.

Treats from the Deli
The sweet aroma of baked apples welcomes visitors to the deli. Fruit compotes and jellies, and rice puddings studded with dried fruit are all available. Apricot leather – a paste of cooked apricots, dried in sheets or strips, and eaten as a confection or warmed with boiling water until it reverts to a thick paste – is also a deli speciality. Dates are coated with coconut or stuffed with nuts and sold in blocks. Delis with a large Middle Eastern clientele have jars of sweet preserves, ready to be spooned out and eaten with plain cake. Green walnuts, cherries, plums and kumquats are stewed in honey and sold in this way.

Sesame seeds can be purchased whole or hulled, raw or toasted. For optimum flavour, buy raw hulled seeds. Just before use, toast them in a heavy, ungreased pan until fragrant and golden. Toasted sesame seeds can be crushed to make halva or tahini, or simmered with honey or sugar to make sumsum, crisp confections that are sold as street food in Israel.

Walnuts are widely used in Ashkenazi cooking and are an essential ingredient in charoset.

HERBS, SPICES AND FLAVOURINGS

The Ashkenazim used the flavourings of Eastern Europe to create their robust and often piquant dishes, while the Sephardim used their own local flavourings to create a cuisine that is richly spiced and aromatic.

HERBS AND SPICES

A special place is reserved for herbs and spices in the rituals of the Jewish table. Both mild and bitter herbs are eaten at Pesach, while the sweet aroma of cinnamon, ginger, nutmeg and cloves is inhaled as part of the havdalah ceremony that signifies the end of Shabbat, the smell of the spices welcoming the week ahead.

Ashkenazim adopted the flavours of Eastern European cooking: young dill fronds, parsley, spring onions (scallions) and tender young garlic. Spices were

added to cakes and breads and occasionally meat dishes. A mixture of herbs and spices was used in pickled vegetables, meats and fish, contributing to their piquant flavours.

Countries with a strong German and Russian heritage introduced Jewish settlers to mustards of various kinds. In delis today you will find a large selection of mustards, such as wholegrain, smooth, sweet and herbed, ready to add their flavour to all manner of Ashkenazi dishes. In Hungary, Ashkenazi Jews encountered paprika, and soon embraced it, making their own versions of dishes dominated by this warm, yet subtle, spice, such as chicken paprikash and meat goulash.

In the same eclectic fashion, Jews embraced other flavours typical of the lands in which they lived: thyme and oregano from the Mediterranean region; cumin and coriander from India; cinnamon and harissa from North Africa and chillies from Mexico.

On the wondrous palette of Middle Eastern cooking, spice mixtures are the culinary colours. They add fragrance and flavour to whatever they touch. Middle Eastern spice blends are many and varied and may be dry ground mixtures or wet pastes made with fresh chillies, garlic and herbs. Spice blends taste much more intense if they are made from freshly roasted and ground spices.

Above (clockwise from top): Cumin and coriander seeds are favoured in the North African kitchen, while paprika is essential in Hungarian Jewish cooking.

Making Harissa

This hot, spicy paste is used extensively in Tunisian and other North African cooking. It is based on medium-sized chillies with a medium hot flavour. The blend is widely sold in jars, but it is easy to make your own.

1 Put 10–15 whole dried chillies in a pan with water to cover. Bring to the boil, then remove from the heat.

2 When the chillies are cool enough to handle, remove the stems, seeds and membrane, then pound to a purée with 10 garlic cloves, 5ml/1 tsp each of ground coriander, caraway and cumin in a mortar with a pestle. Add 2.5ml/½ tsp salt and about 15ml/1 tbsp extra virgin olive oil. Stir in enough cold water to make a thick paste.

> **Karpas and Moror**
>
> These are the herbs that feature at Pesach. Karpas is the mild herb eaten at the Seder meal. It might be leaves of young lettuce, as favoured in the Sephardi tradition, or parsley, as favoured by the Ashkenazim. Moror are the bitter herbs, eaten as a reminder of the tears shed by Hebrew slaves in Egypt. Grated horseradish is often used, or the bitter greens might be represented by chicory (Belgian endive) or watercress.

Right: Fresh dill is used extensively in Ashkenazi cooking and its aroma is redolent of many classic dishes from the Old Country.

Making Hawaij

This wonderfully fragrant mixture of spices comes from Yemen. It is delicious in stews, soups and sauces.

Place 30ml/2 tbsp black peppercorns and 15ml/1 tbsp caraway seeds in a spice grinder, or use a pestle and mortar. Add 10ml/2 tsp each of ground cumin and turmeric, 5ml/1 tsp cardamom seeds and several pinches of saffron threads. Process to a powder and keep in a tightly sealed jar in a cool, dark place.

Making Berbere

This Ethiopian spice mixture is based on hot chillies.

1 Mix 90g/3½oz paprika with 10ml/2 tsp cayenne pepper, the seeds from 20 cardamom pods, 2.5ml/½ tsp ground fenugreek seeds; 1.5ml/¼ tsp each of ground ginger and freshly grated nutmeg, and generous pinches of black pepper, cloves, ground cinnamon and allspice.

2 Lightly toast the mixture in a hot, ungreased pan for less than a minute. When cool, store in a tightly sealed jar.

Making Chermoula

This moist mixture of herbs, spices and aromatics comes from North Africa. It is mainly used as a marinade for fish but is also good with chicken, potatoes and other vegetables.

1 In a bowl, combine 75ml/5 tbsp extra virgin olive oil with 30ml/2 tbsp lemon juice, 4–5 crushed garlic cloves and 10ml/2 tsp ground cumin.

2 Stir 15ml/1 tbsp paprika, 1.5ml/¼ tsp ground ginger and 1 chopped fresh chilli or a pinch of chilli powder into the spice mixture.

3 Add 90ml/6 tbsp chopped fresh coriander (cilantro) leaves and a little flat leaf parsley or mint, if you like, to the bowl, season with salt and mix well or purée to a smooth paste.

Below (clockwise from top left): Rose water, honey and halek are widely used in both sweet and savoury dishes in the Sephardi kitchen.

FLAVOURINGS

There are a number of other flavouring ingredients that play an essential role in Jewish cooking.

Salt is not just used as a seasoning but also plays a role in ritual, especially in kashering. It is seen as a purifying agent and, in biblical times, it was sacrificed at the Temple in Jerusalem. In Morocco, Jews sprinkle salt on newborn babies, to ward off the evil eye. At the Pesach Seder, it is dissolved in water and used to represent the tears of Israelite slaves.

Sour salt (citric acid) is a great favourite in the Ashkenazi kitchen and is used instead of lemon or vinegar to add a sour taste to dishes such as borscht.

Honey has been much loved by Jews since the biblical description of Israel as a land flowing with milk and honey. It is used to represent the sweetness of the year to come at Rosh Hashanah and is also used in baking – most famously in lekach, the Ashkenazi honey cake eaten to celebrate a child's first day at school.

Rose water and orange flower water are fragrant essences used in sweet and savoury dishes. They are added to the syrups poured over sweet pastries, and to savoury tagines and couscous dishes.

Halek, also known as dibis, is a thick date syrup used to flavour sweet and savoury foods. It is readily available in jars, but you can easily make your own. Reconstitute dried dates in water, then boil in a little water until soft. Purée in a food processor, then strain into a clean pan and cook over a medium heat until thickened.

NOODLES, PANCAKES, DUMPLINGS AND SAVOURY PASTRIES

NOODLES

These were once the pride of the Ashkenazi kitchen and housewives were judged on their skills as home-makers (*balaboostas*) by how thin and delicate they could make their noodles. Noodles were cut into a variety of shapes, such as little squares (plaetschen) and small butterflies (varnishkes). Noodles were served in soup, tossed with sour cream or cheese, or layered with other ingredients such as fruit or cheeses and baked into delicious puddings known as kugels. Noodle dough could also be rolled thin and filled to make dumplings, such as the meat-filled kreplach; potato-, kasha- or cabbage-filled pierogi, or cheese- or fruit-filled varenikes.

Noodles were probably introduced to German Ashkenazi kitchens during the 14th century, via the Italian Jews. This was long before they reached the non-Jewish German kitchen during the 16th century. Pasta came to Poland at the same time, possibly through Central Asia, and the Yiddish word for noodles (*lokshen*) comes from the Polish word *lokszyn*. The sauces of the Polish Yiddish kitchen also showed a Central Asian slant. They were based on yogurt, sour cream and fresh cheeses, rather than the rich tomato sauces of Italian extraction. Sephardi cooking showed a more distinctive Italian or Spanish influence as evidenced in kelsonnes, dumplings filled with cheese and eaten at the festival of Shavuot, and calzonicchi, which are filled with spinach and enjoyed for Purim.

Left: Kreplach are meat-filled pasta dumplings that are often enjoyed in chicken soup.

Right: (clockwise from top) Lokshen, farfel, varnishkes and plaetschen are just a few of the classic noodles from the Ashkenazi kitchen.

Making Noodle Dough

Egg noodles are still made at home for special occasions. This is easy to do with a pasta-rolling machine, but they can also be rolled by hand on a well-floured surface with a large rolling pin.

1 Sift 225g/8oz/2 cups plain (all-purpose) flour and 2.5ml/½ tsp salt into a bowl, making a well in the centre.

2 Pour 2 lightly beaten eggs into the flour and mix with a fork, gradually incorporating the eggs into the flour. Continue to stir, using a wooden spoon, until well combined. Alternatively, place all the ingredients in a food processor fitted with the metal blade and mix to form a dough. If the dough is sticky, add a little more flour.

3 Tip the dough on to a floured board and knead until smooth and elastic. Place the dough in a plastic bag, seal and leave for at least 30 minutes.

4 If using a pasta-rolling machine, roll out walnut-size balls of the dough, then, one at a time, feed the dough into the largest opening of the rollers. Fold the flattened dough and repeat, reducing the roller opening until the dough is the desired thickness.

5 If rolling by hand, divide the dough into three equal pieces, then roll out each piece on a floured surface, until it is extremely thin.

Making Noodle Shapes

Lightly sprinkle the sheets of freshly rolled noodle dough with flour, then cut into the desired shape. To cook, drop the pasta into a large pan of boiling salted water and cook for 2–4 minutes.

To make lokshen (flat noodles), roll a sheet of noodle dough into a tight scroll. Using a heavy sharp knife cut the scroll of dough crossways into narrow or wide strips, as desired. Unroll the strips, boil and serve with sauce, in soup or baked with other ingredients in a kugel.

To make plaetschen (little squares), cut a sheet of noodle dough into 1cm/½in squares. Boil and serve in soup.

To make varnishkes (butterflies), cut a sheet of noodle dough into 2.5cm/1in squares. Pinch each square in the centre to form a bow tie or butterfly. Boil and serve in soup or with kasha.

To make farfel (pellets), grate kneaded, unrolled noodle dough through the large holes of a grater to form pellets. Boil and add to soups.

Making Mandlen

These crisp soup garnishes are made from noodle dough. They take their name from the Yiddish word for almond, a reference to their shape and colour.

1 Preheat the oven to 190°C/375°F/ Gas 5. Beat 1 egg with 15ml/1 tbsp vegetable oil. Add 2.5ml/½ tsp salt, then mix in about 115g/4oz/1 cup plain (all-purpose) flour until the dough holds together. Knead for 10 minutes. Cover and leave for 20 minutes.

2 Divide the dough into two to four pieces and form each into a rope, about 1cm/½in wide. Cut each one into 1cm/ ½in pieces and place on an oiled baking sheet. Bake for 35–40 minutes. Alternatively, deep-fry, until just golden.

PANCAKES

Since biblical times pancakes have been popular. In times of plenty, they were made from the finest ingredients and fried in lots of oil. When times were hard, they were made from whatever wild greens and grains could be found and fried in a drop or two of fat.

Pancakes are usually either very thin and filled or thick and crispy. Crêpe-like blintzes are filled with cheese, meat, fruit or vegetables and are often folded into parcels and fried until crisp. Thick, hearty latkes are best known as a treat eaten at Chanukkah, consisting of grated potatoes formed into cakes and fried until golden brown. They can also be enjoyed at any time of year and can be made from spinach, grated apples or a mixture of cottage cheese, matzo meal and eggs. Hearty grains such as kasha can also be used.

Chremslach are thick pancakes eaten at Pesach, made from egg, matzo meal and seasonings. They are good served with a generous spoonful of cooling sour cream or yogurt.

Ataif are Egyptian pancakes, raised with yeast, and served with a sweet syrup and dollops of rich clotted cream. Like other dairy-filled pancakes, they are enjoyed at Shavuot, the festival when dairy products are traditionally eaten in abundance.

Below: Melawah are pancake flat breads eaten by Yemenite Jews, often with chopped tomatoes and spicy zchug.

DUMPLINGS

Generations of Jewish cooks have delighted in dumplings, especially knaidlach made from matzo meal and egg. The word *knaidlach* comes from *knodel,* the German for dumpling. Knaidlach are as much a part of Yiddish cooking as dumplings are of Eastern European peasant food. Because they were made with matzo, knaidlach were eaten for Shabbat and other festivals, especially Pesach, when bread is forbidden.

Different Jewish communities added their distinctive flavour to knaidlach: some added chopped herbs such as parsley or chives, or aromatics such as garlic or grated onions. Others stuffed them with a bit of meat, while the Viennese Jews added a pinch of dried ginger to the mixture. Knaidlach can be big balls or small two-bite wonders and can be tender and light or solid and heavy. Cold cooked knaidlach can be cut into bitesize pieces and browned with eggs and mushrooms.

Sephardi dumplings are made from noodles stuffed with meat, then floated in soup. Alternatively, they may be made from rice as is the case with the Middle Eastern kobeba, meat-filled dumplings much like kibbeh, using rice instead of bulgur wheat.

Below: Knaidlach are the Ashkenazi matzo balls that are traditionally served in chicken soup.

Above: Kibbeh are classic Sephardi dumplings made of pounded bulgur wheat and minced (ground) meat.

SAVOURY PASTRIES

These are popular with both Ashkenazi and Sephardi Jews. Whenever there was something special to celebrate, the women of the community would gather and spend days preparing pastries.

Ashkenazi Pastries

Classic Ashkenazi pastries include knishes (half-moon shaped turnovers), strudels (wafer-thin pastry rolled around fillings) and piroshkis (small pies). They may be filled with kasha, mashed potatoes and onions, minced (ground) meat, browned cabbage, chopped egg and sometimes smoked salmon. The dough can be shortcrust (unsweetened) pastry or puff pastry, but there are also yeast doughs and even doughs made from mashed potato. The pastries may then be baked or fried.

Sephardi Pastries

The Sephardim have a virtually endless number of pastries, with many different types of pastry and filling. They are made in an array of shapes, including cigars, half moons, triangles, rectangles, squares, circles and even cones and round balls, and may be baked or deep-fried in oil.

Borekas are eaten wherever Turkish, Greek and Balkan Jews have settled. These pastries are flaky on the outside, with tender layers within. Borekas can be tiny one-bite pastries or made as tapadas – big trays to cut into individual portions. They are usually filled with aubergine (eggplant) and tomatoes, cheese, spinach or meat.

Iraqi Jews traditionally fill their pastries with mashed chickpeas and chicken. Also from Iraq are sambusaks, crisp shortcrust pastries filled with egg and cheese or vegetables or meat. They are usually topped with sesame seeds or a blend of za'atar herbs containing thyme. Italian Jews fill their savoury burricche with a variety of mixtures, from tuna to liver, and even make sweet pastries with pumpkin and glacé (candied) fruit. Pumpkin pastries are a speciality of Bukharan Jews.

The Spanish and Portuguese Jews have empanadas, crisp little pastries filled with meats, fish or vegetables.

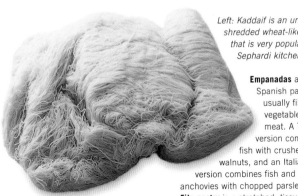

Left: Kaddaif is an unusual, shredded wheat-like pastry that is very popular in the Sephardi kitchen.

Empanadas are crisp Spanish pastries, usually filled with vegetables and meat. A Turkish version combines fish with crushed walnuts, and an Italian version combines fish and anchovies with chopped parsley.

Filo pastry is a stretched, tissue-paper-thin pastry made from flour and water with a touch of oil for elasticity. It is brushed with oil or butter and rolled around a filling before being fried or baked. Filo pastry is bought ready-made as it requires great skill and years of practice to make it successfully.

Kaddaif is a shredded pastry that looks much like shredded wheat. It is also known as konafa. It is usually used for sweet pastries, which are stuffed with nuts, baked, then soaked in syrup. Like filo dough kaddaif is usually purchased ready-made, as preparing it requires great skill and dexterity.

Khatchapuri are yeast dough pastries filled with cheese from Georgia in Russia. Goat's cheese mixed with Gruyère is a very popular filling, sometimes with a little chopped coriander (cilantro).

Bulemas and rodanchas are made by rolling sheets of filo pastry around a filling, then coiling the rolls on a baking sheet. The dough is very delicate and needs to be handled with great care when being rolled around the filling.

Lamahjeen are small pizza-like pastries made with tomato, tamarind and meat; a speciality of the Jews of Aleppo.

A mina is a Sephardi pie made using soaked matzo as a kind of pastry. They are usually served for Pesach when bread and pastry are forbidden. Minas are often served in Mexico, where they are likened to tortillas.

Warka is similar to filo pastry. It is made by quickly tapping a ball of dough on to a hot surface, leaving behind a thin, wispy layer of tissue-thin pastry, which rapidly becomes crisp.

Bishak are Bukharan baked pastries made from pizza dough filled with sweet and peppery cooked pumpkin.

Brik are crisp, fried filo pastries, filled with tuna or meat, and a raw egg.

Borekas, sambusak, pasteles and buricche are crisp shortcrust pastries filled with cheese, aubergine (eggplant), and tomato or meat.

Boyos are little pies made from dough layered with mature (sharp) cheese, fried onions and vegetables.

From the Deli Counter

Sweet noodle kugels may be sold cut into big squares and sold as dessert. Potato latkes can be bought all year round, but are particularly popular at Chanukkah. Blintzes are often sold in delis – hot, freshly cooked blintzes will often be on the menu for brunch, while take-away blintzes can be reheated at home.

Many delis sell hot or cold knishes or piroshkis, ready to eat on the spot or to take home for later, filled with anything from kasha to meat to spinach. Filo pastries can also be found – spinach and cheese is a particularly popular filling. Fresh filo pastry and kaddaif are also sold in delis, especially those with a Middle Eastern influence.

Right: Piroshkis and knishes from the Ashkenazi tradition are particular favourites on the deli counter.

BREADS

The world over, bread is very important to the Jews. A meal without bread is not a meal, according to the dictates of the Jewish religion. Without bread, there can be no hamotzi (blessing over the bread that signals the start of a meal) and neither can there be the Birkat Hamazon (grace that usually concludes a meal). A meal without bread can only really be considered a snack.

ASHKENAZI BREADS

In Jewish bakeries, it is usual for the breads to be pareve – made without butter or milk so that they can be eaten with either meat or dairy foods. There is challah, rye bread, pumpernickel, bagels, Kaiser rolls and onion rolls – the variety is astonishing and, if you happen to have wandered into an ethnic Jewish bakery, you may well encounter some wonderful regional specialities as well as the usual fare.

All ethnic groups have a wide variety of breads, both for everyday use and special occasions. When the Ukrainian Ashkenazim emigrated to America, they brought with them sourdough loaves of seeded rye, dark pumpernickel and onion-crusted

rolls. Walking into one of their bakeries is a joy: the smells of baking – yeast, flour, a whiff of something sweet – mingling with the scent of the wood-burning stove.

Bagels are an Ashkenazi classic that travelled from the shtetlach and ghettos of Eastern Europe and are now enjoyed all over the world. They lend themselves to any number of different fillings and are satisfyingly chewy.

Bagels are usually made in bakeries that bake nothing else, because the procedure for making them is a special one. The dough rings are first briefly poached in huge vats of water before being glazed and baked. This technique creates the distinctive dense, chewy texture that has made bagels so popular. To walk past a bagel bakery without venturing in is just about impossible. The alluring smell inevitably entices you in, and you'll want to get yourself a nice hot bagel before setting off once more.

Right: Pumpernickel, from the Ashkenazi tradition, is dark and sour with a crisp crust.

Above: Challah is the traditional bread of Shabbat and festivals and may be braided, round or shaped like a ladder, depending on the festival.

Sweet challah is the traditional Shabbat and festival bread of the Ashkenazi Jews. The dough is made with eggs and vegetable oil, which gives it a soft texture, similar to that of brioche, and is lightly sweetened with honey or sugar.

The loaves are usually braided, made with three, six or even twelve strands of dough. During Rosh Hashanah challah may be shaped into a round or crown, in honour of the Rosh Hashanah blessing: "The whole world will crown thee." On the eve of Yom Kippur, the challah is shaped like a ladder, raised arms or wings, representing prayers rising heavenwards.

Boulkas are small, individual challah rolls, shaped into rounds, braids or spirals and dusted with poppy seeds, that are frequently served at weddings.

Left: Pitta bread came from the Middle East but is now enjoyed by Ashkenazim, Europeans and Americans alike.

MATZO

This is unleavened bread, made for Pesach, when leavened bread may not be eaten. The flat, brittle sheets are served at the table, and are also ground to make a meal that is transformed into cakes, biscuits and cookies. Matzo meal can be fine or coarse, while matzo farfel is lightly crushed matzo.

For Pesach, matzo is prepared under special guidelines and the packaging is always marked "Kosher for Pesach". Observant Jews often eat schmurah matzo as they are handmade to a very high specification.

SEPHARDI BREADS

These vary greatly and are very different from the breads of the Ashkenazim. Some are risen; some are flat; some, such as melawah, are slightly puffed and fried to a crisp. One Sephardi bread most of us are familiar with is pitta, a flat bread favoured by Jews and Arabs alike, and by many other Middle Easterners as well. Iraqi pitta bread is a particularly large flat bread, which resembles an enormous, thick pancake.

Breads that are especially made for the Sabbath include mouna, lahuhua and kubaneh. A coiled bread from Yemen, kubaneh, is made from a rich yeast dough. It is prepared before the Sabbath begins, then steamed in a very low oven overnight.

Israel produces a marvellous array of breads, from the simple everyday loaf, which is crusty on the outside and beautifully tender inside, to large flat breads, which are used for wrapping around vegetables or meat.

Right: Jews eat unleavened matzos at Pesach but they are also enjoyed during the rest of the year.

From the Deli

Oy what sandwiches! A true Jewish deli sandwich is a thing of mammoth proportions. Piles of thinly sliced salami, billows of roasted turkey, peppery pastrami, corned or salt beef, bologna or steamed knockwurst are just some of the possible ingredients, and most likely there will be a combination of several of the above, at least 350g/12oz per sandwich, layered between thick slices of fresh, crusty, tender bread.

A sandwich from one of the legendary New York delis, such as the Carnegie or Second Avenue Deli, Katz's, the Stage Deli or Juniors will be far too thick for the average eater

to get his or her mouth around. It will be necessary to wrap up at least half for later – much, much later.

The Reuben, assumed by many to be a Jewish classic, is not actually kosher. Slices of seeded rye bread contain both corned beef and Swiss cheese – a forbidden combination.

Choosing the filling for your deli sandwich is taxing enough, but it can be even more difficult to decide precisely which bread to have. One thing everyone agrees on, however, is that a sandwich from the deli is never served on sliced white.

Left: A bagel spread generously with cream cheese and topped with wafer-thin slices of smoked salmon is the quintessential Jewish deli snack.

CAKES, PASTRIES AND SWEETMEATS

For Jews, whenever there is something to celebrate, be it a festival or a family occasion, cakes and other sweet treats are very much in evidence. Precisely what is on the table will largely depend on whether the hosts come from the Ashkenazi or Sephardi traditions, as these take very different approaches when it comes to baking.

During Pesach, the kosher kitchens of both Ashkenazim and Sephardim undergo a transformation. At this time, all food must be free of leaven, and eggs are used as the main raising agent instead. The result is a wealth of featherlight sponge cakes, often made with matzo meal and ground nuts.

THE ASHKENAZI BAKERY

Visit an Eastern European bakery and you will find the shelves filled with a wide selection of delectable pastries, sweetmeats, crisp cookies, cakes and crunchy rolls. No one could possibly walk through without having a "little something". A cup of coffee is never just a cup of coffee: you must have a Danish – a pastry filled with jam and topped with icing (frosting) – or a rugelach, or maybe a mohn cake or strudel, or perhaps an apfelkuchen. The choice and variety is seemingly endless.

Cakes of all kinds are baked in the Ashkenazi kitchen. Kuchen is closer to a sweet fruit bread than a cake. It is made from a moderately sweet dough, filled with fresh or dried fruit. Honey cake, also known as lekach, is

eaten for Rosh Hashanah and Shabbat, while almond cakes, plava and other leaven-free cakes are classic Pesach specialities. For Purim, the traditional treat is hamantashen, triangular cakes filled with seeds and fruit that resemble the three-cornered hat of Haman.

Cookies and sweet biscuits include croissant-shaped rugelach, almond mandelbrot and plain kichel. None of these are very sweet, and they make the perfect accompaniment to tea or coffee. Teiglach, from Lithuania, are rich with honey, so a little goes a very long way.

Candied orange peel known as pomerantzen is a great favourite of all Jews, not just because it tastes so good, but because the peel that might otherwise have been discarded is transformed into an irresistible treat.

Jews love pastries, the most well known being strudel, which originated as a hefty pastry roll filled with

Left: Pomerantzen (candied citrus peel) is a classic Ashkenazi sweetmeat.

Below: Sweet, fruit-filled strudel made with paper-thin pastry is one of the glories of the Eastern European Jews.

vegetables or fruit. It was the Turks, invading Hungary in 1526, who introduced the thin multi-layered pastry that we now know as strudel dough.

Strudel is eaten for many festivals: with cabbage for Simchat Torah; with dried fruit for Tu b'Shevat; with crushed poppy-seed paste for Purim and with cheese for Shavuot. Fruit versions are filled with sliced apple, cherries or rhubarb, alone or with dried fruit.

Left: (left to right) Traditional Ashkenazi rugelach and mandelbrot cookies are delicious with a glass of hot tea.

Making Strudel Pastry

This is very like filo pastry, which can be bought ready-made and makes a good substitute for strudel pastry.

1 In a large bowl, beat 250g/9oz/ generous 1 cup butter with 30ml/2 tbsp sugar and 250ml/8fl oz/1 cup sour cream or softened vanilla ice cream. Add 2.5ml/½ tsp vanilla or almond essence (extract) and 1.5ml/¼ tsp salt, then stir in 500g/1¼lb/5 cups plain (all-purpose) flour. Mix to a soft dough.

2 Divide the dough into three pieces, wrap separately and chill overnight. (It may be frozen for up to 3 months.)

3 If necessary, thaw the dough. Place one piece on a floured board. Flatten it lightly, then, very gently, pull it out with your hands, pulling each side in turn until it is almost paper thin. It is now ready to fill and bake. (Take extra care if you have long fingernails.)

VARIATION
To make a non-dairy pastry, substitute 120ml/4fl oz/½ cup each of sweet wine and vegetable oil for the butter and sour cream or ice cream.

SEPHARDI SWEET SPECIALITIES

These are Mediterranean in their origin. Every Sephardi community produces a wealth of moist, succulent almond and walnut cakes. Often a local dish was adapted for Jewish holidays – Greek Jews eat crisp, fried loukomades for Chanukkah, Israelis eat jam-filled sufganiot (doughnuts) and Tunisians enjoy syrup-soaked cakes for Purim.

During Pesach when leaven (and flour) may not be used, nuts are used to give body to desserts. Almond cakes and coconut macaroons are particularly popular, as is sesame seed halva.

Syrup-soaked filo pastries, such as nut-filled baklava, are popular among Sephardi Jews. Other pastries include kaddaif, a shredded pastry drenched in syrup, and felabis, deep-fried, pretzel-like pastries filled with syrup.

The Deli Cheesecake
This is one of the most popular desserts in the deli cabinet. It is often associated with Ashkenazim from Germany, who were famous for their fresh cheeses. It is eaten at Shavuot, reflecting the legend of the Jews who, on returning to camp after receiving the Torah, found that their milk had turned sour and had to sweeten it with honey.

Cheesecakes can be flavoured and topped with many ingredients from fruit to chocolate and it is not unusual to find delis offering upwards of 30 different types.

Below: Cheesecake is a deli classic, though purists argue that only a simple white cheesecake can be considered the real thing.

Making Simple Baklava

The secret to perfect baklava is to pour very cold syrup over a hot pastry, or very hot syrup over a cold pastry.

1 Preheat the oven to 200°C/400°F/ Gas 6. Layer six sheets of filo pastry in a shallow dish, brushing each layer with melted butter or oil.

2 Sprinkle chopped nuts on top of the pastry, to a depth of 1cm/½in. Sprinkle generously with sugar and cinnamon. Top with six more layers of buttered or oiled filo, then, using a sharp knife, cut the top layer of pastry into triangles.

3 Bake the baklava for 30 minutes until golden. Remove from the oven and pour over hattar, or a light syrup flavoured with orange flower water or rose water.

APPETIZERS

*From chopped liver to herring to aubergine (eggplant) salads, Jewish appetizers
are adored by Jews and non-Jews alike. Festive meals from the weekly Shabbat
to annual holidays almost always include a selection of appetizers. In fact,
what often distinguishes an everyday meal from a celebration is
the serving of these delicacies. Ashkenazim and Sephardim alike
have a wealth of tasty morsels to sharpen the appetite
and enhance the sociability of the occasion.*

CHOPPED CHICKEN LIVERS

IT IS SAID THAT REMNANTS OF THIS CLASSIC DISH WERE FOUND IN SITES DATING BACK TO 1400 AND HAVE BEEN EATEN IN VARIOUS GUISES EVER SINCE. THE FRENCH LOVE OF LIVER-ENRICHED PÂTÉS IS AN INHERITANCE FROM THE JEWS OF ALSACE, STRASBOURG AND THE EAST WHO BROUGHT THEIR SPECIALITIES WITH THEM WHEN THEY FLED, AND SHARED THEM AT THEIR TABLE.

SERVES FOUR TO SIX

INGREDIENTS
  250g/9oz chicken livers
  2–3 onions, chopped, plus ½ onion,
    finely chopped or grated
  60ml/4 tbsp rendered chicken fat or
    vegetable oil
  3–4 spring onions (scallions),
    thinly sliced
  2–3 hard-boiled eggs, roughly
    chopped or diced
  10ml/2 tsp mayonnaise or firm
    chicken fat (optional)
  5–10ml/1–2 tsp chopped fresh dill
  salt and ground black pepper
  chopped fresh dill or parsley, to garnish
  lettuce, thin slices of crisp matzos
    or rye bread and a few slices of dill
    pickle, to serve

1 Grill (broil) the chicken livers lightly to bring the blood out on to the surface and render them kosher. Rinse, place in a pan, cover with cold water and bring to the boil. Reduce the heat, simmer gently for 5–10 minutes, then leave to cool in the water. (The livers should be firm but not dry and brown.)

2 In a large pan, fry the onions in the fat or oil over a medium heat, sprinkling with salt and pepper, until well browned and beginning to crisp, and caramelized around the edges.

3 To hand-chop the livers, use a round-bladed knife and chop the livers finely. Place in a bowl and mix in the fried onions and oil. If using a food processor, put the livers and fried onions in the bowl of the food processor with just enough oil from the fried onions to process to a thick paste.

4 In a bowl, combine the livers with the finely chopped or grated onion, the spring onions, hard-boiled eggs, mayonnaise or chicken fat, if using, and chopped dill. Cover and chill the livers for an hour or so until firm.

5 When ready to serve, mound the chopped livers on plates and garnish with the chopped fresh dill or parsley. Serve with lettuce, matzos or rye bread and dill pickles.

VARIATIONS
• To make traditional chopped liver, use calf's liver in place of the chicken livers.
• For a Hungarian accent, use a combination of onions: lots of very, very browned chopped onions, a little raw chopped onion and a handful of thinly sliced spring onions.

VEGETARIAN CHOPPED LIVER

THERE ARE MANY VEGETARIAN VERSIONS OF THE CLASSIC CHOPPED LIVER, WHICH ARE EXTREMELY POPULAR IN THE ASHKENAZI KITCHEN. THIS MIXTURE OF BROWNED ONIONS, CHOPPED VEGETABLES, HARD-BOILED EGG AND WALNUTS LOOKS AND TASTES SURPRISINGLY LIKE CHOPPED LIVER BUT IS LIGHTER AND FRESHER. IT IS PAREVE SO MAY BE ENJOYED WITH BOTH MEAT AND DAIRY MEALS.

SERVES SIX

INGREDIENTS

   90ml/6 tbsp vegetable oil, plus extra
     if necessary
   3 onions, chopped
   175–200g/6–7oz/1½–scant 1¾ cups
     frozen or fresh shelled peas
   115–150g/4–5oz/1 cup green beans,
     roughly chopped
   15 walnuts, shelled (30 halves)
   3 hard-boiled eggs, shelled
   salt and ground black pepper
   slices of rye bread or crisp matzos,
     to serve

1 Heat the oil in a pan, add the onions and fry until softened and lightly browned. Add the peas and beans and season with salt and pepper to taste. Continue to cook until the beans and peas are tender and the beans are no longer bright green.

2 Put the vegetables in a food processor, add the walnuts and eggs and process until the mixture forms a thick paste. Taste for seasoning and, if the mixture seems a bit dry, add a little more oil and mix in thoroughly. Serve with slices of rye bread or matzos.

BULGARIAN CUCUMBER AND WALNUT APPETIZER

MANY BULGARIAN JEWS CAME TO ISRAEL BRINGING WITH THEM THEIR PASSION FOR EXCELLENT YOGURTS, WHICH ARE OFTEN USED IN SALADS. WHEN MADE WITH VERY THICK GREEK YOGURT, THIS APPETIZER CAN BE SHAPED INTO BALLS AND SERVED ON SALAD LEAVES.

SERVES SIX

INGREDIENTS

1 large cucumber
3–5 garlic cloves, finely chopped
250ml/8fl oz/1 cup sour cream or
  120ml/4fl oz/½ cup Greek
  (US strained plain) yogurt mixed
  with 120ml/4fl oz/½ cup double
  (heavy) cream
250ml/8fl oz/1 cup yogurt, preferably
  thick Greek or Bulgarian sheep's
  milk yogurt
2–3 large pinches of dried dill or
  30–45ml/2–3 tbsp chopped
  fresh dill
45–60ml/3–4 tbsp chopped walnuts
salt
sprig of dill, to garnish (optional)

1 Do not peel the cucumber. Using a sharp knife, dice it finely and place in a large mixing bowl.

2 Add the garlic, sour cream or yogurt and cream, yogurt, dill and salt. Mix together, then cover and chill.

3 To serve, pile the mixture into a bowl and sprinkle with walnuts. Garnish with dill, if you like.

MINT AND PARSLEY TAHINI SALAD

TAHINI IS A CREAMY SESAME SEED PASTE THAT IS WIDELY USED IN ISRAELI AND ARAB COOKING. ITS ALMOST DRY FLAVOUR COMBINES WONDERFULLY WITH FRESH HERBS AND SUBTLE SPICES IN THIS SALAD TO MAKE A LIGHT AND REFRESHING APPETIZER.

SERVES FOUR TO SIX

INGREDIENTS

115g/4oz/½ cup tahini
3 garlic cloves, chopped
½ bunch (about 20g/¾oz) fresh
  mint, chopped
½ bunch (about 20g/¾oz) fresh
  coriander (cilantro), chopped
½ bunch (about 20g/¾oz) fresh flat
  leaf parsley, chopped
juice of ½ lemon, or to taste
pinch of ground cumin
pinch of ground turmeric
pinch of ground cardamom seeds
cayenne pepper, to taste
salt
extra virgin olive oil, warmed pitta
  bread, olives and raw vegetables,
  to serve

1 Combine the tahini with the chopped garlic, fresh herbs and lemon juice in a bowl. Taste and add a little more lemon juice, if you like. Stir in a little water if the mixture seems too dense and thick. Alternatively, place the ingredients in a food processor. Process briefly, then stir in a little water if required.

2 Stir in the cumin, turmeric and cardamom to taste, then season with salt and cayenne pepper.

3 To serve, spoon into a shallow bowl or on to plates and drizzle with olive oil. Serve with warmed pitta bread, olives and raw vegetables.

BABA GHANOUSH

THE QUANTITIES IN THIS RICHLY FLAVOURED MIDDLE EASTERN AUBERGINE DIP CAN BE VARIED
ACCORDING TO TASTE. ADJUST THE AMOUNT OF AUBERGINE, GARLIC AND LEMON JUICE DEPENDING
ON HOW CREAMY, GARLICKY OR TART YOU WANT THE DIP TO BE.

2 Put the aubergine(s) in a plastic bag or in a bowl and seal tightly. Leave to cool for 30–60 minutes.

3 Peel off the blackened skin from the aubergine(s), reserving the juices. Chop the aubergine flesh, either by hand for a textured result or in a food processor for a smooth purée. Put the aubergine in a bowl and stir in the reserved juices.

4 Add the garlic and tahini to the aubergine and stir until smooth and well combined. Stir in the lemon juice, which will thicken the mixture. If the mixture becomes too thick, add 15–30ml/1–2 tbsp water or more lemon juice, if you like. Season with cumin and salt to taste.

SERVES TWO TO FOUR

INGREDIENTS
1 large or 2 medium
  aubergines (eggplant)
2–4 garlic cloves, chopped, to taste
90–150ml/6–10 tbsp tahini
juice of 1 lemon, or to taste
1.5ml/¼ tsp ground cumin, or
  to taste
salt
extra virgin olive oil, for drizzling
coriander (cilantro) leaves, hot
  pepper sauce and a few olives
  and/or pickled cucumbers and
  (bell) peppers, to garnish
pitta bread or chunks of crusty
  French bread, to serve

1 Place the aubergine(s) directly over the flame of a gas stove or on the coals of a barbecue. Turn the aubergine(s) fairly frequently until deflated and the skin is evenly charred. Remove from the heat with a pair of tongs.

5 Spoon the mixture into a serving bowl. Drizzle with olive oil and garnish with fresh coriander leaves, hot pepper sauce and olives and/or pickled cucumbers and peppers. Serve at room temperature with pitta bread or chunks of crusty French bread.

SMOKY AUBERGINE AND PEPPER SALAD

COOKING THE AUBERGINES WHOLE, OVER AN OPEN FLAME, GIVES THEM A DISTINCTIVE SMOKY FLAVOUR AND AROMA, AS WELL AS TENDER, CREAMY FLESH. THE SUBTLE FLAVOUR OF THE ROASTED AUBERGINE CONTRASTS WONDERFULLY WITH THE STRONG, SWEET FLAVOUR OF THE PEPPERS.

SERVES FOUR TO SIX

INGREDIENTS
   2 aubergines (eggplant)
   2 red (bell) peppers
   3–5 garlic cloves, chopped, or more
      to taste
   2.5ml/½ tsp ground cumin
   juice of ½–1 lemon, to taste
   2.5ml/½ tsp sherry or wine vinegar
   45–60ml/3–4 tbsp extra virgin
      olive oil
   1–2 shakes of cayenne pepper,
      Tabasco or other hot pepper sauce
   coarse sea salt
   chopped fresh coriander (cilantro),
      to garnish
   pitta bread wedges or thinly sliced
      French bread or ciabatta bread,
      sesame seed crackers and cucumber
      slices, to serve

1 Place the aubergines and peppers directly over a medium-low gas flame or on the coals of a barbecue. Turn the vegetables frequently until deflated and the skins are evenly charred.

2 Put the aubergines and peppers in a plastic bag or in a bowl and seal tightly. Leave to cool for 30–40 minutes.

3 Peel the vegetables, reserving the juices, and roughly chop the flesh. Put the flesh in a bowl and add the juices, garlic, cumin, lemon juice, vinegar, olive oil, hot pepper seasoning and salt. Mix well to combine. Turn the mixture into a serving bowl and garnish with coriander. Serve with bread, sesame seed crackers and cucumber slices.

SUN-DRIED TOMATO AND PEPPER SALAD

THIS APPETIZER IS VERY NEW-WAVE TEL AVIV – MODERN MEDITERRANEAN FOOD THAT BRIDGES THE GAP BETWEEN MIDDLE EASTERN AND CONTEMPORARY EUROPEAN STYLES. IT IS GOOD SERVED WITH SLICES OF VERY FRESH BREAD OR WEDGES OF FLAT BREAD.

SERVES FOUR TO SIX

INGREDIENTS

10–15 sun-dried tomatoes
60–75ml/4–5 tbsp olive oil
3 yellow (bell) peppers, cut into
  bitesize pieces
6 garlic cloves, chopped
400g/14oz can chopped tomatoes
5ml/1 tsp fresh thyme leaves, or
  more to taste
large pinch of sugar
15ml/1 tbsp balsamic vinegar
2–3 capers, rinsed and drained
15ml/1 tbsp chopped fresh parsley,
  or more to taste
salt and ground black pepper
fresh thyme, to garnish (optional)

1 Put the sun-dried tomatoes in a bowl and pour over boiling water to cover. Leave to stand for at least 30 minutes until plumped up and juicy, then drain and cut the tomatoes into halves or quarters.

2 Heat the olive oil in a pan, add the peppers and cook for 5–7 minutes until lightly browned but not too soft.

3 Add half the garlic, the tomatoes, thyme and sugar and cook over a high heat, stirring occasionally, until the mixture is reduced to a thick paste. Season with salt and pepper to taste. Stir in the sun-dried tomatoes, balsamic vinegar, capers and the remaining chopped garlic. Leave to cool to room temperature.

4 Serve the salad at room temperature, heaped into a serving bowl and sprinkled with chopped fresh parsley. Garnish with thyme, if you like.

LIBYAN SPICY PUMPKIN DIP

THIS SPICY SEPHARDI DIP FROM A LIBYAN-JEWISH RESTAURANT IN JAFFA IS THE COLOUR OF THE SEASON AND IS GREAT TO SERVE AT A THANKSGIVING FEAST. IT CAN BE STORED FOR AT LEAST A WEEK IN THE REFRIGERATOR. SERVE IT WITH CHUNKS OF BREAD OR RAW VEGETABLES TO DIP INTO IT.

SERVES SIX TO EIGHT

INGREDIENTS

45–60ml/3–4 tbsp olive oil
1 onion, finely chopped
5–8 garlic cloves, roughly chopped
675g/1½lb pumpkin, peeled
   and diced
5–10ml/1–2 tsp ground cumin
5ml/1 tsp paprika
1.5–2.5ml/¼–½ tsp ground ginger
1.5–2.5ml/¼–½ tsp curry powder
75g/3oz chopped canned tomatoes or
   diced fresh tomatoes and 15–30ml/
   1–2 tbsp tomato purée (paste)
½–1 red jalapeño or serrano chilli,
   chopped, or cayenne pepper,
   to taste
pinch of sugar, if necessary
juice of ½ lemon, or to taste
salt
30ml/2 tbsp chopped fresh coriander
   (cilantro) leaves, to garnish

1 Heat the oil in a frying pan, add the onion and half the garlic and fry until softened. Add the pumpkin, then cover and cook for about 10 minutes, or until half-tender.

2 Add the spices to the pan and cook for 1–2 minutes. Stir in the tomatoes, chilli, sugar and salt and cook over a medium-high heat until the liquid has evaporated.

3 When the pumpkin is tender, mash to a coarse purée. Add the remaining garlic and taste for seasoning, then stir in the lemon juice to taste. Serve at room temperature, sprinkled with the chopped fresh coriander.

VARIATION
Use butternut squash, or any other winter squash, in place of the pumpkin.

MUHAMMARA

*THIS THICK, ROASTED RED PEPPER AND WALNUT PURÉE IS BELOVED ON THE SEPHARDI TABLE,
ESPECIALLY IN SYRIA. SERVE IT AS A DIP WITH SPEARS OF COS OR ROMAINE LETTUCE, WEDGES
OF PITTA BREAD, CHUNKS OF TOMATO AND SLICES OF MOZZARELLA CHEESE.*

SERVES FOUR

INGREDIENTS

1½ slices Granary (whole-wheat)
 bread, day-old or toasted
3 red (bell) peppers, roasted, skinned
 and chopped
2 very mild chillies, roasted, skinned
 and chopped
115g/4oz/1 cup walnut pieces
3–4 garlic cloves, chopped
15–30ml/1–2 tbsp balsamic vinegar
 or pomegranate molasses
juice of ½ lemon
2.5–5ml/½–1 tsp ground cumin
2.5ml/½ tsp sugar, or to taste
105ml/7 tbsp extra virgin olive oil
salt

1 Break the Granary bread into small
pieces and place in a food processor
or blender with all the remaining
ingredients except the extra virgin olive
oil. Blend together until the ingredients
are finely chopped.

2 With the motor running, slowly drizzle
the extra virgin olive oil into the food
processor or blender and process until
the mixture forms a smooth paste.
Tip the muhammara into a serving dish.
Serve at room temperature.

HUMMUS

THIS CLASSIC MIDDLE EASTERN DISH IS MADE FROM COOKED CHICKPEAS, GROUND TO A PASTE AND FLAVOURED WITH GARLIC, LEMON JUICE, TAHINI, OLIVE OIL AND CUMIN. IT IS DELICIOUS SERVED WITH WEDGES OF TOASTED PITTA BREAD OR CRUDITÉS.

SERVES FOUR TO SIX

INGREDIENTS
    400g/14oz can chickpeas, drained
    60ml/4 tbsp tahini
    2–3 garlic cloves, chopped
    juice of ½–1 lemon
    cayenne pepper
    small pinch to 1.5ml/¼ tsp ground
      cumin, or more to taste
    salt and ground black pepper

VARIATION
Process 2 roasted red (bell) peppers with the chickpeas, then continue as above. Serve sprinkled with lightly toasted pine nuts and paprika mixed with olive oil.

1 Using a potato masher or food processor, coarsely mash the chickpeas. If you prefer a smoother purée, process them in a food processor or blender until smooth.

2 Mix the tahini into the chickpeas, then stir in the garlic, lemon juice, cayenne, cumin and salt and pepper to taste. If needed, add a little water. Serve at room temperature.

BRIK À L'OEUF

THESE PASTRIES ARE SOLD IN THE MARKETPLACES OF ISRAEL. MEN BALANCING FULL TRAYS OF BRIKS WILL NEGOTIATE THE CROWDS IN A BID TO SELL THEIR CRISPY PASTRIES BEFORE THE MARKET CLOSES FOR THE LONG AFTERNOON SIESTA. TRADITIONALLY, BRIKS ARE MADE WITH A THIN PASTRY CALLED WARKA BUT FILO PASTRY MAKES AN EXCELLENT ALTERNATIVE.

2 Preheat the oven to 200°C/400°F/ Gas 6. Heat the oil in a pan until it browns a cube of bread in 30 seconds.

3 Working quickly, break an egg into a small bowl or cup, then carefully tip it into the corner of the pastry sheet with the onion. Quickly fold over the pastry to form a triangle and enclose the egg completely.

4 Carefully slide the parcel into the oil and fry until golden brown. (The egg inside should be lightly cooked and still soft.)

5 Remove the brik from the pan with a slotted spoon, drain on kitchen paper, then transfer to a baking sheet. Make three more pastries in the same way.

6 Bake the pastries for 5 minutes, or until crisp and golden brown. Do not overcook as the egg yolk must be served runny. Serve immediately, accompanied by hot sauce for dipping or drizzling over.

MAKES FOUR

INGREDIENTS
1 onion, finely chopped
30–45ml/2–3 tbsp chopped
  fresh parsley or coriander
  (cilantro), or a mixture
  of both
a pinch of chopped fresh
  chilli (optional)
4 filo pastry sheets
90–115g/3½–4oz can tuna,
  well drained
vegetable oil, for deep-frying
4 eggs
hot sauce, such as zchug, harissa
  or Tabasco, to serve

1 In a bowl, combine the onion, herbs and chilli, if using. Lay a sheet of pastry on some baking parchment. Put one-quarter of the onion mixture at one corner, then add one-quarter of the tuna.

REBECCHINE <u>DE</u> JERUSALEMME

THESE STUFFED POLENTA FRITTERS COME FROM THE JEWISH COMMUNITY OF ITALY. POLENTA, COOKED TO A THICK CONSISTENCY AND POURED OUT TO COOL INTO A FIRM BREAD-LIKE MIXTURE, IS THE "BREAD" OF THESE TINY FRIED SANDWICHES. ANCHOVIES ARE THE TRADITIONAL FILLING BUT HERE A LITTLE TOMATO, ROSEMARY AND CHEESE HAVE BEEN USED. PORCINI MUSHROOMS ALSO MAKE A GOOD FILLING.

SERVES SIX

INGREDIENTS

250g/9oz/1½ cups polenta
30–45ml/2–3 tbsp tomato
   purée (paste)
30–45ml/2–3 tbsp diced ripe fresh or
   canned chopped tomatoes
30ml/2 tbsp chopped fresh rosemary
30–45 ml/2–3 tbsp freshly grated
   Parmesan or pecorino cheese
130g/4½oz mozzarella, Gorgonzola
   or fontina cheese, finely chopped
half vegetable and half olive oil,
   for frying
1–2 eggs, lightly beaten
plain (all-purpose) flour, for dusting
salt
diced red (bell) pepper, shredded
   lettuce and rosemary sprigs, to garnish

1 In a large pan, combine the polenta with 250ml/8fl oz/1 cup cold water and stir. Add 750ml/1¼ pints/3 cups boiling water and cook, stirring constantly, for about 30 minutes until the mixture is very thick and no longer grainy. If the mixture is thick but still not cooked through, stir in a little more boiling water and simmer until soft. Season.

2 Pour the mixture into an oiled baking dish, forming a layer about 1cm/½in thick. Lightly cover the polenta, then chill.

3 Using a 6–7.5cm/2½–3in plain pastry (cookie) cutter or the rim of a glass, cut the polenta into rounds.

4 In a small bowl, combine the tomato purée with the diced tomatoes. Spread a little of the mixture on the soft, moist side of a polenta round, sprinkle with rosemary and a little of the grated and chopped cheeses, then top with another round of polenta, the moist soft side against the filling. Press the edges together to help seal the sandwiches. Fill the remaining polenta rounds in the same way.

5 Heat the oil in a wide, deep frying pan, to a depth of about 5cm/2in until it is hot enough to brown a cube of bread in 30 seconds.

6 Dip a sandwich into the beaten egg, then coat in the flour. Gently lower it into the hot oil and fry for 4–5 minutes, turning once. Drain on kitchen paper. Cook the remaining polenta sandwiches in the same way. Serve warm, garnished with pepper, lettuce and rosemary.

COOK'S TIPS
• If the polenta is too thin the fritters will fall apart; if too thick they will be heavy.
• Do not use instant polenta as the sandwiches will fall apart on cooking.
• The fritters can be cooked ahead of time and reheated in the oven at 200°C/ 400°F/Gas 6 for 5–10 minutes.

MUSHROOM CAVIAR ON GARLIC-RUBBED RYE TOASTS

MIXTURES OF FINELY CHOPPED VEGETABLES, SERVED WITH FRESH BREAD OR TOAST, ARE VERY POPULAR IN THE JEWISH KITCHEN. THE NAME CAVIAR SIMPLY REFERS TO THE DARK COLOUR AND RICH TEXTURE, RATHER THAN THE ACTUAL CONTENT, OF THE DISH.

SERVES FOUR

INGREDIENTS

10–15g/¼–½oz dried porcini or
  other well-flavoured dried mushrooms
120ml/4fl oz/½ cup water
45ml/3 tbsp olive or vegetable oil
450g/1lb mushrooms, roughly chopped
5–10 shallots, chopped
5 garlic cloves, 4 chopped and
  1 whole
30ml/2 tbsp port
juice of ¼ lemon, or to taste
12–16 slices cocktail rye bread or
  2 ordinary slices, cut in halves,
  quarters or fingers
salt
2–3 spring onions (scallions), thinly
  shredded and/or 15ml/1 tbsp
  chopped fresh parsley and
  1 roughly chopped hard-boiled egg,
  or sour cream, to garnish

1 Break up the dried mushrooms, put in a bowl and soak in the water for about 30 minutes.

2 Heat the oil in a pan, add the fresh mushrooms, shallots and chopped garlic and fry until browned. Season with salt. Add the soaked mushrooms and water and cook until all the liquid has evaporated. Add the port and lemon juice.

3 Continue cooking until the port and lemon juice have evaporated and the mixture is brown and dry.

4 Put the mixture in a food processor or blender and process briefly until a chunky paste is formed.

5 Toast the rye bread until golden on both sides, then rub with the whole garlic clove. Spoon the mushroom caviar into dishes and serve with the toast, or top each piece of garlic toast with the mushroom mixture and heat gently under the grill (broiler). Serve garnished with the spring onions, parsley, hard-boiled egg, or sour cream.

COOK'S TIP
Depending on the size and strength of the shallots, you may wish to vary the quantity according to your own taste.

HERRING SALAD <u>WITH</u> BEETROOT AND SOUR CREAM

THIS SALAD, SERVED WITH BLACK PUMPERNICKEL BREAD, IS THE QUINTESSENTIAL SHABBAT MORNING DISH AFTER SERVICES. SERVE IT WITH COLD BOILED POTATOES AND ALLOW YOUR GUESTS TO CUT THEM UP AND ADD TO THE SALAD AS THEY LIKE.

SERVES EIGHT

INGREDIENTS

1 large tangy cooking apple
500g/1¼lb matjes herrings
  (schmaltz herrings), drained and
  cut into slices
2 small pickled cucumbers, diced
10ml/2 tsp caster (superfine) sugar,
  or to taste
10ml/2 tsp cider vinegar or white
  wine vinegar
300ml/½ pint/1¼ cups sour cream
2 cooked beetroot (beets), diced
lettuce, to serve
sprigs of fresh dill and chopped
  onion or onion rings, to garnish

1 Peel, core and dice the apple. Put in a bowl, add the herrings, cucumbers, sugar and cider or white wine vinegar and mix together. Add the sour cream and mix well to combine.

2 Add the beetroot to the herring mixture and chill in the refrigerator. Serve the salad on a bed of lettuce leaves, garnished with fresh dill and chopped onion or onion rings.

SOUPS

Throughout Jewish history, soups have provided sustenance in times of scarcity and deprivation. Clear, golden chicken soup is perhaps the most famous, but warming, stew-like soups made of root vegetables, and light summer soups based on sorrel and beetroot are evocative of the shtetl life of the Ashkenazim, and the spicy soups of the Yemenite Jews are reminiscent of the exotic lands settled by the Sephardim.

HUNGARIAN CHERRY SOUP

SOUPS MADE FROM SEASONAL FRUITS ARE A FAVOURITE CENTRAL EUROPEAN TREAT, AND CHERRY SOUP IS ONE OF THE GLORIES OF THE HUNGARIAN TABLE. IT IS OFTEN SERVED AT THE START OF A DAIRY MEAL, SUCH AS AT THE FESTIVAL OF SHAVUOT WHEN DAIRY FOODS ARE TRADITIONALLY FEASTED UPON, AND IS DELICIOUS SERVED WITH AN EXTRA SPOONFUL OR TWO OF SOUR CREAM.

SERVES SIX

INGREDIENTS

1kg/2¼lb fresh, frozen or canned sour cherries, such as Morello or Montmorency, pitted
250ml/8fl oz/1 cup water
175–250g/6–9oz/about 1 cup sugar, to taste
1–2 cinnamon sticks, each about 5cm/2in long
750ml/1¼ pints/3 cups dry red wine
5ml/1 tsp almond essence (extract), or to taste
250ml/8fl oz/1 cup single (light) cream
250ml/8fl oz/1 cup sour cream or crème fraîche

1 Put the pitted cherries, water, sugar, cinnamon and wine in a large pan. Bring to the boil, reduce the heat and simmer for 20–30 minutes until the cherries are tender. Remove from the heat and add the almond essence.

2 In a bowl, stir a few tablespoons of single cream into the sour cream or crème fraîche to thin it down, then stir in the rest until the mixture is smooth. Stir the mixture into the cherry soup, then chill until ready to serve.

SWEET AND SOUR CABBAGE, BEETROOT AND TOMATO BORSCHT

THERE ARE MANY VARIATIONS OF THIS CLASSIC ASHKENAZI SOUP, WHICH MAY BE SERVED HOT OR COLD. THIS VERSION INCLUDES PLENTIFUL AMOUNTS OF CABBAGE, TOMATOES AND POTATOES.

SERVES SIX

INGREDIENTS

1 onion, chopped
1 carrot, chopped
4–6 raw or vacuum-packed (cooked, not pickled) beetroot (beets), 3–4 diced and 1–2 coarsely grated
400g/14oz can tomatoes
4–6 new potatoes, cut into bitesize pieces
1 small white cabbage, thinly sliced
1 litre/1¾ pints/4 cups vegetable stock
45ml/3 tbsp sugar
30–45ml/2–3 tbsp white wine, cider vinegar or sour salt (citric acid)
45ml/3 tbsp chopped fresh dill, plus extra to garnish
salt and ground black pepper
sour cream, to garnish
buttered rye bread, to serve

1 Put the onion, carrot, diced beetroot, tomatoes, potatoes, cabbage and stock in a large pan. Bring to the boil, reduce the heat and simmer for 30 minutes, or until the potatoes are tender.

VARIATION
To make meat borscht, place 1kg/2¼lb chopped beef in a large pan. Pour over water to cover and crumble in 1 beef stock (bouillon) cube. Bring to the boil, then reduce the heat and simmer until tender. Skim any fat from the surface, then add the vegetables and proceed as above. For Kashrut, omit the sour cream and serve with unbuttered rye bread.

2 Add the grated beetroot, sugar and wine, vinegar or sour salt to the soup and cook for 10 minutes. Taste for a good sweet-sour balance and add more sugar and/or vinegar if necessary. Season.

3 Stir the chopped dill into the soup and ladle into warmed bowls immediately. Garnish each bowl with a generous spoonful of sour cream and more dill and serve with buttered rye bread.

CHICKEN SOUP WITH KNAIDLACH

A BOWL OF CHICKEN SOUP CAN HEAL THE SOUL AS WELL AS THE BODY, AS ANYONE WHO HAS EVER SUFFERED FROM FLU AND BEEN COMFORTED, OR SUFFERED GRIEF AND BEEN CONSOLED, WILL KNOW. THIS IS WHY THIS WARMING SOUP IS OFTEN KNOWN AS THE JEWISH ANTIBIOTIC.

SERVES SIX TO EIGHT

INGREDIENTS
1–1.5kg/2¼–3¼lb chicken, cut
   into portions
2–3 onions
3–4 litres/5–7 pints/12–16 cups water
3–5 carrots, thickly sliced
3–5 celery sticks, thickly sliced
1 small parsnip, cut in half
30–45ml/2–3 tbsp roughly chopped
   fresh parsley
30–45ml/2–3 tbsp chopped fresh dill
1–2 pinches ground turmeric
2 chicken stock (bouillon) cubes
2 garlic cloves, finely chopped
   (optional)
salt and ground black pepper
For the knaidlach
175g/6oz/¾ cup medium matzo meal
2 eggs, lightly beaten
45ml/3 tbsp vegetable oil or rendered
   chicken fat
1 garlic clove, finely chopped (optional)
30ml/2 tbsp chopped fresh parsley,
   plus extra to garnish
½ onion, finely grated
1–2 pinches of chicken stock
   (bouillon) cube or powder (optional)
about 90ml/6 tbsp water
salt and ground black pepper

1 Put the chicken pieces in a very large pan. Keeping them whole, cut a large cross in the stem end of each onion and add to the pan with the water, carrots, celery, parsnip, parsley, half the fresh dill, the turmeric, and salt and black pepper.

2 Cover the pan and bring to the boil, then immediately lower the heat to a simmer. Skim and discard the scum that surfaces to the top. (Scum will continue to form but it is only the first scum that rises that will detract from the clarity and flavour of the soup.)

3 Add the crumbled stock cubes and simmer for 2–3 hours. When the soup is flavourful, skim off the fat. Alternatively, chill the soup and remove the layer of solid fat that forms.

4 To make the knaidlach, in a large bowl combine the matzo meal with the eggs, oil or fat, chopped garlic, if using, parsley, onion, salt and pepper. Add only a little chicken stock cube or powder, if using, as these are salty. Add the water and mix together until the mixture is of the consistency of a thick, soft paste.

5 Cover the matzo batter and chill for 30 minutes, during which time the mixture will become firm.

6 Bring a pan of water to the boil and have a bowl of water next to the stove. Dip two tablespoons into the water, then take a spoonful of the matzo batter. With wet hands, roll it into a ball, then slip it into the boiling water and reduce the heat so that the water simmers. Continue with the remaining matzo batter, working relatively quickly, then cover the pan and cook for 15–20 minutes.

7 Remove the knaidlach from the pan with a slotted spoon and transfer to a plate for about 20 minutes to firm up.

8 To serve, reheat the soup, adding the remaining dill and the garlic, if using. Put two to three knaidlach in each bowl, pour over the hot soup and garnish.

VARIATIONS
• Instead of knaidlach, the soup can be served over rice, noodles or kreplach.
• To make lighter knaidlach, separate the eggs and add the yolks to the matzo mixture. Whisk the whites until stiff, then fold into the mixture.

TOMATO SOUP WITH ISRAELI COUSCOUS

ISRAELI COUSCOUS IS A TOASTED, ROUND PASTA, WHICH IS MUCH LARGER THAN REGULAR COUSCOUS.
IT MAKES A WONDERFUL ADDITION TO THIS WARM AND COMFORTING SOUP. IF YOU LIKE YOUR SOUP
REALLY GARLICKY, ADD AN EXTRA CLOVE OF CHOPPED GARLIC JUST BEFORE SERVING.

SERVES FOUR TO SIX

INGREDIENTS
    30ml/2 tbsp olive oil
    1 onion, chopped
    1–2 carrots, diced
    400g/14oz can chopped tomatoes
    6 garlic cloves, roughly chopped
    1.5 litres/2½ pints/6¼ cups
        vegetable or chicken stock
    200–250g/7–9oz/1–1½ cups
        Israeli couscous
    2–3 mint sprigs, chopped, or several
        pinches of dried mint
    1.5ml/¼ tsp ground cumin
    ¼ bunch fresh coriander (cilantro),
        or about 5 sprigs, chopped
    cayenne pepper, to taste
    salt and ground black pepper

1 Heat the oil in a large pan, add the onion and carrots and cook gently for about 10 minutes until softened. Add the tomatoes, half the garlic, stock, couscous, mint, ground cumin, coriander, and cayenne pepper, salt and pepper to taste.

2 Bring the soup to the boil, add the remaining chopped garlic, then reduce the heat slightly and simmer gently for 7–10 minutes, stirring occassionally, or until the couscous is just tender. Serve piping hot, ladled into individual serving bowls.

LUBIYA

THIS DELICIOUS SEPHARDI ISRAELI SOUP, OF BLACK-EYED BEANS AND TURMERIC-TINTED TOMATO BROTH, IS FLAVOURED WITH TANGY LEMON AND SPECKLED WITH CHOPPED FRESH CORIANDER. IT IS IDEAL FOR SERVING AT PARTIES — SIMPLY MULTIPLY THE QUANTITIES AS REQUIRED.

SERVES FOUR

INGREDIENTS

175g/6oz/1 cup black-eyed
  beans (peas)
15ml/1 tbsp olive oil
2 onions, chopped
4 garlic cloves, chopped
1 medium-hot or 2–3 mild fresh
  chillies, chopped
5ml/1 tsp ground cumin
5ml/1 tsp ground turmeric
250g/9oz fresh or canned
  tomatoes, diced
600ml/1 pint/2½ cups chicken,
  beef or vegetable stock
25g/1oz fresh coriander (cilantro)
  leaves, roughly chopped
juice of ½ lemon
pitta bread, to serve

1 Put the beans in a pan, cover with cold water, bring to the boil, then cook for 5 minutes. Remove from the heat, cover and leave to stand for 2 hours. Drain the beans, return to the pan, cover with fresh cold water, then simmer for 35–40 minutes, or until the beans are tender. Drain and set aside.

2 Heat the oil in a pan, add the onions, garlic and chilli and cook for 5 minutes, or until the onion is soft. Stir in the cumin, turmeric, tomatoes, stock, half the coriander and the beans and simmer for 20–30 minutes. Stir in the lemon juice and remaining coriander and serve at once with pitta bread.

A POTAGE OF LENTILS

THIS SOUP IS SOMETIMES KNOWN AS ESAU'S SOUP AND MAY BE SERVED AS PART OF A MEAL FOR SHABBAT OR AS A MEZE THE NEXT DAY. RED LENTILS AND VEGETABLES ARE COOKED AND PURÉED, THEN SHARPENED WITH LOTS OF LEMON JUICE.

SERVES FOUR

INGREDIENTS
45ml/3 tbsp olive oil
1 onion, chopped
2 celery sticks, chopped
1–2 carrots, sliced
8 garlic cloves, chopped
1 potato, peeled and diced
250g/9oz/generous 1 cup red lentils
1 litre/1¾ pints/4 cups
  vegetable stock
2 bay leaves
1–2 lemons, halved
2.5ml/½ tsp ground cumin, or
  to taste
cayenne pepper or Tabasco sauce,
  to taste
salt and ground black pepper
lemon slices and chopped
  fresh flat leaf parsley leaves,
  to serve

1 Heat the oil in a large pan. Add the onion and cook for about 5 minutes, or until softened. Stir in the celery, carrots, half the garlic and all the potato. Cook for a few minutes until beginning to soften.

2 Add the lentils and stock to the pan and bring to the boil. Reduce the heat, cover and simmer for about 30 minutes, until the potato and lentils are tender.

3 Add the bay leaves, remaining garlic and half the lemons to the pan and cook the soup for a further 10 minutes. Remove the bay leaves. Squeeze the juice from the remaining lemons, then stir into the soup, to taste.

4 Pour the soup into a food processor or blender and process until smooth. (You may need to do this in batches.) Tip the soup back into the pan, stir in the cumin, cayenne pepper or Tabasco sauce, and season with salt and pepper.

5 Ladle the soup into bowls and top each portion with lemon slices and a sprinkling of chopped fresh flat leaf parsley.

VARIATION
On a hot day, serve this soup cold, with even more lemon juice.

RUSSIAN SPINACH AND ROOT VEGETABLE SOUP WITH DILL

THIS IS A TYPICAL RUSSIAN SOUP, TRADITIONALLY PREPARED WHEN THE FIRST VEGETABLES OF SPRINGTIME APPEAR. EARTHY ROOT VEGETABLES, COOKED WITH FRESH SPINACH LEAVES, ARE ENLIVENED WITH A TART, FRESH TOPPING OF DILL, LEMON AND SOUR CREAM.

SERVES FOUR TO SIX

INGREDIENTS
    1 small turnip, cut into chunks
    2 carrots, sliced or diced
    1 small parsnip, cut into large dice
    1 potato, peeled and diced
    1 onion, chopped or cut into chunks
    1 garlic clove, finely chopped
    ¼ celeriac bulb, diced
    1 litre/1¾ pints/4 cups vegetable or
      chicken stock
    200g/7oz spinach, washed and
      roughly chopped
    1 small bunch fresh dill, chopped
    salt and ground black pepper
For the garnish
    2 hard-boiled eggs, sliced
    1 lemon, cut into slices
    250ml/8fl oz/1 cup sour cream
    30ml/2 tbsp fresh parsley and dill

1 Put the turnip, carrots, parsnip, potato, onion, garlic, celeriac and stock into a large pan. Bring to the boil, then simmer for 25–30 minutes, or until the vegetables are very tender.

COOK'S TIP
For the best results, use a really good quality vegetable stock.

2 Add the spinach to the pan and cook for a further 5 minutes, or until the spinach is tender but still green and leafy. Season with salt and pepper.

3 Stir the dill into the soup, then ladle into bowls and serve garnished with egg, lemon, sour cream and a sprinkling of parsley and dill.

FRAGRANT BEETROOT AND VEGETABLE SOUP WITH SPICED LAMB KUBBEH

THE JEWISH COMMUNITY FROM COCHIN IN INDIA IS SCATTERED NOW BUT THEY ARE STILL FAMOUS FOR THEIR CUISINE. THIS TANGY SOUP IS SERVED WITH DUMPLINGS MADE OF BRIGHT YELLOW PASTA WRAPPED AROUND A SPICY LAMB FILLING AND A DOLLOP OF FRAGRANT GREEN HERB PASTE.

SERVES SIX TO EIGHT

INGREDIENTS
    15ml/1 tbsp vegetable oil
    ½ onion, finely chopped
    6 garlic cloves
    1 carrot, diced
    1 courgette (zucchini), diced
    ½ celery stick, diced (optional)
    4–5 cardamom pods
    2.5ml/½ tsp curry powder
    4 vacuum-packed beetroot (beets)
        (cooked not pickled), finely diced
        and juice reserved
    1 litre/1¾ pints/4 cups
        vegetable stock
    400g/14oz can chopped tomatoes
    45–60ml/3–4 tbsp chopped fresh
        coriander (cilantro) leaves
    2 bay leaves
    15ml/1 tbsp sugar
    salt and ground black pepper
    15–30ml/1–2 tbsp white wine
        vinegar, to serve
For the kubbeh
    2 large pinches of saffron threads
    15ml/1 tbsp hot water
    15ml/1 tbsp vegetable oil
    1 large onion, chopped
    250g/9oz lean minced (ground) lamb
    5ml/1 tsp vinegar
    ½ bunch fresh mint, chopped
    115g/4oz/1 cup plain (all-purpose) flour
    2–3 pinches of salt
    2.5–5ml/½–1 tsp ground turmeric
    45–60ml/3–4 tbsp cold water
For the ginger and coriander paste
    4 garlic cloves, chopped
    15–25ml/1–1½ tbsp chopped
        fresh root ginger
    ½–4 fresh mild chillies
    ½ large bunch fresh coriander
        (cilantro)
    30ml/2 tbsp white wine vinegar
    extra virgin olive oil

COOK'S TIP
Serve any leftover paste with meatballs or spread on sandwiches.

1 To make the paste, put the garlic, ginger and chillies in a food processor and process. Add the coriander, vinegar, oil and salt and process to a purée. Set aside.

2 To make the kubbeh filling, place the saffron and hot water in a small bowl and leave to infuse (steep). Meanwhile, heat the oil in a pan and fry the onion until softened. Put the onion and saffron water in a food processor and blend. Add the lamb, season and blend. Add the vinegar and mint, then chill.

3 To make the kubbeh dough, put the flour, salt and ground turmeric in a food processor, then gradually add the water, processing until it forms a sticky dough. Knead on a floured surface for 5 minutes, wrap in a plastic bag and leave to stand for 30 minutes.

4 Divide the dough into 10–15 pieces. Roll each into a ball, then, using a pasta machine, roll into very thin rounds.

5 Lay the rounds on a well-floured surface. Place a spoonful of filling in the middle of each. Dampen the edges of the dough, then bring them together and seal. Set aside on a floured surface.

6 To make the soup, heat the oil in a pan, add the onion and fry for about 10 minutes, or until softened but not browned. Add half the garlic, the carrot, courgette, celery, if using, cardamom pods and curry powder, and cook for 2–3 minutes.

7 Add three of the diced beetroot, the stock, tomatoes, coriander, bay leaves and sugar to the pan. Bring to the boil, then reduce the heat and simmer for about 20 minutes.

8 Add the remaining beetroot, beetroot juice and garlic to the soup. Season with salt and pepper to taste and set aside until ready to serve.

9 To serve, reheat the soup and poach the dumplings in a large pan of salted boiling water for about 4 minutes. Using a slotted spoon, remove the dumplings from the water as they are cooked and place on a plate to keep warm.

10 Ladle the soup into bowls, adding a dash of vinegar to each bowl, then add two or three dumplings and a small spoonful of the ginger and coriander paste to each. Serve immediately.

OLD COUNTRY MUSHROOM, BEAN AND BARLEY SOUP

THIS HEARTY ASHKENAZI SOUP IS PERFECT ON A FREEZING COLD DAY. SERVE IN WARMED BOWLS, WITH PLENTY OF RYE OR PUMPERNICKEL BREAD.

SERVES SIX TO EIGHT

INGREDIENTS

30–45ml/2–3 tbsp small haricot
(navy) beans, soaked overnight
45–60ml/ 3–4 tbsp green split peas
45–60ml/3–4 tbsp yellow split peas
90–105ml/6–7 tbsp pearl barley
1 onion, chopped
2 carrots, sliced
3 celery sticks, diced or sliced
½ baking potato, peeled and cut
into chunks
10g/¼oz or 45ml/3 tbsp mixed
flavourful dried mushrooms
5 garlic cloves, sliced
2 litres/3½ pints/8 cups water
2 vegetable stock (bouillon) cubes
salt and ground black pepper
30–45ml/2–3 tbsp chopped fresh
parsley, to garnish

1 In a large pan, put the beans, green and yellow split peas, pearl barley, onion, carrots, celery, potato, mushrooms, garlic and water.

2 Bring the mixture to the boil, then reduce the heat, cover and simmer gently for about 1½ hours, or until the beans are tender.

3 Crumble the stock cubes into the soup and taste for seasoning. Ladle into warmed bowls, garnish with parsley and serve with rye or pumpernickel bread.

COOK'S TIP
Do not add the stock cubes until the end of cooking as the salt will prevent the beans from becoming tender.

CHAMIM

THIS SEPHARDI SHABBAT DISH OF SAVOURY MEATS AND BEANS IS BAKED IN A VERY LOW OVEN FOR SEVERAL HOURS. A PARCEL OF RICE IS OFTEN ADDED TO THE BROTH PART WAY THROUGH COOKING, WHICH PRODUCES A LIGHTLY PRESSED RICE WITH A SLIGHTLY CHEWY TEXTURE.

SERVES EIGHT

INGREDIENTS
    250g/9oz/1 cup chickpeas,
      soaked overnight
    45ml/3 tbsp olive oil
    1 onion, chopped
    10 garlic cloves, chopped
    1 parsnip, sliced
    3 carrots, sliced
    5–10ml/1–2 tsp ground cumin
    2.5ml/½ tsp ground turmeric
    15ml/1 tbsp chopped fresh root ginger
    2 litres/3½ pints/8 cups beef stock
    1 potato, peeled and cut into chunks
    ½ marrow (large zucchini), sliced or
      cut into chunks
    400g/14oz fresh or canned
      tomatoes, diced
    45–60ml/3–4 tbsp brown or
      green lentils
    2 bay leaves
    250g/9oz salted meat such as
      salt beef (or double the quantity
      of lamb)
    250g/9oz piece of lamb
    ½ large bunch fresh coriander
      (cilantro), chopped
    200g/7oz/1 cup long grain rice
    1 lemon, cut into wedges and a spicy
      sauce such as zchug or fresh
      chillies, finely chopped, to serve

1 Preheat the oven to 120°C/250°F/ Gas ½. Drain the chickpeas.

2 Heat the oil in a large flameproof casserole, add the onion, garlic, parsnip, carrots, cumin, turmeric and ginger and cook for 2–3 minutes. Add the chickpeas, stock, potato, marrow, tomatoes, lentils, bay leaves, salted meat, lamb and coriander. Cover and cook in the oven for about 3 hours.

COOK'S TIP
Add 1–2 pinches of bicarbonate of soda (baking soda) to the soaking chickpeas to make them tender, but do not add too much as it can make them mushy.

3 Put the rice on a double thickness of muslin (cheesecloth) and tie together at the corners, allowing enough room for the rice to expand while it is cooking.

4 Two hours before the end of cooking, remove the casserole from the oven. Place the rice parcel in the casserole, anchoring the edge of the muslin parcel under the lid so that the parcel is held above the soup and allowed to steam. Return the casserole to the oven and continue cooking for a further 2 hours.

5 Carefully remove the lid and the rice. Skim any fat off the top of the soup and ladle the soup into bowls with a scoop of the rice and one or two pieces of meat. Serve with lemon wedges and a spoonful of hot sauce or chopped fresh chillies.

DELI AND BRUNCH

New York deli culture, combined with the growing prosperity of American Jews who no longer needed to work on Sundays, gave way to the Sunday brunch. Each week, families throughout America buy bags of bagels from the bakery, schmears to spread on them, and perhaps a few salads from the deli and gather together for brunch. Smoked salmon might be scrambled into eggs or piled on to bagels, matzos may be browned up with eggs into matzo brei, or smoked whitefish flaked into salad with mayonnaise and sour cream.

NEW YORK EGG CREAM

NO EGGS, NO CREAM, JUST THE BEST CHOCOLATE SODA YOU WILL EVER SIP. THIS LEGENDARY DRINK IS EVOCATIVE OF OLD NEW YORK. NO ONE KNOWS WHY IT IS CALLED EGG CREAM BUT SOME SAY IT WAS A WITTY WAY OF DESCRIBING RICHNESS AT A TIME WHEN NO ONE COULD AFFORD TO PUT BOTH EXPENSIVE EGGS AND CREAM TOGETHER IN A DRINK.

SERVES ONE

INGREDIENTS
   45–60ml/3–4 tbsp good quality
      chocolate syrup
   120ml/4fl oz/½ cup chilled milk
   175ml/6fl oz/¾ cup chilled
      carbonated water
   cocoa powder, to sprinkle

1 Carefully pour the chocolate syrup into the bottom of a tall glass.

2 Pour the chilled milk on to the chocolate syrup. Pour the carbonated water into the glass, sip up any foam that rises to the top of the glass and continue to add the remaining water. Dust with cocoa powder and serve. Stir well before drinking.

COOK'S TIP
An authentic egg cream is made with an old-fashioned seltzer dispenser that you press and *shpritz*.

SCHAV

*THIS REFRESHINGLY SHARP, CHILLED SORREL SOUP IS SOLD IN GLASS BOTTLES IN MANY NEW YORK
DELIS. THE SORREL GIVES IT A WONDERFUL PALE GREEN COLOUR AND TANGY FLAVOUR AND THE
ADDITION OF LEMON JUICE GIVES IT A TART EDGE.*

SERVES FOUR TO SIX

INGREDIENTS
500g/1¼lb sorrel leaves,
   stems removed
1 medium-large onion, thinly sliced
1.5 litres/2½ pints/6¼ cups
   vegetable stock
15–30ml/1–2 tbsp sugar
60ml/4 tbsp lemon juice
2 eggs
150ml/¼ pint/⅔ cup sour cream
salt
3–4 spring onions (scallions), thinly
   sliced, to serve

COOK'S TIP
Shred the sorrel across the grain. This
will help to prevent it from becoming
stringy when it is cooked.

1 Finely shred the sorrel, then put in
a large pan with the onion and stock.
Bring to the boil, then reduce the heat
and simmer for 10–15 minutes.

2 Add the sugar and half the lemon
juice to the pan, stir and simmer for
a further 5–10 minutes.

3 In a bowl, beat the eggs and mix in
the sour cream, then stir in about 250ml/
8fl oz/1 cup of the hot soup. Add
another 250ml/8fl oz/1 cup of soup,
stirring to ensure a smooth texture.

4 Slowly pour the egg mixture into
the hot soup, stirring all the time to
prevent the eggs curdling and ensure
a smooth texture. Cook for just a few
moments over a low heat until the soup
thickens slightly. Season with a little
salt to taste and stir in the remaining
lemon juice.

5 Leave the soup to cool, then chill
for at least 2 hours. Taste again for
seasoning (it may need more salt or
lemon juice) and serve sprinkled with
the spring onions.

CHOPPED EGG AND ONIONS

THIS ASHKENAZI DISH, ALTHOUGH THE ESSENCE OF MODERN WESTERN DELI FOOD, IS IN FACT ONE OF THE OLDEST DISHES IN JEWISH HISTORY. SOME SAY THAT IT GOES BACK TO EGYPTIAN TIMES. IT IS DELICIOUS PILED ON TO TOAST OR USED AS A SANDWICH OR BAGEL FILLING.

SERVES FOUR TO SIX

INGREDIENTS
8–10 eggs
6–8 spring onions (scallions) and/or
   1 yellow or white onion, very finely
   chopped, plus extra to garnish
60–90ml/4–6 tbsp mayonnaise or
   rendered chicken fat
mild French wholegrain mustard, to
   taste (optional if using mayonnaise)
15ml/1 tbsp chopped fresh parsley
salt and ground black pepper
rye toasts or crackers, to serve

COOK'S TIP
The amount of rendered chicken fat or
mayonnaise required will depend on how
much onion you use in this dish.

1 Put the eggs in a large pan and cover with cold water. Bring the water to the boil and when it boils, reduce the heat and simmer over a low heat for 10 minutes.

2 Hold the eggs under cold running water, then remove the shells, dry the eggs and chop roughly.

3 Place the chopped eggs in a large bowl, add the onions, season generously with salt and pepper and mix well. Add enough mayonnaise or chicken fat to bind the mixture together. Stir in the mustard, if using, and the chopped parsley, or sprinkle the parsley on top to garnish. Chill before serving with rye toasts or crackers.

ISRAELI WHITE CHEESE AND GREEN OLIVES

THE DAIRY SHELVES OF ISRAEL BOAST AN EVER-INCREASING ARRAY OF CHEESES, FROM KASHKAVAL TO GOAT'S CHEESES AND MILD WHITE CHEESES SPIKED WITH SEASONINGS SUCH AS THIS ONE WITH PIQUANT GREEN OLIVES. SERVE IT WITH DRINKS AND LITTLE CRACKERS OR TOAST, OR AS A BRUNCH SPREAD WITH CHUNKS OF BREAD OR BAGELS.

SERVES FOUR

INGREDIENTS
175–200g/6–7oz soft white
   (farmer's) cheese
65g/2½oz feta cheese, preferably
   sheep's milk, lightly crumbled
20–30 pitted green olives, some
   chopped, the rest halved or quartered
2–3 large pinches of fresh thyme,
   plus extra to garnish
2–3 garlic cloves, finely
   chopped (optional)
crackers, toast or bagels, to serve

VARIATION
Add 115g/4oz chopped smoked salmon
and 2 thinly sliced spring onions
(scallions) to the cheese mixture.

1 Place the soft cheese in a mixing bowl and stir with the back of a spoon until soft and smooth.

2 Add the crumbled feta cheese to the blended soft cheese and stir until thoroughly combined.

3 Add the olives, thyme and chopped garlic to the cheese mixture and mix well to combine.

4 Spoon the mixture into a bowl, sprinkle with thyme and serve with crackers, toast, chunks of bread or bagels.

SWEET AND SOUR CUCUMBER WITH FRESH DILL

THIS IS HALF PICKLE, HALF SALAD, AND TOTALLY DELICIOUS SERVED AS A BRUNCH OR AS AN
APPETIZER BEFORE A HOMELY, ROASTED MEAT MAIN COURSE. SERVE WITH THIN SLICES OF
PUMPERNICKEL OR OTHER COARSE, DARK, FULL-FLAVOURED BREAD.

SERVES FOUR

INGREDIENTS
    1 large or 2 small cucumbers,
       thinly sliced
    3 onions, thinly sliced
    45ml/3 tbsp sugar
    75–90ml/5–6 tbsp white wine vinegar
       or cider vinegar
    30–45ml/2–3 tbsp water
    30–45ml/2–3 tbsp chopped
       fresh dill
    salt

COOK'S TIP
This salad can be kept in the refrigerator
for up to a week.

1 In a bowl, mix together the sliced
cucumber and onion, season with salt
and toss together until thoroughly
combined. Leave to stand in a cool
place for 5–10 minutes.

2 Add the sugar, white wine or cider
vinegar, water and chopped dill to the
cucumber mixture. Toss together until
well combined, then chill for a few
hours, or until ready to serve.

SWEET AND SOUR RED CABBAGE

CABBAGE USED TO BE THE MOST IMPORTANT VEGETABLE IN THE ASHKENAZI KITCHEN AND OFTEN IT WAS THE ONLY VEGETABLE. LUCKILY CABBAGE IS VERY VERSATILE, IS DELICIOUS PREPARED PAREVE, AND IS ALSO VERY GOOD FOR YOU. THIS DISH CAN BE MADE AHEAD OF TIME AND REHEATED AT THE LAST MINUTE TO SERVE WITH EITHER A MEAT OR DAIRY MEAL.

SERVES FOUR TO SIX

INGREDIENTS
  30ml/2 tbsp vegetable oil
  ½ large or 1 small red
  cabbage, cored and
  thinly sliced
  1 large onion, chopped
  2–3 handfuls of raisins
  1 small apple, finely diced
  15ml/1 tbsp sugar
  120ml/4fl oz/½ cup dry red wine
  juice of 1 lemon or 50ml/2fl oz/
  ¼ cup lemon juice and cider vinegar
  mixed together
salt and ground black pepper

1 Heat the oil in a large flameproof casserole, add the cabbage and onion and fry for 3–5 minutes, stirring, until the vegetables are well coated in the oil and the cabbage has softened slightly.

2 Add the raisins, apple, sugar and red wine to the pan and cook for about 30 minutes, or until very tender. Check occasionally and add more water or red wine if the liquid has evaporated and there is a risk of the cabbage burning.

3 Towards the end of the cooking time, add the lemon juice, and vinegar if using, and season with salt and pepper to taste. Serve hot or cold.

COOK'S TIP
This makes a great side dish, served alongside a Shabbat long-braised brisket, with rye bread and boiled potatoes.

NEW YORK DELI COLESLAW

EVERY DELI SELLS COLESLAW BUT THERE IS BORING COLESLAW AND EXCITING COLESLAW. THE KEY TO GOOD COLESLAW IS A ZESTY DRESSING AND AN INTERESTING SELECTION OF VEGETABLES.

SERVES SIX TO EIGHT

INGREDIENTS
  1 large white or green cabbage, very
    thinly sliced
  3–4 carrots, coarsely grated
  ½ red (bell) pepper, chopped
  ½ green (bell) pepper, chopped
  1–2 celery sticks, finely chopped or
    5–10ml/1–2 tsp celery seeds
  1 onion, chopped
  2–3 handfuls of raisins or sultanas
    (golden raisins)
  45ml/3 tbsp white wine vinegar or
    cider vinegar
  60–90ml/4–6 tbsp sugar, to taste
  175–250ml/6–8fl oz/¾–1 cup
    mayonnaise, to bind
  salt and ground black pepper

1 Put the cabbage, carrots, peppers, celery or celery seeds, onion, and raisins or sultanas in a salad bowl and mix to combine well. Add the vinegar, sugar, salt and ground black pepper and toss together. Leave to stand for about 1 hour.

2 Stir enough mayonnaise into the salad to lightly bind the ingredients together. Taste the salad for seasoning and sweet-and-sour flavour, adding more sugar, salt and pepper if needed. Chill. Drain off any excess liquid before serving.

DELI POTATO SALAD WITH EGG, MAYONNAISE AND OLIVES

POTATO SALAD IS SYNONYMOUS WITH DELI FOOD AND THERE ARE MANY VARIETIES, SOME WITH SOUR CREAM, SOME WITH VINAIGRETTE AND OTHERS WITH VEGETABLES. THIS VERSION INCLUDES A PIQUANT MUSTARD MAYONNAISE, CHOPPED EGGS AND GREEN OLIVES.

SERVES SIX TO EIGHT

INGREDIENTS
  1kg/2¼lb waxy salad
    potatoes, scrubbed
  1 red, brown or white onion,
    finely chopped
  2–3 celery sticks, finely chopped
  60–90ml/4–6 tbsp chopped
    fresh parsley
  15–20 pimiento-stuffed olives, halved
  3 hard-boiled eggs, chopped
  60ml/4 tbsp extra virgin olive oil
  60ml/4 tbsp white wine vinegar
  15–30ml/1–2 tbsp mild or
    wholegrain mustard
  celery seeds, to taste (optional)
  175–250ml/6–8fl oz/
    ¾–1 cup mayonnaise
  salt and ground black pepper
  paprika, to garnish

1 Cook the potatoes in a pan of salted boiling water until tender. Drain, return to the pan and leave for 2–3 minutes to cool and dry a little.

2 When the potatoes are cool enough to handle but still very warm, cut them into chunks or slices and place in a salad bowl.

3 Sprinkle the potatoes with salt and pepper, then add onion, celery, parsley, olives and the chopped eggs. In a jug (pitcher), combine the olive oil, vinegar mustard and celery seeds, if using, pour over the salad and toss to combine. Add enough mayonnaise to bind the salad together. Chill before serving, sprinkled with a little paprika.

MARINATED HERRINGS

THIS IS A CLASSIC ASHKENAZI DISH, SWEET-AND-SOUR AND LIGHTLY SPICED. IT IS DELICIOUS FOR SUNDAY BRUNCH AND IS ALWAYS WELCOMED AT A SHABBAT MIDDAY KIDDUSH RECEPTION.

SERVES FOUR TO SIX

INGREDIENTS
  2–3 herrings, filleted
  1 onion, sliced
  juice of 1½ lemons
  30ml/2 tbsp white wine vinegar
  25ml/1½ tbsp sugar
  10–15 black peppercorns
  10–15 allspice berries
  1.5ml/¼ tsp mustard seeds
  3 bay leaves, torn
  salt

1 Soak the herrings in cold water for 5 minutes, then drain. Pour over water to cover and soak for 2–3 hours, then drain. Pour over water to cover and leave to soak overnight.

2 Hold the soaked herrings under cold running water and rinse very well, both inside and out.

3 Cut each fish into bitesize pieces, then place the pieces in a glass bowl or shallow dish.

4 Sprinkle the onion over the fish, then add the lemon juice, vinegar, sugar, peppercorns, allspice, mustard seeds, bay leaves and salt. Add enough water to just cover. Cover the bowl and chill for 2 days to allow the flavours to blend before serving.

WHITEFISH SALAD

*SMOKED WHITEFISH IS ONE OF THE GLORIES OF DELI FOOD AND, MADE INTO A SALAD WITH
MAYONNAISE AND SOUR CREAM, IT BECOMES INDISPENSABLE AS A BRUNCH DISH. EAT IT WITH A STACK
OF BAGELS, PUMPERNICKEL OR RYE BREAD. IF YOU CAN'T FIND SMOKED WHITEFISH, USE ANY OTHER
SMOKED FIRM WHITE FISH SUCH AS HALIBUT OR COD.*

SERVES FOUR TO SIX

INGREDIENTS

   1 smoked whitefish, skinned
     and boned
   2 celery sticks, chopped
   ½ red, white or yellow onion
     or 3–5 spring onions
     (scallions), chopped
   45ml/3 tbsp mayonnaise
   45ml/3 tbsp sour cream or Greek
     (US strained plain) yogurt
   juice of ½–1 lemon
   1 round lettuce
   ground black pepper
   5–10ml/1–2 tsp chopped fresh
     parsley, to garnish

1 Break the smoked fish into bitesize pieces. In a bowl, combine the chopped celery, onion or spring onion, mayonnaise, and sour cream or yogurt, and add lemon juice to taste.

2 Fold the fish into the mixture and season with pepper. Arrange the lettuce leaves on serving plates, then spoon the whitefish salad on top. Serve chilled, sprinkled with parsley.

KASHA <u>AND</u> MUSHROOM KNISHES

MADE IN TINY, ONE-BITE PASTRIES, KNISHES ARE DELICIOUS COCKTAIL OR APPETIZER FARE; MADE IN BIG, HANDFUL-SIZED PASTRIES THEY ARE THE PERFECT ACCOMPANIMENT TO A LARGE BOWL OF BORSCHT. THEY CAN BE FILLED WITH DAIRY, MEAT OR PAREVE FILLINGS, THOUGH WITH MEAT FILLINGS, OR FOR A MEAT MEAL, A DAIRY-FREE PASTRY MUST BE USED.

MAKES ABOUT FIFTEEN

INGREDIENTS
  40g/1½oz/3 tbsp butter (for a dairy
    meal), 45ml/3 tbsp rendered chicken
    or duck fat (for a meat meal), or
    vegetable oil (for a pareve filling)
  2 onions, finely chopped
  200g/7oz/scant 3 cups mushrooms,
    diced (optional)
  200–250g/7–9oz/1–1¼ cups
    buckwheat, cooked
  handful of mixed dried mushrooms,
    broken into small pieces
  200ml/7fl oz/scant 1 cup hot stock,
    preferably mushroom
  1 egg, lightly beaten
  salt and ground black pepper
For the sour cream pastry
  250g/9oz/2¼ cups plain
    (all-purpose) flour
  5ml/1 tsp baking powder
  2.5ml/½ tsp salt
  2.5ml/½ tsp sugar
  130g/4½oz/generous ½ cup plus
    15ml/1 tbsp unsalted (sweet)
    butter, cut into small pieces
  75g/3oz sour cream or Greek
    (US strained plain) yogurt

1 To make the pastry, sift together the flour, baking powder, salt and sugar, then rub in the butter until the mixture resembles fine breadcrumbs. Add the sour cream or yogurt and mix together to form a dough. Add 5ml/1 tsp water if necessary. Wrap the dough in a plastic bag and chill for about 2 hours.

VARIATIONS
• To make chopped liver knishes, replace the sour cream pastry with 500g/1¼lb pareve puff or shortcrust pastry and fill with chopped liver.
• To make smoked salmon knishes, roll puff pastry into rounds about 4–5cm/ 1½ –2in in diameter and fill with a little soft (cream) cheese, shreds of smoked salmon, a sprinkling of thinly sliced spring onions (scallions) and fresh dill.

2 To make the filling, heat the butter, fat or oil in a pan, add the onions and fresh mushrooms, if using, and fry until soft and browned. Add the buckwheat and cook until slightly browned. Add the dried mushrooms and stock and cook over a medium-high heat until the liquid has been absorbed. Leave to cool, then stir in the egg and season well.

3 Preheat the oven to 200°C/400°F/ Gas 6. Roll out the pastry on a lightly floured surface to about 3mm/⅛in thickness, then cut into rectangles (about 7.5 × 16cm/3 × 6¼in). Place 2–3 spoonfuls of the filling in the middle of each piece and brush the edges with water, fold up and pinch together to seal. Bake for 15 minutes.

PIROSHKI

YOU CAN MAKE THESE LITTLE RUSSIAN PIES WITH VARIOUS PASTRIES, SUCH AS PUFF OR SHORTCRUST,
BUT THIS RECIPE USES THE TRADITIONAL YEAST DOUGH.

MAKES ABOUT FORTY

INGREDIENTS
  40g/1½oz/3 tbsp unsalted (sweet)
    butter or margarine
  1 onion, chopped
  150g/5oz salmon fillet, diced
  30ml/2 tbsp mixed dried mushrooms,
    broken into pieces
  105ml/7 tbsp mushroom stock
  30ml/2 tbsp crème fraîche
  30ml/2 tbsp chopped fresh dill
  30ml/2 tbsp chopped fresh chives or
    spring onions (scallions)
  salt and ground black pepper
For the dough
  375g/13oz/3¼ cups plain
    (all-purpose) flour
  7.5ml/1½ tsp salt
  7g packet easy-blend (rapid-rise)
    dried yeast
  150ml/¼ pint/⅔ cup milk or
    lukewarm water (for a meat meal)
  115g/4oz/½ cup unsalted (sweet)
    butter or margarine (for a meat
    meal), melted
  2 eggs, beaten, plus extra to seal

1 To make the dough, put the flour (reserving 30ml/2 tbsp), the salt and yeast in a bowl and mix together. Make a well in the centre and add the liquid, fat and eggs. Mix to form a soft dough.

2 Knead on a surface dusted with the reserved flour for 10–15 minutes. Form the dough into a ball and put in an oiled bowl. Cover with a dishtowel and leave in a warm place for 1–1½ hours until doubled in size. Knock back (punch down), then cover and put in the refrigerator for 2–3 hours or overnight.

3 To make the mushroom and salmon filling, melt 25g/1oz/2 tbsp of the butter in a frying pan, add the onion and fry until softened, then transfer to a bowl.

4 Add the remaining butter to the pan, then add the salmon and fry for 20–30 seconds until it begins to turn opaque. Add to the onions and season.

5 Add the mushrooms to the pan with any juices from the onions and salmon, and the stock. Cook over a medium heat for 5 minutes, or until the mushrooms are reconstituted. Leave to cool, then remove the mushrooms from the stock, chop roughly and add to the onions and salmon.

6 Strain the stock, return it to the pan and boil rapidly until reduced to 15ml/ 1 tbsp. Remove from the heat and stir in the crème fraîche, the onions, salmon and mushrooms, the dill and chives. Season to taste.

7 Preheat the oven to 200°C/400°F/ Gas 6. Lightly oil several baking sheets. Cut the dough into about four pieces. Roll out one piece to a thickness of about 3mm/⅛in, then cut into rounds measuring about 7.5cm/3in in diameter. Gather up the scraps and re-roll the dough to make more rounds.

8 Brush the edges of the dough with egg and water, then place 10–15ml/2–3 tsp of the filling in the centre of each round.

9 Bring up the sides around the filling. Pinch the edges together to seal, then place on the baking sheets.

10 Leave the pastries in a warm place for 15 minutes to rise, then bake for 15–20 minutes until golden brown. Serve hot or warm.

SCRAMBLED EGGS <u>WITH</u> LOX <u>AND</u> ONIONS

SERVE THIS QUINTESSENTIAL NEW YORK SUNDAY BRUNCH WITH PILES OF FRESHLY TOASTED BAGELS, MUGS OF COFFEE AND A SELECTION OF SUNDAY NEWSPAPERS.

SERVES FOUR

INGREDIENTS
40g/1½oz/3 tbsp unsalted
  (sweet) butter
2 onions, chopped
150–200g/5–7oz smoked
  salmon trimmings
6–8 eggs, lightly beaten
ground black pepper
45ml/3 tbsp chopped fresh chives,
  plus whole chives, to garnish
bagels, to serve

VARIATIONS
Substitute 200–250g/7–9oz diced
kosher salami for the smoked salmon
and cook in oil or pareve margerine.

1 Heat half the unsalted butter in a frying pan, add the chopped onions and fry until softened and just beginning to brown. Add the smoked salmon trimmings to the onions and mix well to combine.

2 Pour the eggs into the pan and stir until soft curds form. Add the remaining butter and stir off the heat until creamy. Season with pepper. Spoon on to serving plates and garnish with chives. Serve with bagels.

MATZO BREI

EVERY ASHKENAZI FAMILY HAS ITS OWN VERSION OF THIS DISH OF SOAKED MATZOS, MIXED WITH EGG AND FRIED UNTIL CRISP. SOME RECIPES USE WATER, SOME MILK, OTHERS USE LOTS OF EGG, A VERY LITTLE EGG, OR EVEN NONE AT ALL. THIS VERSION IS CRISP, SALTY AND BROKEN INTO PIECES.

SERVES ONE

INGREDIENTS
 3 matzos, broken into bitesize pieces
 2 eggs, lightly beaten
 30–45ml/2–3 tbsp olive oil or
  25–40g/1–1½oz/2–3 tbsp butter
 salt
 sour cream and fresh dill,
  to serve (optional)

VARIATION
To make a sweet matzo brei pancake, soak the matzos in 250ml/8fl oz/1 cup milk for 5–10 minutes. Add the eggs, a large pinch of ground cinnamon, 15–30ml/1–2 tbsp sugar and 2.5ml/½ tsp vanilla essence (extract). Fry the mixture in the oil or butter, turning once. Serve with jam or cinnamon sugar and sour cream.

1 Put the matzos in a large bowl and pour over cold water to cover. Leave for 2–3 minutes, then drain. Add the eggs.

2 Heat the oil or butter in a frying pan, then add the matzo mixture. Lower the heat and cook for 2–3 minutes until the bottom is golden brown.

3 Break up the matzo brei into pieces, turn them over and brown their other side. Turn once or twice again until the pieces are crisp. (The more times you turn them, the smaller the pieces will become.) Sprinkle with a little salt and serve immediately, with sour cream and dill if you like.

FISH DISHES

Fish is pareve and so may be eaten with either meat or dairy
foods. This provides great variety and flexibility within the
otherwise demanding laws of Kashrut. Having fish as a main
course means that you can serve an elegant entertaining menu that
has butter, cheeses and rich dairy desserts, without worrying
about the lack of meat. Both Ashkenazim and
Sephardim have many traditional fish dishes,
from the fried fish of London's East End
to whole fish baked with
fragrant spices in
Israel.

CLASSIC ASHKENAZI GEFILTE FISH

GEFILTE MEANS STUFFED AND ORIGINALLY THIS MIXTURE OF CHOPPED FISH WAS STUFFED BACK INTO THE SKIN OF THE FISH BEFORE COOKING. OVER THE CENTURIES, IT HAS EVOLVED INTO THE CLASSIC BALLS OF CHOPPED FISH THAT ARE SERVED AT THE START OF MOST JEWISH FESTIVITIES, INCLUDING SHABBAT, PESACH AND ROSH HASHANAH.

SERVES EIGHT

INGREDIENTS
 1kg/2¼lb of 2–3 varieties of fish
  fillets, such as carp, whitefish,
  yellow pike, haddock and cod
 2 eggs
 120ml/4fl oz/½ cup cold water
 30–45ml/2–3 tbsp medium
  matzo meal
 15–45ml/1–3 tbsp sugar
 fish stock, for simmering
 2–3 onions
 3 carrots
 1–2 pinches of ground cinnamon
 salt and ground black pepper
 chrain or horseradish and beetroot
  (beets), to serve

1 Place the fish fillets on a plate, sprinkle with salt and chill for 1 hour, or until the flesh has firmed. Rinse the fish well, then put in a food processor or blender and process until minced (ground).

2 Put the fish into a bowl, add the eggs, mix, then gradually add the water. Stir in the matzo meal, then the sugar and seasoning. Beat until light and aerated; cover and chill for 1 hour.

3 Take 15–30ml/1–2 tbsp of the mixture and, with wet hands, roll into a ball. Continue with the remaining mixture.

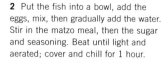

4 Bring a large pan of fish stock to the boil, reduce to a simmer, then add the fishballs. Return to the boil, then simmer for 1 hour. (Add more water, if necessary, to keep the balls covered.)

5 Add the onions, carrots, cinnamon and a little extra sugar, if you like, to the pan and simmer, uncovered, for 45–60 minutes. Add more water, if necessary, to keep the balls covered.

6 Leave the fish to cool slightly, then remove from the liquid with a slotted spoon. Serve warm or cold with chrain or horseradish and beetroot.

BRITISH FRIED FISH PATTIES

THESE PATTIES ARE THE FRIED VERSION OF GEFILTE FISH AND ARE PROBABLY THE ORIGINAL WAY THAT THEY WERE MADE WHEN BROUGHT TO ENGLAND BY PORTUGUESE JEWS IN THE SIXTEENTH CENTURY.

2 The batter should be firm enough to shape into a soft patty. If it is too thin, add a little more matzo meal and if too thick, add 15–30ml/1–2 tbsp water. Cover and chill for at least 1 hour.

3 Form the mixture into round patties measuring about 6cm/2½in in diameter and 2cm/¾in thick.

4 Put some matzo meal on a plate and use to coat each patty. Place the coated patties on another plate.

5 Heat the oil in a pan until it is hot enough to brown a cube of bread in 30 seconds. Add the patties, taking care not to overcrowd the pan, and fry for 7–8 minutes, turning occasionally, until they are golden brown on both sides. Place on kitchen paper to drain. Serve hot or cold with one or more spicy condiments.

MAKES TWELVE TO FOURTEEN

INGREDIENTS
   450g/1lb haddock fillet, skinned
   450g/1lb cod fillet, skinned
   2 eggs
   50–65g/2–2½oz matzo meal, plus
     extra for coating
   10ml/2 tsp salt
   5ml/1 tsp sugar
   15ml/1 tbsp vegetable oil
   15ml/1 tbsp chopped fresh parsley
   2 onions, chopped
   vegetable oil, for frying
   ground black pepper
   chrain or other spicy condiment,
    to serve

1 Mince (grind) or finely chop the fish in a food processor or by hand. Add the eggs, matzo meal, salt, sugar, oil, parsley, onions and a little pepper. Combine to form a batter.

VARIATION
To make a Sephardi version, add a little chopped garlic to the fish mixture and fry the patties in olive oil.

GINGER FISHBALLS IN TOMATO AND PRESERVED LEMON SAUCE

THESE SPICY BALLS OF MINCED FISH AND GINGER, COOKED IN A SAUCE OF TOMATOES AND PRESERVED LEMON, ARE A SPECIALITY OF THE JEWS OF MOROCCO. ENJOY THEM ACCOMPANIED BY FLAT BREAD TO SCOOP UP THE DELICIOUS SAUCE AND LEMON, OR WITH COUSCOUS COOKED IN FISH STOCK.

SERVES SIX

INGREDIENTS
  65g/2½oz bread (about 2 slices)
  1kg/2¼lb minced (ground) fish such
    as cod, haddock or whiting
  2 onions, chopped
  8 garlic cloves, chopped
  2.5–5ml/½–1 tsp ground turmeric
  2.5ml/½ tsp ground ginger
  2.5ml/½ tsp ras al hanout or
    garam masala
  1 bunch fresh coriander (cilantro),
    chopped, plus extra to garnish
  1 egg
  cayenne pepper, to taste
  150ml/¼ pint/⅔ cup vegetable or
    olive oil or a combination of both
  4 ripe tomatoes, diced
  5ml/1 tsp paprika
  1 preserved lemon, rinsed and cut
    into small strips
  salt and ground black pepper
  ½ lemon, cut into wedges, to serve

4 Add the diced tomatoes, paprika and half the remaining coriander to the pan and cook over a medium heat until the tomatoes have formed a sauce consistency. Stir in the strips of preserved lemon.

5 With wet hands, roll walnut-size lumps of the fish mixture into balls and flatten slightly. Place in the sauce. Cook gently, for 15–20 minutes, turning twice. Garnish with coriander and serve with lemon wedges for squeezing.

1 Remove the crusts from the bread, put the bread in a bowl and pour over cold water. Leave to soak for about 10 minutes, then squeeze dry.

2 Add the fish to the bread with half the onions, half the garlic, half the turmeric, the ginger, half the ras al hanout or garam masala, half the coriander, the egg and cayenne pepper and seasoning. Mix together and chill while you make the sauce.

3 To make the sauce, heat the oil in a pan, add the remaining onion and garlic and fry for about 5 minutes, or until softened. Sprinkle in the remaining turmeric and ras al hanout or garam masala and warm through.

VARIATION
Use a fresh lemon, instead of the preserved lemon, if you prefer. Cut it into small dice and add with the tomatoes.

MOROCCAN GRILLED FISH BROCHETTES

SERVE THESE DELICIOUS SKEWERS WITH POTATOES, AUBERGINE SLICES AND STRIPS OF RED PEPPERS,
WHICH CAN BE COOKED ON THE BARBECUE ALONGSIDE THE FISH BROCHETTES. ACCOMPANY WITH
A BOWL OF ZCHUG AND A STACK OF WARM, SOFT PITTA BREADS OR FLOUR TORTILLAS.

SERVES FOUR TO SIX

INGREDIENTS

5 garlic cloves, chopped
2.5ml/½ tsp paprika
2.5ml/½ tsp ground cumin
2.5–5ml/½–1 tsp salt
2–3 pinches of cayenne pepper
60ml/4 tbsp olive oil
30ml/2 tbsp lemon juice
30ml/2 tbsp chopped fresh coriander
   (cilantro) or parsley
675g/1½lb firm-fleshed white fish,
   such as haddock, halibut, sea bass,
   snapper or turbot, cut into
   2.5–5cm/1–2in cubes
3–4 green (bell) peppers, cut into
   2.5–5cm/1–2in pieces
2 lemon wedges, to serve

1 Put the garlic, paprika, cumin, salt, cayenne pepper, oil, lemon juice and coriander or parsley in a large bowl and mix together. Add the fish and toss to coat. Leave to marinate for at least 30 minutes, and preferably 2 hours, at room temperature, or chill overnight.

2 About 40 minutes before you are going to cook the brochettes, light the barbecue. The barbecue is ready when the coals have turned white and grey.

3 Meanwhile, thread the fish cubes and pepper pieces alternately on to wooden or metal skewers.

4 Grill the brochettes on the barbecue for 2–3 minutes on each side, or until the fish is tender and lightly browned. Serve with lemon wedges.

COOK'S TIP
If you are using wooden skewers for the brochettes, soak them in cold water for 30 minutes before using to prevent them from burning.

PERUVIAN WHITEBAIT ESCABECHE

ANY TYPE OF TINY WHITE FISH, FRIED UNTIL CRISP, THEN MARINATED WITH VEGETABLES, IS A FAVOURITE FOOD IN PERU, ESPECIALLY AMONG THE JEWS. SERVE THESE TANGY MORSELS AS AN APPETIZER WITH DRINKS OR AS A MAIN COURSE WITH CAUSA, A SALAD OF COLD MASHED POTATOES DRESSED WITH ONIONS, CHILLIES, OLIVE OIL AND LOTS OF LEMON JUICE.

3 Fry the fish, in small batches, until golden brown, then put in a shallow serving dish and set aside.

4 In a separate pan, heat 30ml/2 tbsp of oil. Add the onions, cumin seeds, carrots, chillies and garlic and fry for 5 minutes, until the onions are softened. Add the vinegar, oregano and coriander, stir well and cook for 1–2 minutes.

5 Pour the onion mixture over the fried fish and leave to cool. Serve the fish at room temperature, garnished with slices of corn on the cob, black olives and coriander leaves.

SERVES FOUR

INGREDIENTS
    800g/1¾lb whitebait or tiny white fish
    juice of 2 lemons
    5ml/1 tsp salt
    plain (all-purpose) flour, for dusting
    vegetable oil, for frying
    2 onions, chopped or thinly sliced
    2.5–5ml/½–1 tsp cumin seeds
    2 carrots, thinly sliced
    2 jalapeño chillies, chopped
    8 garlic cloves, roughly chopped
    120ml/4fl oz/½ cup white wine or
        cider vinegar
    2–3 large pinches of dried oregano
    15–30ml/1–2 tbsp chopped fresh
        coriander (cilantro) leaves
    slices of corn on the cob, black olives
        and coriander (cilantro), to garnish

1 Put the fish in a bowl, add the lemon juice and salt and leave to marinate for 30–60 minutes. Remove the fish from the bowl and dust with flour.

2 Heat the oil in a deep-frying pan until hot enough to turn a cube of bread golden brown in 30 seconds.

COOK'S TIPS
• When selecting whitebait or any other smelt, make sure the fish are very tiny as they are eaten whole.
• If you prefer, use chunks of any firm white fish such as cod or halibut instead of tiny whole fish. Simply flour the chunks of fish and fry as above.

FILO-WRAPPED FISH

This delicious dish comes from Jerusalem, where whole fish are wrapped in filo pastry and served with a zesty tomato sauce. The choice of fish can be varied according to what is in season and what is freshest on the day of purchase.

SERVES THREE TO FOUR

INGREDIENTS
450g/1lb salmon or cod steaks
   or fillets
1 lemon
30ml/2 tbsp olive oil, plus extra
   for brushing
1 onion, chopped
2 celery sticks, chopped
1 green (bell) pepper, diced
5 garlic cloves, chopped
400g/14oz fresh or canned
   tomatoes, chopped
120ml/4fl oz/½ cup passata
   (bottled strained tomatoes)
30ml/2 tbsp chopped fresh flat
   leaf parsley
2–3 pinches of ground allspice or
   ground cloves
cayenne pepper, to taste
pinch of sugar
about 130g/4½oz filo pastry
   (6–8 large sheets)
salt and ground black pepper

1 Sprinkle the salmon or cod steaks or fillets with salt and black pepper and a squeeze of lemon juice. Set aside while you prepare the sauce.

2 Heat the olive oil in a pan, add the chopped onion, celery and pepper and fry for about 5 minutes, until the vegetables are softened. Add the garlic and cook for a further 1 minute, then add the tomatoes and passata and cook until the tomatoes are of a sauce consistency.

3 Stir the parsley into the sauce, then season with allspice or cloves, cayenne pepper, sugar and salt and pepper.

4 Preheat the oven to 200°C/400°F/Gas 6. Take a sheet of filo pastry, brush with a little olive oil and cover with a second sheet. Place a piece of fish on top of the pastry, towards the bottom edge, then top with 1–2 spoonfuls of the sauce, spreading it evenly.

5 Roll the fish in the pastry, taking care to enclose the filling completely. Arrange on a baking sheet and repeat with the remaining fish and pastry. You should have about half the sauce remaining, to serve with the fish.

6 Bake for 10–15 minutes, or until golden. Meanwhile, reheat the remaining sauce if necessary. Serve immediately with the remaining sauce.

TONNO CON PISELLI

This Jewish Italian dish of fresh tuna and peas is especially enjoyed at Pesach, which falls in spring. Before the days of the freezer, spring was the time for little seasonal peas. At other times of the year chickpeas were used instead.

2 Sprinkle the tuna steaks on each side with salt and pepper. Add to the pan and cook for 2–3 minutes on each side until lightly browned. Transfer the tuna steaks to a shallow baking dish, in a single layer.

3 Add the canned tomatoes along with their juice and the wine or fish stock to the onions and cook over a medium heat for 5–10 minutes, stirring, until the flavours blend together and the mixture thickens slightly.

4 Stir the tomato purée, sugar, if needed, and salt and pepper, into the tomato sauce, then add the fresh or frozen peas. Pour the mixture over the fish steaks and bake, uncovered, for about 10 minutes, or until tender.

SERVES FOUR

INGREDIENTS

60ml/4 tbsp olive oil
1 onion, chopped
4–5 garlic cloves, chopped
45ml/3 tbsp chopped fresh flat
  leaf parsley
1–2 pinches of fennel seeds
350g/12oz tuna steaks
400g/14oz can chopped tomatoes
120ml/4fl oz/½ cup dry white wine
  or fish stock
30–45ml/2–3 tbsp tomato
  purée (paste)
pinch of sugar, if needed
350g/12oz/3 cups fresh shelled or
  frozen peas
salt and ground black pepper

1 Preheat the oven to 190°C/375°F/ Gas 5. Heat the olive oil in a large frying pan, then add the chopped onion, garlic, flat leaf parsley and fennel seeds, and fry over a low heat for about 5 minutes, or until the onion is softened but not browned.

VARIATIONS

This recipe works well with other fish. Use tuna fillets in place of the steaks or try different fish steaks, such as salmon or swordfish.

YEMENITE POACHED FISH
IN SPICY TOMATO HERB SAUCE

THIS TRADITIONAL JEWISH DISH IS KNOWN AS SAMAK. YEMENITE SPICING IS REFRESHING IN THE
SULTRY HEAT OF THE MIDDLE EAST AND IS VERY POPULAR WITH ISRAELIS. SERVE THIS DISH WITH
FLAT BREADS SUCH AS PITTA OR MATZOS, AND HILBEH, A TOMATO AND FENUGREEK RELISH.

SERVES EIGHT

INGREDIENTS

300ml/½ pint/1¼ cups passata
(bottled strained tomatoes)
150ml/¼ pint/⅔ cup fish stock
1 large onion, chopped
60ml/4 tbsp chopped fresh coriander
(cilantro) leaves
60ml/4 tbsp chopped fresh parsley
5–8 garlic cloves, crushed
chopped fresh chilli or chilli paste,
to taste
large pinch of ground ginger
large pinch of curry powder
1.5ml/¼ tsp ground cumin
1.5ml/¼ tsp ground turmeric
seeds from 2–3 cardamom pods
juice of 2 lemons, plus extra
if needed
30ml/2 tbsp vegetable or olive oil
1.5kg/3¼lb mixed white fish fillets
salt and ground black pepper

1 Put the passata, stock, onion, herbs, garlic, chilli, ginger, curry powder, cumin, turmeric, cardamom, lemon juice and oil in a pan and bring to the boil.

VARIATIONS
• This dish is just as good using only one type of fish, such as cod or flounder.
• Instead of poaching the fish, wrap each piece in puff pastry and bake at 190°C/375°F/Gas 5 for 20 minutes, then serve with the tomato sauce.

2 Remove the pan from the heat and add the fish fillets to the hot sauce. Return to the heat and allow the sauce to boil briefly again. Reduce the heat and simmer very gently for about 5 minutes, or until the fish is tender. (Test the fish with a fork. If the flesh flakes easily, then it is cooked.)

3 Taste the sauce and adjust the seasoning, adding more lemon juice if necessary. Serve hot or warm.

BAKED SALMON WITH WATERCRESS SAUCE

WHOLE BAKED SALMON IS A CLASSIC DISH SERVED AT BAR AND BAT MITZVAH FEASTS, WEDDING PARTIES AND ANY BIG SIMCHA. BAKING THE SALMON IN FOIL PRODUCES A FLESH RATHER LIKE THAT OF A POACHED FISH BUT WITH THE EASE OF BAKING. DECORATING THE FISH WITH THIN SLICES OF CUCUMBER LOOKS PRETTY AND WILL CONCEAL ANY FLESH THAT MAY LOOK RAGGED AFTER SKINNING.

SERVES SIX TO EIGHT

INGREDIENTS
2–3kg/4½–6¾lb salmon, cleaned with head and tail left on
3–5 spring onions (scallions), thinly sliced
1 lemon, thinly sliced
1 cucumber, thinly sliced
fresh dill sprigs, to garnish
lemon wedges, to serve
For the watercress sauce
3 garlic cloves, chopped
200g/7oz watercress leaves, finely chopped
40g/1½oz fresh tarragon, finely chopped
300g/11oz mayonnaise
15–30ml/1–2 tbsp freshly squeezed lemon juice
200g/7oz/scant 1 cup unsalted (sweet) butter
salt and ground black pepper

3 Remove the fish from the oven and leave to stand, still wrapped in the foil, for about 15 minutes, then unwrap the parcel and leave the fish to cool.

4 When the fish is cool, carefully lift it on to a large plate, still covered with lemon slices. Cover the fish tightly with clear film (plastic wrap) and chill for several hours.

5 Before serving, discard the lemon slices around the fish. Using a blunt knife to lift up the edge of the skin, carefully peel the skin away from the flesh, avoiding tearing the flesh, and pull out any fins at the same time.

6 Arrange the cucumber slices in overlapping rows along the length of the fish, to resemble large fish scales.

COOK'S TIP
Do not prepare the sauce more than a few hours ahead of serving as the watercress will discolour the sauce.

7 To make the sauce, put the garlic, watercress, tarragon, mayonnaise and lemon juice in a food processor or blender or a bowl, and process or mix to combine.

8 Melt the butter, then add to the watercress mixture, a little at a time, processing or stirring, until the butter has been incorporated and the sauce is thick and smooth. Cover and chill before serving. Serve the fish, garnished with dill, with the sauce and lemon wedges.

VARIATION
Instead of cooking a whole fish, prepare 6–8 salmon steaks. Place each fish steak on an individual square of foil, then top with a slice of onion and a slice of lemon and season generously with salt and ground black pepper. Loosely wrap the foil up around the fish, fold the edges to seal and place the parcels on a baking sheet. Bake as above for 10–15 minutes, or until the flesh is opaque. Serve cold with watercress sauce, garnished with slices of cucumber.

1 Preheat the oven to 180°C/350°F/Gas 4. Rinse the salmon and lay it on a large piece of foil. Stuff the fish with the sliced spring onions and layer the lemon slices inside and around the fish, then sprinkle with plenty of salt and ground black pepper.

2 Loosely fold the foil around the fish and fold the edges over to seal. Bake for about 1 hour.

SINIYA

THE NAME OF THIS CLASSIC SEPHARDI DISH SIMPLY MEANS FISH AND TAHINI SAUCE. IN THIS VERSION, THE FISH IS FIRST WRAPPED IN VINE LEAVES, THEN SPREAD WITH TAHINI AND BAKED. A FINAL SPRINKLING OF POMEGRANATE SEEDS ADDS A FRESH, INVIGORATING FLAVOUR.

SERVES FOUR

INGREDIENTS
4 small fish, such as trout, sea
   bream or red mullet, each weighing
   about 300g/11oz, cleaned
at least 5 garlic cloves, chopped
juice of 2 lemons
75ml/5 tbsp olive oil
about 20 brined vine leaves
tahini, for drizzling
1–2 pomegranates
fresh mint and coriander (cilantro)
   sprigs, to garnish

VARIATION
Instead of whole fish, use fish fillets or
steaks such as fresh tuna. Make a bed
of vine leaves and top with the fish and
marinade. Bake for 5–10 minutes until
the fish is half cooked, then top with the
tahini as above and grill (broil) until
golden brown and lightly crusted on top.

1 Preheat the oven to 180°C/350°F/
Gas 4. Put the fish in a shallow, ovenproof
dish, large enough to fit the whole fish
without touching each other. In a bowl,
combine the garlic, lemon juice and oil;
spoon over the fish. Turn the fish to coat.

2 Rinse the vine leaves well under cold
water, then wrap the fish in the leaves.
Arrange the fish in the same dish and
spoon any marinade in the dish over
the top of each. Bake for 30 minutes.

3 Drizzle the tahini over the top of each
wrapped fish, making a ribbon so that
the tops and tails of the fish and some
of the vine leaf wrapping still show.
Return to the oven and bake for a
further 5–10 minutes until the top is
golden and slightly crusted.

4 Meanwhile, cut the pomegranates in
half and scoop out the seeds. Sprinkle
the seeds over the fish, garnish with
mint and coriander, and serve.

DAG ᴴᴬ SFARIM

A WHOLE FISH, COOKED IN SPICES, IS A FESTIVAL TREAT. IT IS ESPECIALLY POPULAR AT ROSH HASHANAH, WHEN THE SEPHARDI COMMUNITY EAT WHOLE FISH. THE WHOLENESS SYMBOLIZES THE FULL YEAR TO COME AND THE HEAD SYMBOLIZES THE WISDOM THAT WE ASK TO BE ENDOWED WITH.

SERVES SIX TO EIGHT

INGREDIENTS

1–1.5kg/2¼–3¼lb fish, such as snapper, cleaned, with head and tail left on (optional)
2.5ml/½ tsp salt
juice of 2 lemons
45–60ml/3–4 tbsp extra virgin olive oil
2 onions, sliced
5 garlic cloves, chopped
1 green (bell) pepper, seeded and chopped
1–2 fresh green chillies, seeded and finely chopped
2.5ml/½ tsp ground turmeric
2.5ml/½ tsp curry powder
2.5 ml/½ tsp ground cumin
120ml/4fl oz/½ cup passata (bottled strained tomatoes)
5–6 fresh or canned tomatoes, chopped
45–60ml/3–4 tbsp chopped fresh coriander (cilantro) leaves and/or parsley
65g/2½oz pine nuts, toasted
parsley, to garnish

1 Prick the fish all over with a fork and rub with the salt. Put the fish in a roasting pan or dish and pour over the lemon juice. Leave to stand for 2 hours.

VARIATION
The spicy tomato sauce is very good served with fish patties. Omit step 1 and simply warm fried patties through in the spicy sauce.

2 Preheat the oven to 180°C/350°F/ Gas 4. Heat the oil in a pan, add the onions and half the garlic and fry for about 5 minutes, or until softened.

3 Add the pepper, chillies, turmeric, curry powder and cumin to the pan and cook gently for 2–3 minutes. Stir in the passata, tomatoes and herbs.

4 Sprinkle half of the pine nuts over the base of an ovenproof dish, top with half of the sauce, then add the fish and its marinade. Sprinkle the remaining garlic over the fish, then add the remaining sauce and the remaining pine nuts. Cover tightly with a lid or foil and bake for 30 minutes, or until the fish is tender. Garnish with parsley.

MEAT AND POULTRY

To the Ashkenazim, meat was the most important of foods but, for the Jews of the
shtetl, eating meat tended to be little more than a smear of chicken fat on a piece
of rye bread or a few shreds of brisket cooked with potatoes. The price of
meat was high, reflecting the trained skills of the shochet and the high
taxes that were made on kosher meat. Classic Ashkenazi meat dishes
are rich with robust flavours: meats braised with onions and eaten
with kasha, and beef minced (ground) with onions and made into
croquettes or stewed into a cholent. Jewish meat dishes can also be
aromatic, flavoured with the spices of the Eastern,
or Sephardi, kitchen, particularly the
grilled meats from Israel and
the Middle East.

JERUSALEM BARBECUED LAMB KEBABS

IN THE EARLY DAYS OF THE MODERN STATE OF ISRAEL, THE DAYS OF AUSTERITY, "LAMB" KEBABS WOULD HAVE BEEN MADE WITH TURKEY AND A LITTLE LAMB FAT, AND "VEAL" KEBABS WITH CHICKEN AND A SMALL AMOUNT OF VEAL. TURKEY, CHICKEN, BEEF AND VEAL CAN ALL BE COOKED IN THIS WAY.

SERVES FOUR TO SIX

INGREDIENTS

800g/1¾lb tender lamb, cubed
1.5ml/¼ tsp ground allspice
1.5ml/¼ tsp ground cinnamon
1.5ml/¼ tsp ground black pepper
1.5ml/¼ tsp ground cardamom
45–60ml/3–4 tbsp chopped
  fresh parsley
2 onions, chopped
5–8 garlic cloves, chopped
juice of ½ lemon or 45ml/3 tbsp dry
  white wine
45ml/3 tbsp extra virgin olive oil
sumac, for sprinkling (optional)
30ml/2 tbsp pine nuts
salt
For serving
  flat breads, such as pitta bread,
    tortillas or naan bread
  tahini
  crunchy vegetable salad

1 Put the lamb, allspice, cinnamon, black pepper, cardamom, half the parsley, half the onions, the garlic, lemon juice or wine and olive oil in a bowl and mix together. Season with salt now, if you prefer, or sprinkle on after cooking. Set aside and leave to marinate.

2 Meanwhile, light the barbecue and leave for about 40 minutes. When the coals are white and grey, the barbecue is ready for cooking. If using wooden skewers, soak them in water for about 30 minutes to prevent them from burning.

3 Thread the cubes of meat on to wooden or metal skewers, then cook on the barbecue for 2–3 minutes on each side, turning occasionally, until cooked evenly and browned.

4 Transfer the kebabs to a serving dish and sprinkle with the reserved onions, parsley, sumac, if using, pine nuts and salt, if you like. Serve the kebabs with warmed flat breads to wrap the kebabs in, a bowl of tahini for drizzling over and a vegetable salad.

COOK'S TIPS

• If sumac is available, its tangy flavour is fresh and invigorating, and its red colour is appealing.

• These kebabs can also be cooked under a hot grill (broiler).

KOFTA KEBABS

These spicy patties of minced lamb are spiked with aromatic herbs and seasonings. They are very popular in both Jewish communities and non-Jewish communities from the Middle East through to the Indian subcontinent. Serve with flatbread and a selection of salads, such as oranges sprinkled with cayenne or paprika, onions sprinkled with sumac, and tomato wedges with herbs and chillies.

SERVES FOUR

INGREDIENTS

    450g/1lb minced (ground) lamb
    1–2 large slices of French bread,
        very finely crumbled
    ½ bunch fresh coriander (cilantro),
        finely chopped
    5 garlic cloves, chopped
    1 onion, finely chopped
    juice of ½ lemon
    5ml/1 tsp ground cumin
    5ml/1 tsp paprika
    15ml/1 tbsp curry powder
    pinch each of ground cardamom,
        turmeric and cinnamon
    15ml/1 tbsp tomato purée (paste)
    cayenne pepper or chopped fresh
        chillies (optional)
    1 egg, beaten, if needed
    salt and ground black pepper
    flat bread and salads, to serve

1 Put the lamb, crumbled bread, coriander, garlic, onion, lemon juice, spices, tomato purée, cayenne pepper or chillies and seasoning in a large bowl. Mix well. If the mixture does not bind together, add the beaten egg and a little more bread.

2 With wet hands, shape the mixture into four large or eight small patties.

3 Heat a heavy non-stick frying pan, add the patties and cook, taking care that they do not fall apart, turning once or twice, until browned. Serve hot with flat bread and salads.

VARIATION

Mix a handful of raisins or sultanas (golden raisins) into the meat mixture before shaping it into patties.

LAMB POT-ROASTED WITH TOMATOES, BEANS AND ONIONS

THIS SLOW-BRAISED DISH OF LAMB AND TOMATOES, SPICED WITH CINNAMON AND STEWED WITH GREEN BEANS, SHOWS A GREEK INFLUENCE. IT IS ALSO GOOD MADE WITH COURGETTES INSTEAD OF BEANS.

SERVES EIGHT

INGREDIENTS

1kg/2¼lb lamb on the bone
8 garlic cloves, chopped
2.5–5ml/½–1 tsp ground cumin
45ml/3 tbsp olive oil
juice of 1 lemon
2 onions, thinly sliced
about 500ml/17fl oz/2¼ cups
  lamb, beef or vegetable stock
75–90ml/5–6 tbsp tomato
  purée (paste)
1 cinnamon stick
2–3 large pinches of ground
  allspice or ground cloves
15–30ml/1–2 tbsp sugar
400g/14oz/scant 3 cups runner
  (green) beans
salt and ground black pepper
15–30ml/1–2 tbsp chopped
  fresh parsley, to garnish

1 Preheat the oven to 160°C/325°F/Gas 3. Coat the lamb with the garlic, cumin, olive oil, lemon juice, salt and pepper.

2 Heat a flameproof casserole. Sear the lamb on all sides. Add the onions and pour the stock over the meat to cover. Stir in the tomato purée, spices and sugar. Cover and cook in the oven for 2–3 hours.

3 Remove the casserole from the oven and pour the stock into a pan. Move the onions to the side of the dish and return to the oven, uncovered, for 20 minutes.

4 Meanwhile, add the beans to the hot stock and cook until the beans are tender and the sauce has thickened. Slice the meat and serve with the pan juices and beans. Garnish with parsley.

MOROCCAN LAMB WITH HONEY AND PRUNES

THIS DISH IS EATEN BY MOROCCAN JEWS AT ROSH HASHANAH, WHEN SWEET FOODS ARE TRADITIONALLY SERVED IN ANTICIPATION OF A SWEET NEW YEAR TO COME.

SERVES SIX

INGREDIENTS

130g/4½oz/generous ½ cup
  pitted prunes
350ml/12fl oz/1½ cups hot tea
1kg/2¼lb stewing or braising
  lamb such as shoulder, cut into
  chunky portions
1 onion, chopped
75–90ml/5–6 tbsp chopped
  fresh parsley
2.5ml/½ tsp ground ginger
2.5ml/½ tsp curry powder or
  ras al hanout
pinch of freshly grated nutmeg
10ml/2 tsp ground cinnamon
1.5ml/¼ tsp saffron threads
30ml/2 tbsp hot water
75–120ml/5–9 tbsp honey, to taste
250ml/8fl oz/1 cup beef or lamb stock
115g/4oz/1 cup blanched
  almonds, toasted
30ml/2 tbsp chopped fresh coriander
  (cilantro) leaves
3 hard-boiled eggs, cut into wedges
salt and ground black pepper

1 Preheat the oven to 180°C/350°F/ Gas 4. Put the prunes in a bowl, pour over the tea and cover. Leave to soak and plump up.

2 Meanwhile, put the lamb, chopped onion, parsley, ginger, curry powder or ras al hanout, nutmeg, cinnamon, salt and a large pinch of ground black pepper in a roasting pan. Cover and cook in the oven for about 2 hours, or until the meat is tender.

3 Drain the prunes; add their liquid to the lamb. Combine the saffron and hot water and add to the pan with the honey and stock. Bake, uncovered, for 30 minutes, turning the lamb occasionally.

4 Add the prunes to the pan and stir gently to mix. Serve sprinkled with the toasted almonds and chopped coriander, and topped with the wedges of hard-boiled egg.

LAMB <u>WITH</u> GLOBE ARTICHOKES

IN THIS ITALIAN JEWISH DISH, A GARLIC-STUDDED LEG OF LAMB IS COOKED WITH RED WINE AND ARTICHOKE HEARTS, MAKING IT NOT ONLY ELEGANT BUT A DISH WORTHY OF ANY SPECIAL FEAST OR GATHERING. ITALIAN JEWS FAVOURED ARTICHOKES FOR MILLENNIA AND THE CLASSIC ROMAN DISH OF FRIED ARTICHOKES ALLA GIUDIA ACTUALLY CAME FROM THE OLD GHETTO IN ROME.

SERVES SIX TO EIGHT

INGREDIENTS
1 leg of lamb, about 2kg/4½lb
1–2 garlic heads, divided into cloves,
    peeled and thinly sliced, leaving
    5–6 peeled but whole
handful of fresh rosemary, stalks
    removed (about 25g/1oz)
500ml/17fl oz/2¼ cups dry
    red wine
30–60ml/2–4 tbsp olive oil
4 globe artichokes
a little lemon juice
5 shallots, chopped
250ml/8fl oz/1 cup beef stock
salt and ground black pepper
crisp green salad with garlic-rubbed
    croûtons, to serve (optional)

2 Put the lamb in a non-metallic dish and pour half the wine and all of the olive oil over the top. Set aside and leave to marinate until you are ready to roast the meat.

3 Preheat the oven to 230°C/450°F/ Gas 8. Put the meat and its juices in a roasting pan and surround with the remaining whole garlic cloves. Roast in the oven for 10–15 minutes, then reduce the temperature to 160°C/325°F/ Gas 3 and cook for a further 1 hour, or until the lamb is cooked to your liking. Test with a sharp knife.

4 Meanwhile, prepare the artichokes. Pull back their tough leaves and let them snap off. Trim the rough ends off the base. With a sharp knife, cut the artichokes into quarters and cut out the inside thistle heart. Immediately place the quarters into a bowl of water to which you have added the lemon juice. (The acidulated water will prevent the artichokes from discolouring.)

5 About 20 minutes before the lamb is cooked, drain the globe artichokes and place them around the meat.

6 When the lamb is cooked, transfer the meat and artichokes to a serving dish. Carefully pour the meat juices and roasted garlic into a pan.

7 Spoon off the fat from the pan juices and add the chopped shallots and the remaining red wine to the pan. Cook over a high heat until the liquid has reduced to a very small amount, then add the beef stock and cook, stirring constantly, until the pan juices are rich and flavourful.

8 To serve, coat the lamb and artichokes with the roasted garlic and red wine sauce and garnish with extra rosemary, if you wish. Serve immediately with green salad and garlic croûtons, if you like.

1 Using a sharp knife, make incisions all over the leg of lamb. Into each incision, put a sliver of garlic and as many rosemary leaves as you can stuff in. Season the lamb with salt and plenty of black pepper.

COOK'S TIPS
• Choose garlic heads that are plump and whose cloves are full and not shrivelled. Avoid any that are beginning to sprout.
• If you do not have access to a kosher leg of lamb with the sciatic nerve removed, use lamb riblets or shoulder of lamb instead.
• If you wish, you can marinate the lamb ahead of time. Cover and store the meat in the refrigerator for up to 1 day.

HOLISHKES

THESE STUFFED CABBAGE LEAVES ARE A TRADITIONAL DISH FOR SUKKOT, THE HARVEST FESTIVAL IN THE AUTUMN. THE STUFFING SYMBOLIZES ABUNDANCE. VERSIONS OF THIS DISH HAVE LONG BEEN ENJOYED BY JEWISH COMMUNITIES IN THE MIDDLE EAST, EUROPE AND RUSSIA.

SERVES SIX TO EIGHT

INGREDIENTS

1kg/2¼lb lean minced (ground) beef
75g/3oz/scant ½ cup long grain rice
4 onions, 2 chopped and 2 sliced
5–8 garlic cloves, chopped
2 eggs
45ml/3 tbsp water
1 large head of white or
  green cabbage
2 × 400g/14oz cans chopped tomatoes
45ml/3 tbsp demerara (raw) sugar
45ml/3 tbsp white wine vinegar,
  cider vinegar or lemon juice
pinch of ground cinnamon
salt and ground black pepper
lemon wedges, to serve

1 Put the beef, rice, 5ml/1 tsp salt, pepper, chopped onions and garlic in a bowl. Beat the eggs with the water, and combine with the meat mixture. Chill.

2 Cut the core from the cabbage in a cone shape and discard. Bring a very large pan of water to the boil, lower the cabbage into the water and blanch for 1–2 minutes, then remove from the pan. Peel one or two layers of leaves off the head, then re-submerge the cabbage. Repeat until all the leaves are removed.

3 Preheat the oven to 150°C/300°F/ Gas 2. Form the beef mixture into ovals, the size of small lemons, and wrap each in one to two cabbage leaves, folding and overlapping the leaves so that the mixture is completely enclosed.

4 Lay the cabbage rolls in the base of a large ovenproof dish, alternating with the sliced onions. Pour the tomatoes over and add the sugar, vinegar or lemon juice, salt, pepper and cinnamon. Cover and bake for 2 hours.

5 During cooking, remove the holishkes from the oven and baste them with the tomato juices two or three times.

6 After 2 hours, uncover the dish and cook for a further 30–60 minutes, or until the tomato sauce has thickened and is lightly browned on top. Serve hot with wedges of lemon.

COOK'S TIP

Any leaves that are too small to stuff, or that are left over when the stuffing has been used up, can be tucked into the side of the dish, alongside the stuffed cabbage rolls. Serve the cabbage leaves with the holishkes.

HUNGARIAN CHOLENT

A CHOLENT IS A LONG-SIMMERED OR BAKED DISH OF BEANS, GRAINS, MEATS AND VEGETABLES, LEFT IN A WARM OVEN OVERNIGHT OR FOR THE AFTERNOON. IT IS THE PERFECT SHABBAT DISH, TO BE EATEN AFTER RETURNING HOME FROM THE SYNAGOGUE ON A COLD NIGHT.

SERVES FOUR TO SIX

INGREDIENTS

250g/9oz/1⅓ cups white haricot
 (navy) or butter (wax) beans, soaked
 in water overnight
90ml/6 tbsp rendered chicken fat,
 goose fat, duck fat or olive oil
2 onions, chopped
14 garlic cloves, half chopped and
 half left whole
130g/4½oz pearl barley
25ml/1½ tbsp paprika
2–3 shakes of cayenne pepper
400g/14oz can chopped tomatoes
1 celery stick, chopped
3 carrots, sliced
1 small turnip, diced
2–3 baking potatoes, peeled and cut
 into large chunks and 1 potato,
 sliced (optional)
500g/1¼lb beef brisket, whole or
 cut into chunks
250g/9oz piece of smoked beef
250g/9oz stewing beef
4–6 eggs
1 litre/1¾ pints/4 cups water and
 500ml/17fl oz/2¼ cups beef stock
 or 1.5 litres/2½ pints/6¼ cups
 water and 1–2 stock (bouillon) cubes
stuffed kishke or helzel (optional)
a handful of rice (optional)
salt and ground black pepper

1 Preheat the oven to 120°C/250°F/ Gas ½. Drain the beans. Heat the fat or oil in a flameproof casserole, add the onions and chopped garlic and cook for 5 minutes. Add the beans.

2 Add the whole garlic cloves, barley, paprika, cayenne pepper, tomatoes, celery, carrots, turnip, chopped potatoes, brisket, smoked beef, stewing beef, the eggs in their shells, water and stock or stock cubes to the casserole and season well. Cover and bake for 3 hours.

3 Place the kishke or helzel, if using, on top of the stew. Check if the cholent needs more water. (There should still be a little liquid on top.) Add a little water if necessary, or, if there is too much liquid, add the extra sliced potato or a handful of rice. Cover and bake for a further 1–2 hours. Season and serve hot, making sure each portion contains a whole egg.

VARIATION

To make a Russian cholent, add kasha to the stew. Lightly toast 130g/4½oz buckwheat in a heavy, dry frying pan, then add it to the cholent in place of the pearl barley.

S W E E T <u>AND</u> S O U R T O N G U E

Tongue is a favourite meat in the Ashkenazi kitchen, although in recent years it has rather gone out of fashion. It is wonderful served hot with a sweet-and-sour sauce and leftovers are good cold, without the sauce, thinly sliced for sandwiches or a salad.

SERVES ABOUT EIGHT

INGREDIENTS
    1kg/2¼lb fresh ox tongue
    2–3 onions, 1 sliced and
        1–2 chopped
    3 bay leaves
    ½–1 stock (bouillon) cube or a
        small amount of stock powder
        or bouillon
    45ml/3 tbsp vegetable oil
    60ml/4 tbsp potato flour
    120ml/4fl oz/½ cup honey
    150g/5oz/1 cup raisins
    2.5ml/½ tsp salt
    2.5ml/½ tsp ground ginger
    1 lemon, sliced
    fresh rosemary sprigs, to garnish

1 Put the tongue, sliced onion and bay leaves in a large pan. Pour over cold water to cover and add the stock cube, powder or bouillon. Bring to the boil, reduce the heat, cover and simmer gently for 2–3 hours. Leave to cool.

2 In a small frying pan, heat the oil, add the chopped onion and cook for about 5 minutes, until softened.

3 Stir the potato flour into the onions and gradually add about 500ml/17fl oz/ 2¼ cups of the stock, stirring constantly to prevent lumps forming.

4 Stir the honey, raisins, salt and ginger into the sauce and continue to cook until it has thickened and is smooth. Add the lemon slices and set the sauce aside.

5 Slice the tongue thinly and serve generously coated with the sweet-and-sour sauce. Garnish with rosemary.

POT-ROASTED BRISKET

THIS BIG, POT-ROASTED MEAT DISH INCLUDES THE TRADITIONAL KISHKE, A HEAVY, SAUSAGE-SHAPED DUMPLING, WHICH IS ADDED TO THE POT AND COOKED WITH THE MEAT. SERVE WITH KASHA VARNISHKES — MEAT GRAVY WITH KASHA IS ONE OF LIFE'S PERFECT COMBINATIONS.

SERVES SIX TO EIGHT

INGREDIENTS
5 onions, sliced
3 bay leaves
1–1.6kg/2¼–3½lb beef brisket
1 garlic head, broken into cloves
4 carrots, thickly sliced
5–10ml/1–2 tsp paprika
about 500ml/17fl oz/2¼ cups
   beef stock
3–4 baking potatoes, peeled
   and quartered
salt and ground black pepper
For the kishke
   about 90cm/36in sausage casing
      (see Cook's Tip)
   250g/9oz/2¼ cups plain
      (all-purpose) flour
   120ml/4fl oz/½ cup semolina
      or couscous
   10–15ml/2–3 tsp paprika
   1 carrot, grated and 2 carrots,
      diced (optional)
   250ml/8fl oz/1 cup rendered
      chicken fat
   30ml/2 tbsp crisp, fried onions
   ½ onion, grated and 3 onions,
      thinly sliced
   3 garlic cloves, chopped
   salt and ground black pepper

2 Pour in enough stock to fill the dish to about 5–7.5cm/2–3in and cover with foil. Cook in the oven for 2 hours.

3 Meanwhile, make the kishke. In a bowl, combine all the ingredients and stuff the mixture into the casing, leaving enough space for the mixture to expand. Tie into sausage-shaped lengths.

4 When the meat has cooked for about 2 hours, add the kishke and potatoes to the pan, re-cover and cook for a further 1 hour, or until the meat and potatoes are tender.

5 Remove the foil from the dish and increase the oven temperature to 190–200°C/375–400°F/Gas 5–6. Move the onions away from the top of the meat to the side of the dish and return to the oven for a further 30 minutes, or until the meat, onions and potatoes are beginning to brown and become crisp. Serve hot or cold.

COOK'S TIP
Traditionally, sausage casings are used for kishke but, if unavailable, use cooking-strength clear film (plastic wrap) or a piece of muslin (cheesecloth).

1 Preheat the oven to 180°C/350°F/ Gas 4. Put one-third of the onions and a bay leaf in an ovenproof dish, then top with the brisket. Sprinkle over the garlic, carrots and the remaining bay leaves, sprinkle with salt, pepper and paprika, then top with the remaining onions.

BACHI'S BRAISED MINCED BEEF PATTIES WITH ONIONS

THIS IS ONE OF THE DISHES MY NEW YORKER GRANDMOTHER USED TO MAKE. SHE OFTEN ADDED EXTRA VEGETABLES WITH THE ONIONS, SUCH AS SLICED GREEN PEPPERS, BROCCOLI OR MUSHROOMS.

SERVES FOUR

INGREDIENTS

500g/1¼lb lean minced
  (ground) beef
4–6 garlic cloves, coarsely chopped
4 onions, 1 finely chopped and
  3 sliced
15–30ml/1–2 tbsp soy sauce
15–30ml/1–2 tbsp vegetable oil
  (optional)
2–3 green (bell) peppers, sliced
  lengthways into strips
ground black pepper

COOK'S TIP

If the patties and onions become slightly
dry during cooking, add a little water or
beef stock.

1 Place the minced beef, garlic and
chopped onions in a bowl and mix well.
Season with soy sauce and pepper and
form into four large or eight small patties.

2 Heat a non-stick pan, add a little oil,
if you like, then add the patties and cook
until browned. Splash over soy sauce.

3 Cover the patties with the sliced onions
and peppers, add a little soy sauce,
then cover the pan. Reduce the heat to
very low; braise for 20–30 minutes.

4 When the onions are turning golden
brown, remove the pan from the heat.
Serve the patties, piled with onions.

ISRAELI BARBECUED CHICKEN

BARBECUED CHICKEN IS UBIQUITOUS TO ISRAEL AND IT SEEMS THAT EVERY STREET CORNER KIOSK AND STALL SELLS A VERSION OF THIS AROMATIC TREAT. IN THIS RECIPE, THE EGYPTIAN-INSPIRED MARINADE IS STRONGLY SCENTED WITH CUMIN AND CINNAMON.

SERVES FOUR

INGREDIENTS
    5 garlic cloves, chopped
    30ml/2 tbsp ground cumin
    7.5ml/1½ tsp ground cinnamon
    5ml/1 tsp paprika
    juice of 1 lemon
    30ml/2 tbsp olive oil
    1.3kg/3lb chicken, cut into
        8 portions
    salt and ground black pepper
    fresh coriander (cilantro) leaves,
        to garnish
    warmed pitta bread, salad and
        lemon wedges, to serve

VARIATION
For a Yemenite flavour, use 7.5ml/
1½ tsp turmeric and a pinch of ground
cardamom in place of the cinnamon.

1 In a bowl, combine the garlic, cumin, cinnamon, paprika, lemon juice, oil, salt and pepper. Add the chicken and turn to coat thoroughly. Leave to marinate for at least 1 hour or cover and place in the refrigerator overnight.

2 Light the barbecue. After about 40 minutes it will be ready for cooking.

3 Arrange the dark meat on the grill and cook for 10 minutes, turning once.

4 Place the remaining chicken on the grill and cook for 7–10 minutes, turning occasionally, until golden brown and the juices run clear when pricked with a skewer. Serve immediately, with pitta breads, lemon wedges and salad.

SEPHARDI SPICED CHICKEN RICE
WITH LEMON AND MINT RELISH

THIS IS A LIGHTER, QUICKER VERSION OF HAMEEN, THE LONG-SIMMERED SHABBAT STEW. THIS MODERN VERSION IS MORE REFRESHING THAN THE HEAVIER ORIGINAL.

SERVES FOUR

INGREDIENTS
  250g/9oz chicken, skinned and diced
  3 garlic cloves, chopped
  5ml/1 tsp ground turmeric
  30–45ml/2–3 tbsp olive oil
  2 small-medium carrots, diced
    or chopped
  seeds from 6–8 cardamom pods
  500g/1¼lb/2½ cups long grain rice
  250g/9oz tomatoes, chopped
  750ml/1¼ pints/3 cups
    chicken stock
For the lemon and mint relish
  3 tomatoes, diced
  1 bunch or large handful of fresh
    mint, chopped
  5–8 spring onions (scallions),
    thinly sliced
  juice of 2 lemons
  salt

1 To make the relish, put all the ingredients in a bowl and mix together. Chill until ready to serve.

2 Mix the diced chicken with half the garlic and the turmeric. Heat a little of the oil in a pan, add the chicken and fry briefly until the chicken has changed colour and is almost cooked. Remove from the pan and set aside.

3 Add the carrots to the pan with the remaining oil, then stir in the remaining garlic, cardamom seeds and the rice. Cook for 1–2 minutes.

4 Add the tomatoes and chicken stock to the pan and bring to the boil. Cover and simmer for about 10 minutes, until the rice is tender. A few minutes before the rice is cooked, fork in the chicken. Serve with the relish.

VARIATIONS
• Use the same quantity of pumpkin or butternut squash in place of the carrots.
• To make a vegetarian version, omit the chicken and add a 400g/14oz can of drained chickpeas to the rice just before the end of cooking.
• Dark chicken meat, such as thighs, are good in this recipe and less expensive than breast meat.

PETTI DI POLLO ALL'EBRAICA

THIS ITALIAN DISH STRONGLY REFLECTS THE TRADITIONS OF BOTH MEDITERRANEAN AND JEWISH COOKING. JEWS FAVOUR THE ENRICHMENT OF MEAT SAUCES WITH EGG BECAUSE OF THE LAWS OF THE KASHRUT, WHICH FORBIDS THE ADDITION OF CREAM TO MEAT DISHES.

SERVES FOUR

INGREDIENTS

4 skinless, boneless chicken
  breast portions
plain (all-purpose) flour, for dusting
30–45ml/2–3 tbsp olive oil
1–2 onions, chopped
¼ fennel bulb, chopped (optional)
15ml/1 tbsp chopped fresh parsley,
  plus extra to garnish
7.5ml/1½ tsp fennel seeds
75ml/5 tbsp dry Marsala
120ml/4fl oz/½ cup chicken stock
300g/11oz/2¼ cups petits pois
  (baby peas)
juice of 1½ lemons
2 egg yolks
salt and ground black pepper

1 Season the chicken with salt and pepper, then dust generously with flour. Shake off the excess flour; set aside.

2 Heat 15ml/1 tbsp oil in a pan, add the onions, fennel, if using, parsley and fennel seeds. Cook for 5 minutes.

3 Add the remaining oil and the chicken to the pan and cook for 2–3 minutes on each side, until lightly browned. Remove the chicken and onion mixture from the pan and set aside.

4 Deglaze the pan by pouring in the Marsala and cooking over a high heat until reduced to about 30ml/2 tbsp, then pour in the stock. Add the peas and return the chicken and onion mixture to the pan. Cook over a very low heat while you prepare the egg mixture.

5 In a bowl, beat the lemon juice and egg yolks together, then slowly add about 120ml/4fl oz/½ cup of the hot liquid from the chicken and peas, stirring well to combine.

6 Return the mixture to the pan and cook over a low heat, stirring, until the mixture thickens slightly. (Do not allow the mixture to boil or the eggs will curdle and spoil the sauce.) Serve the chicken immediately, sprinkled with a little extra chopped fresh parsley.

ROASTED CHICKEN WITH GRAPES AND FRESH ROOT GINGER

THIS DISH, WITH ITS BLEND OF SPICES AND SWEET FRUIT, IS INSPIRED BY MOROCCAN FLAVOURS.
SERVE WITH COUSCOUS, MIXED WITH A HANDFUL OF COOKED CHICKPEAS.

SERVES FOUR

INGREDIENTS
1–1.6kg/2¼–3½ lb chicken
115–130g/4–4½ oz fresh root
   ginger, grated
6–8 garlic cloves, roughly chopped
juice of 1 lemon
about 30ml/2 tbsp olive oil
2–3 large pinches of ground cinnamon
500g/1¼ lb seeded red and
   green grapes
500g/1¼ lb seedless green grapes
5–7 shallots, chopped
about 250ml/8fl oz/1 cup chicken stock
salt and ground black pepper

1 Rub the chicken with half of the ginger, the garlic, half of the lemon juice, the olive oil, cinnamon, salt and lots of pepper. Leave to marinate.

2 Meanwhile, cut the red and green seeded grapes in half, remove the seeds and set aside. Add the whole green seedless grapes to the halved ones.

3 Preheat the oven to 180°C/350°F/ Gas 4. Heat a heavy frying pan or flameproof casserole until hot.

4 Remove the chicken from the marinade, add to the pan and cook until browned on all sides. (There should be enough oil on the chicken to brown it but, if not, add a little extra.)

5 Put some of the shallots into the chicken cavity with the garlic and ginger from the marinade and as many of the red and green grapes that will fit inside. Roast in the oven for 40–60 minutes, or until the chicken is tender.

VARIATIONS
• This dish is good made with duck in place of the chicken. Marinate and roast as above, adding 15–30ml/1–2 tbsp honey to the pan sauce as it cooks.
• Use boneless chicken breast portions, with the skin still attached, instead of a whole chicken. Pan-fry the chicken portions, rather than roasting them.

6 Remove the chicken from the pan and keep warm. Pour off any oil from the pan, reserving any sediment in the base of the pan. Add the remaining shallots to the pan and cook for about 5 minutes until softened.

7 Add half the remaining red and green grapes, the remaining ginger, the stock and any juices from the roast chicken and cook over a medium-high heat until the grapes have cooked down to a thick sauce. Season with salt, ground black pepper and the remaining lemon juice to taste.

8 Serve the chicken on a warmed serving dish, surrounded by the sauce and the reserved grapes.

COOK'S TIP
Seeded Italia or muscat grapes have a delicious, sweet fragrance and are perfect for using in this recipe.

TURKEY OR CHICKEN SCHNITZEL

SCHNITZEL IS A POUNDED-FLAT, CRISP-COATED, FRIED STEAK OF TURKEY, CHICKEN OR VEAL. IN THE OLD COUNTRY OF AUSTRIA, SCHNITZEL WAS MADE FROM VEAL. TODAY IN ISRAEL IT IS USUALLY MADE OF TURKEY AND IS IMMENSELY POPULAR. SERVE WITH A SELECTION OF VEGETABLES.

SERVES FOUR

INGREDIENTS

4 boneless turkey or chicken breast
  fillets, each weighing about 175g/6oz
juice of 1 lemon
2 garlic cloves, chopped
plain (all-purpose) flour, for dusting
1–2 eggs
15ml/1 tbsp water
about 50g/2oz/½ cup matzo meal
paprika
a mixture of vegetable and olive oil,
  for shallow frying
salt and ground black pepper
lemon wedges and a selection of
  vegetables, to serve (optional)

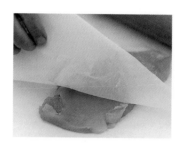

1 Lay each piece of meat between two sheets of greaseproof (waxed) paper and pound with a mallet or the end of a rolling pin until it is about half its original thickness and fairly even.

2 In a bowl, combine the lemon juice, garlic, salt and pepper. Coat the meat in it, then leave to marinate.

3 Meanwhile, arrange three wide plates or shallow dishes in a row. Fill one plate or dish with flour, beat the egg and water together in another and mix the matzo meal, salt, pepper and paprika together on the third.

4 Working quickly, dip each fillet into the flour, then the egg, then the matzo meal. Pat everything in well, then arrange the crumbed fillets on a plate and chill for at least 30 minutes, and up to 2 hours.

5 In a large, heavy frying pan, heat the oil until it will turn a cube of bread dropped into the oil golden brown in 30–60 seconds. Carefully add the crumbed fillets (in batches if necessary) and fry until golden brown, turning once. Remove and drain on kitchen paper. Serve immediately with lemon wedges and a selection of vegetables.

CHICKEN, SPLIT PEA AND AUBERGINE KORESH

THIS IS A CALIFORNIAN VERSION OF THE TRADITIONAL PERSIAN KORESH, A THICK, SAUCY STEW SERVED WITH RICE, WHICH IS A MAINSTAY OF THE PERSIAN TABLE. IN IRAN, LAMB WAS OFTEN THE MEAT OF CHOICE BUT IN SUNNY CALIFORNIA THIS HEARTY MEAT DISH HAS BEEN TRANSFORMED TO A LIGHT CHICKEN, TOMATO AND SPLIT PEA STEW.

SERVES FOUR TO SIX

INGREDIENTS
50g/2oz/¼ cup green split peas
45–60ml/3–4 tbsp olive oil
1 large or 2 small onions,
  finely chopped
500g/1¼lb boneless
  chicken thighs
500ml/17fl oz/2¼ cups
  chicken stock
5ml/1 tsp ground turmeric
2.5ml/½ tsp ground cinnamon
1.5ml/¼ tsp grated nutmeg
2 aubergines (eggplant), diced
8–10 ripe tomatoes, diced
2 garlic cloves, crushed
30ml/2 tbsp dried mint
salt and ground black pepper
fresh mint, to garnish
rice, to serve

1 Put the split peas in a bowl, pour over cold water to cover, then leave to soak for about 4 hours. Drain well.

2 Heat a little of the oil in a pan, add two-thirds of the onions and cook for about 5 minutes. Add the chicken and cook until golden brown on all sides.

3 Add the soaked split peas to the chicken mixture, then the stock, turmeric, cinnamon and nutmeg. Cook over a medium-low heat for about 40 minutes, until the split peas are tender.

VARIATION
To make a traditional lamb koresh, use 675g/1½lb lamb stew chunks in place of the chicken. Add to the onions, pour over water to cover and cook for 1½ hours until tender, then proceed as above.

4 Heat the remaining oil in a pan, add the aubergines and remaining onions and cook until lightly browned. Add the tomatoes, garlic and mint. Season.

5 Just before serving, stir the aubergine mixture into the chicken and split pea stew. Garnish with fresh mint leaves and serve with rice.

DORO WAT

LONG-SIMMERED ETHIOPIAN STEWS, KNOWN AS WATS, ARE OFTEN MADE FOR SHABBAT. THEY ARE TRADITIONALLY SERVED WITH THE PANCAKE-LIKE FLAT BREAD, INJERA, WHICH IS MADE BEFORE THE SABBATH AND WRAPPED IN A CLEAN CLOTH UNTIL THE WAT IS READY TO EAT. THE EGGS ARE AN INTRINSIC PART OF THE DISH SO MAKE SURE EVERYONE RECEIVES ONE IN THEIR PORTION.

SERVES FOUR

INGREDIENTS
90ml/6 tbsp vegetable oil
6–8 onions, chopped
6 garlic cloves, chopped
10ml/2 tsp chopped fresh root ginger
250ml/8fl oz/1 cup water or
    chicken stock
250ml/8fl oz/1 cup passata (bottled
    strained tomatoes) or 400g/14oz
    can chopped tomatoes
1.3kg/3lb chicken, cut into
    8–12 portions
seeds from 5–8 cardamom pods
2.5ml/½ tsp ground turmeric
large pinch of ground cinnamon
large pinch of ground cloves
large pinch of grated nutmeg
cayenne pepper, hot paprika or
    berbere, to taste
4 hard-boiled eggs
salt and ground black pepper
fresh coriander (cilantro) and
    onion rings, to garnish
injera, flat bread or rice, to serve

3 Add the chicken and spices to the pan and turn the chicken in the sauce. Reduce the heat, then cover and simmer, stirring occasionally, for about 1 hour, or until the chicken is tender. Add a little more liquid if the mixture seems too thick.

4 Remove the shells from the eggs and then prick the eggs once or twice with a fork. Add the eggs to the sauce and heat gently until the eggs are warmed through. Garnish with coriander and onion rings and serve with injera, flat bread or rice.

1 Heat the oil in a pan, add the onions and cook for 10 minutes until softened but not browned. Add the garlic and ginger and cook for 1–2 minutes.

2 Add the water or chicken stock and the passata or chopped tomatoes to the pan. Bring to the boil and cook, stirring continuously, for about 10 minutes, or until the liquid has reduced and the mixture has thickened. Season.

MILD GREEN CALCUTTA CURRY OF CHICKEN AND VEGETABLES

THE ADDITION OF COCONUT MILK CREATES A RICH SAUCE THAT IS SWEET WITH DRIED AND FRESH FRUIT AND FRAGRANT WITH HERBS. IT IS PERFECT FOR THOSE KEEPING KASHRUT AS IT HAS A CREAMY CHARACTER YET CONTAINS NO DAIRY PRODUCTS. SERVE WITH HOT NAAN OR STEAMED RICE.

SERVES FOUR

INGREDIENTS

4 garlic cloves, chopped
15ml/1 tbsp chopped fresh
  root ginger
2–3 chillies, chopped
½ bunch fresh coriander (cilantro)
  leaves, roughly chopped
1 onion, chopped
juice of 1 lemon
pinch of cayenne pepper
2.5ml/½ tsp curry powder
2.5ml/½ tsp ground cumin
2–3 pinches of ground cloves
large pinch of ground coriander
3 boneless chicken breast portions
  or thighs, skinned and cut into
  bitesize pieces
30ml/2 tbsp vegetable oil
2 cinnamon sticks
250ml/8fl oz/1 cup chicken stock
250ml/8fl oz/1 cup coconut milk
15–30ml/1–2 tbsp sugar
1–2 bananas
¼ pineapple, peeled and chopped
handful of sultanas (golden raisins)
handful of raisins or currants
2–3 sprigs of fresh mint, thinly sliced
juice of ¼–½ lemon
salt

1 Purée the garlic, ginger, chillies, fresh coriander, onion, lemon juice, cayenne pepper, curry powder, cumin, cloves, ground coriander and salt in a food processor or blender.

2 Toss together the chicken pieces with about 15–30ml/1–2 tbsp of the spice mixture and set aside.

3 Heat the oil in a wok or frying pan, then add the remaining spice mixture and cook over a medium heat, stirring, for 10 minutes, or until the paste is lightly browned.

4 Stir the cinnamon sticks, stock, coconut milk and sugar into the pan, bring to the boil, then reduce the heat and simmer for 10 minutes.

5 Stir the chicken into the sauce and cook for 2 minutes, or until the chicken becomes opaque.

6 Meanwhile, thickly slice the bananas. Stir all the fruit into the curry and cook for 1–2 minutes. Stir in the mint and lemon juice. Check the seasoning and add more salt, spice and lemon juice if necessary. Serve immediately.

VEGETARIAN DISHES

The Jewish table has a tradition of vegetarianism. When meat cannot be eaten, for example when kosher meat is unavailable or when there are no kosher pans to cook it in, vegetarian dishes are often chosen. The repertoire of Jewish vegetarian dishes is wide and varied, including dishes based on aubergine (eggplant), eggs, rice, beans, chickpeas, tahini and even tofu. Vegetable cutlets and schnitzel are popular Israeli dishes, as are the many zesty vegetable stews.

SPLIT PEA <u>OR</u> LENTIL FRITTERS

THESE SPICY FRITTERS CALLED PIAJU COME FROM THE INDIAN SUBCONTINENT. THEY ARE, NO DOUBT, COUSINS OF TA'AMIA AND FALAFEL. SERVE WITH A WEDGE OF LEMON AND A SPOONFUL OF HOT, FRAGRANT CHUTNEY SUCH AS MINT.

SERVES FOUR TO SIX

INGREDIENTS

   250g/9oz/generous 1 cup yellow split
     peas or red lentils, soaked overnight
   3–5 garlic cloves, chopped
   30ml/2 tbsp roughly chopped fresh
     root ginger
   120ml/4fl oz/½ cup chopped fresh
     coriander (cilantro) leaves
   2.5–5ml/½–1 tsp ground cumin
   1.5–2.5ml/¼–½tsp ground turmeric
   large pinch of cayenne pepper or
     ½–1 fresh green chilli, chopped
   120ml/4fl oz/½ cup gram (besan) flour
   5ml/1 tsp baking powder
   30ml/2 tbsp couscous
   2 large or 3 small onions, chopped
   vegetable oil, for frying
   salt and ground black pepper
   lemon wedges, to serve

1 Drain the split peas or lentils, reserving a little of the soaking water. Put the chopped garlic and ginger in a food processor or blender and process until finely minced (ground). Add the drained peas or lentils, 15–30ml/ 1–2 tbsp of the reserved soaking water and the chopped coriander, and process to form a purée.

2 Add the cumin, turmeric, cayenne or chilli, 2.5ml/½ tsp salt, 2.5ml/½ tsp pepper, the gram flour, baking powder and couscous to the mixture and combine. The mixture should form a thick batter. If it seems too thick, add a spoonful of soaking water and if it is too watery, add a little more flour or couscous. Mix in the onions.

3 Heat the oil in a wide, deep frying pan, to a depth of about 5cm/2in, until it is hot enough to brown a cube of bread in 30 seconds. Using two spoons, form the mixture into two-bitesize balls and slip each one gently into the hot oil. Cook until golden brown on the underside, then turn and cook the second side until golden brown.

4 Remove the fritters from the hot oil with a slotted spoon and drain well on kitchen paper. Transfer the fritters to a baking sheet and keep warm in the oven until all the mixture is cooked. Serve hot or at room temperature with lemon wedges.

FALAFEL

THESE DEEP-FRIED CHICKPEA FRITTERS ARE CLASSIC ISRAELI SNACK FOOD. THE SECRET TO GOOD FALAFEL IS USING WELL-SOAKED, BUT NOT COOKED, CHICKPEAS. DO NOT USE CANNED CHICKPEAS AS THE TEXTURE WILL BE MUSHY AND THE FALAFEL WILL FALL APART WHEN THEY ARE FRIED.

SERVES SIX

INGREDIENTS
250g/9oz/generous 1⅓ cups
   dried chickpeas
1 litre/1¾ pints/4 cups water
45–60ml/3–4 tbsp bulgur wheat
1 large or 2 small onions,
   finely chopped
5 garlic cloves, crushed
75ml/5 tbsp chopped fresh parsley
75ml/5 tbsp chopped fresh coriander
   (cilantro) leaves
45ml/3 tbsp ground cumin
15ml/1 tbsp ground coriander
5ml/1 tsp baking powder
5m/1 tsp salt
small pinch to 1.5ml/¼ tsp ground
   black pepper
small pinch to 1.5ml/¼ tsp
   cayenne pepper
5ml/1 tsp curry powder with a pinch
   of cardamom seeds added (optional)
45–60ml/3–4 tbsp gram (besan) flour
crumbled wholemeal (whole-wheat)
   bread or flour, if necessary
vegetable oil, for deep-frying
6 pitta breads, hummus, Chopped
   Vegetable Salad Relish, tahini,
   Tabasco or other hot pepper sauce,
   pickles, olives and salads, such as
   shredded cabbage, to serve

1 Place the chickpeas in a large bowl and pour over the water. Leave to soak for at least 4 hours, then drain and grind in a food processor.

2 Put the ground chickpeas in a bowl and stir in the bulgur wheat, onion, garlic, parsley, fresh coriander, ground cumin and coriander, baking powder, salt, black pepper and cayenne pepper, and curry powder, if using. Stir in 45ml/ 3 tbsp water and leave to stand for about 45 minutes.

3 Stir the gram flour into the falafel batter, adding a little water if it is too thick or a little crumbled wholemeal bread or flour if it is too thin.

4 Using a wet tablespoon and wet hands, shape heaped tablespoons of the falafel mixture into 12–18 balls.

5 Heat the oil for deep-frying in a pan until it is hot enough to brown a cube of bread in 30 seconds. Lower the heat.

6 Add the falafel to the hot oil in batches and cook for 3–4 minutes until golden brown. Remove the cooked falafel with a slotted spoon and drain on kitchen paper before adding more to the oil.

7 Serve the freshly cooked falafel tucked into warmed pitta bread with a spoonful of hummus, vegetable relish and a drizzle of tahini. Accompany with hot pepper sauce, pickles, olives and some salads.

COOK'S TIP
If you wish to prepare the falafel ahead of time, undercook them, then arrange them on a baking sheet and finish cooking them in the oven at 190°C/ 375°F/Gas 5 for about 10 minutes.

SEPHARDI STUFFED ONIONS, POTATOES AND COURGETTES

THE VEGETARIAN FILLING OF THESE VEGETABLES IS TOMATO-RED, YEMENITE-SPICED AND ACCENTED WITH THE TART TASTE OF LEMON. THEY ARE DELICIOUS COLD AND ARE GOOD SERVED AS AN APPETIZER AS WELL AS A MAIN COURSE.

SERVES FOUR

INGREDIENTS

- 4 potatoes, peeled
- 4 onions, skinned
- 4 courgettes (zucchini),
  halved widthways
- 2–4 garlic cloves, chopped
- 45–60ml/3–4 tbsp olive oil
- 45–60ml/3–4 tbsp tomato
  purée (paste)
- 1.5ml/¼ tsp ras al hanout or
  curry powder
- large pinch of ground allspice
- seeds of 2–3 cardamom pods
- juice of ½ lemon
- 30–45ml/2–3 tbsp chopped
  fresh parsley
- 90–120ml/6–8 tbsp vegetable stock
- salt and ground black pepper
- salad, to serve (optional)

1 Bring a large pan of salted water to the boil. Starting with the potatoes, then the onions and finally the courgettes, add to the boiling water and cook until they become almost tender but not cooked through. Allow about 10 minutes for the potatoes, 8 minutes for the onions and 4–6 minutes for the courgettes. Remove the vegetables from the pan and leave to cool.

COOK'S TIP
Use a small melon baller or apple corer to hollow out the vegetables.

2 When the vegetables are cool enough to handle, hollow them out. Preheat the oven to 190°C/375°F/Gas 5.

3 Finely chop the cut-out vegetable flesh and put it in a bowl. Add the garlic, half the olive oil, the tomato purée, ras al hanout or curry powder, allspice, cardamom seeds, lemon juice, parsley, salt and pepper and mix well together. Use the stuffing mixture to fill the hollowed vegetables.

4 Arrange the stuffed vegetables in a baking tin (pan) and drizzle with the stock and the remaining oil. Roast for 35–40 minutes, or until golden brown. Serve warm with a salad, if you like.

STUFFED VINE LEAVES <u>WITH</u> CUMIN, LEMON <u>AND</u> HERBS

THE IMPORTANT INGREDIENTS IN THESE STUFFED VINE LEAVES ARE THE FLAVOURINGS AND FRESH HERBS THAT GIVE THE BROWN RICE FILLING ITS ZEST AND SPECIAL TASTE.

SERVES SIX TO EIGHT

INGREDIENTS

250g/9oz/1¼ cups brown rice
30–45ml/2–3 tbsp natural
  (plain) yogurt
3 garlic cloves, chopped
1 egg, lightly beaten
5–10ml/1–2 tsp ground cumin
2.5ml/½ tsp ground cinnamon
several handfuls of raisins
3–4 spring onions (scallions),
  thinly sliced
½ bunch fresh mint or 10ml/2 tsp
  dried mint, plus extra to garnish
about 25 preserved or fresh
  vine leaves
salt, if necessary
For cooking
8–10 unpeeled garlic cloves
juice of ½–1 lemon
90ml/6 tbsp olive oil
For serving
1 lemon, cut into wedges or half slices
15–25 Greek black olives
150ml/¼ pint/⅔ cup natural
  (plain) yogurt

1 Put the rice in a pan with 300ml/ ½ pint/1¼ cups water. Bring to the boil, reduce the heat, cover and simmer for 30 minutes, or until just tender. Drain well and leave to cool slightly.

2 Put the cooked rice in a bowl, add the yogurt, garlic, egg, ground cumin and cinnamon, raisins, spring onions and mint and mix together.

3 If you are using preserved vine leaves, rinse them well. If using fresh vine leaves, blanch in salted boiling water for 2–3 minutes, then rinse under cold water and drain.

VARIATIONS
For a twist to the classic stuffed vine leaf, other herbs such as dill or parsley can be used, and a handful of pine nuts can be added to the stuffing.

4 Lay the leaves on a board, shiny side down. Place 15–30ml/1–2 tbsp of the mixture near the stalk of each leaf. Fold each one up, starting at the bottom, then the sides, and finally rolling up towards the top to enclose the filling.

5 Carefully layer the rolls in a steamer and stud with the whole garlic cloves. Fill the base of the steamer with water and drizzle the lemon juice and olive oil evenly over the rolls.

6 Cover the steamer tightly and cook over a medium-high heat for about 40 minutes, adding more water to the steamer if necessary.

7 Remove the steamer from the heat and set aside to cool slightly. Arrange the vine leaves on a serving dish and serve hot or, alternatively, leave to cool further. Garnish and serve with lemon wedges or half slices, olives, and a bowl of yogurt, for dipping.

THREE VEGETABLE KUGEL

GRATED SEASONAL VEGETABLES, BAKED UNTIL CRISP ON TOP AND CREAMY AND TENDER INSIDE, MAKE A WONDERFUL MODERN KUGEL. THIS VERSION COMBINES THE TRADITIONAL FLAVOURS AND METHOD BUT USES A MORE CONTEMPORARY COMBINATION OF VEGETABLES.

SERVES FOUR

INGREDIENTS

2 courgettes (zucchini),
  coarsely grated
2 carrots, coarsely grated
2 potatoes, peeled and
  coarsely grated
1 onion, grated
3 eggs, lightly beaten
3 garlic cloves, chopped
pinch of sugar
15ml/1 tbsp finely chopped
  fresh parsley
2–3 pinches of dried basil
30–45ml/2–3 tbsp matzo meal
105ml/7 tbsp olive or vegetable oil
salt and ground black pepper

1 Preheat the oven to 180°C/350°F/ Gas 4. Put the courgettes, carrots, potatoes, onion, eggs, garlic, sugar, parsley, basil, salt and pepper in a bowl and combine. Add the matzo meal and mix together to form a thick batter.

2 Pour half the oil into an ovenproof dish, spoon in the vegetable mixture, then pour over the remaining oil. Bake for 40–60 minutes, or until the vegetables are tender and the top is golden brown. Serve hot.

BROCCOLI AND CHEESE MINA

A MINA IS A TYPE OF PIE, PREPARED FROM LAYERED MATZOS AND A SAVOURY SAUCE, AND TOPPED WITH BEATEN EGG, WHICH HOLDS IT ALL TOGETHER AS IT BAKES.

2 Wet four matzos and leave to soak for 2–3 minutes. Butter a baking sheet that is large enough to hold four matzo pieces in a single layer. If necessary, use two baking sheets.

3 Place the dampened matzos on the baking sheet, then top evenly with the broccoli, onion, Cheddar cheese, cottage cheese, Parmesan cheese, spring onions and dill.

4 In a bowl, lightly beat together the eggs and water, then pour about half the egg over the cheese and broccoli mixture. Wet the remaining matzos and place on top of the broccoli. Pour the remaining beaten egg over the top, dot with half the butter and sprinkle half the chopped garlic over the top.

5 Bake the mina for 20 minutes. Dot the remaining butter on top and sprinkle over the remaining chopped garlic. Return to the oven and bake for about 10 minutes more, or until the mina is golden brown and crisp on top. Serve hot or warm.

SERVES FOUR

INGREDIENTS
1 large broccoli head
pinch of salt
pinch of sugar
8 matzo squares
50g/2oz/½ cup butter, plus extra
  for greasing
1 onion, chopped
250g/9oz/2¼ cups grated
  Cheddar cheese
250g/9oz/generous 1 cup
  cottage cheese
65g/2½oz/¾ cup freshly grated
  Parmesan cheese
2 spring onions (scallions), chopped
30–45ml/2–3 tbsp chopped fresh dill
4 eggs
30ml/2 tbsp water
8 garlic cloves, chopped

1 Preheat the oven to 190°C/375°F/ Gas 5. Remove the tough part of the stem from the broccoli, then cut the broccoli head into even-size florets. Cook the broccoli by either steaming above or boiling in water to which you have added a pinch of salt and sugar. Cook until bright green, then remove from the pan with a slotted spoon.

BALKAN AUBERGINES WITH CHEESE

THIS WONDERFUL DISH OF AUBERGINES IS CLOAKED IN A THICK CHEESE SAUCE THAT, WHEN COOKED, HAS A TOPPING SLIGHTLY LIKE A SOUFFLÉ. IT IS DELICIOUS HOT BUT EVEN BETTER COLD AND, ALTHOUGH IT TAKES A WHILE TO PREPARE, IS THE PERFECT DISH TO MAKE AHEAD OF TIME FOR FESTIVALS, SHABBAT OR A PICNIC.

SERVES FOUR TO SIX

INGREDIENTS

2 large aubergines (eggplant), cut
   into 5mm/¼in thick slices
about 60ml/4 tbsp olive oil
25g/1oz/2 tbsp butter
30ml/2 tbsp plain (all-purpose) flour
500ml/17fl oz/2¼ cups hot milk
about ⅛ of a nutmeg, freshly grated
cayenne pepper
4 large (US extra large) eggs,
   lightly beaten
400g/14oz/3½ cups grated cheese,
   such as kashkaval, Gruyère, or a
   mixture of Parmesan and Cheddar
salt and ground black pepper

1 Layer the aubergine slices in a bowl or colander, sprinkling each layer with salt, and leave to drain for at least 30 minutes. Rinse well, then pat dry with kitchen paper.

2 Heat the oil in a frying pan, then fry the aubergine slices until golden brown on both sides. Remove from the pan and set aside.

3 Melt the butter in a pan, then add the flour and cook for I minute, stirring. Remove from the heat and gradually stir in the hot milk. Return to the heat and slowly bring to the boil, stirring constantly, until the sauce thickens and becomes smooth. Season with nutmeg, cayenne pepper, salt and black pepper and leave to cool.

4 When the sauce is cool, beat in the eggs, then mix in the grated cheese, reserving a little to sprinkle on top of the dish. Preheat the oven to 180°C/350°F/Gas 4.

5 In an ovenproof dish, arrange a layer of the aubergine, then pour over some sauce. Repeat, ending with sauce. Sprinkle with the cheese. Bake for 35–40 minutes until golden and firm.

MUSHROOM STROGANOFF

THIS CREAMY SAUCE, STUDDED WITH MUSHROOMS, IS IDEAL FOR A DINNER PARTY. SERVE IT WITH KASHA, BROWN RICE OR A MIXTURE OF WILD RICES.

SERVES FOUR

INGREDIENTS

40–50g/1½–2oz/3–4 tbsp butter
500g/1¼lb button (white)
  mushrooms, quartered
250g/9oz assorted wild or interesting,
  unusual mushrooms, cut into
  bitesize pieces
6 garlic cloves, chopped
2 onions, chopped
30ml/2 tbsp plain (all-purpose) flour
120ml/4fl oz/½ cup dry white wine
250ml/8fl oz/1 cup vegetable stock
2.5ml/½ tsp dried basil
250g/9oz crème fraîche
large pinch of freshly grated nutmeg
juice of about ¼ lemon
salt and ground black pepper
chopped fresh parsley or chives,
  to garnish
buckwheat, brown rice or wild rice,
  to serve

3 Remove the pan from the heat and gradually stir in the wine and half the stock. Return to the heat and slowly bring to the boil, stirring constantly, until the sauce thickens and becomes smooth. Gradually stir in the remaining stock and continue to cook until the sauce is thick.

4 Add the basil and mushrooms, including their juices, to the pan. Put the crème fraîche in a bowl and stir in a little sauce, then stir the mixture into the sauce. Season with nutmeg, lemon juice, salt and pepper. Serve hot, garnished with parsley or chives and accompanied by buckwheat or rice.

1 Melt a little of the butter in a pan and quickly fry the mushrooms, in batches, over a high heat, until brown. During cooking, sprinkle the mushrooms with a little of the garlic, reserving about half for use later. Transfer the mushrooms to a plate after cooking each batch.

2 Heat the remaining butter in the pan, add the chopped onions and fry for about 5 minutes until softened. Add the remaining garlic and cook for a further 1–2 minutes, then sprinkle over the flour and cook for 1 minute more, stirring continuously.

HATZILIM PILPEL

IN HEBREW, THE WORD HATZILIM MEANS AUBERGINE AND PILPEL MEANS SPICY AND PEPPERY. IN THIS RECIPE THEY COMBINE TO MAKE A FIERY TOMATO AND AUBERGINE STEW THAT IS TYPICAL OF ISRAELI COOKING, FOR WHICH AUBERGINES AND ALL THINGS HOT AND SPICY ARE STAPLES.

SERVES FOUR TO SIX

INGREDIENTS
about 60ml/4 tbsp olive oil
1 large aubergine (eggplant) cut
   into bitesize chunks
2 onions, thinly sliced
3–5 garlic cloves, chopped
1–2 green (bell) peppers, thinly
   sliced or chopped
1–2 fresh hot chillies, chopped
4 fresh or canned tomatoes, diced
30–45ml/2–3 tbsp tomato purée
   (paste), if using fresh tomatoes
5ml/1 tsp ground turmeric
pinch of curry powder or
   ras al hanout
cayenne pepper, to taste
400g/14oz can chickpeas, drained
   and rinsed
juice of ½–1 lemon
30–45ml/2–3 tbsp chopped fresh
   coriander (cilantro) leaves
salt

2 Heat the remaining oil in the pan, add the onions, garlic, peppers and chillies and fry until softened. Add the diced tomatoes, tomato purée, if using, spices and salt, and cook, stirring, until the mixture is of a sauce consistency. Add a little water if necessary.

3 Add the chickpeas to the sauce and cook for about 5 minutes, then add the aubergine, stir to mix and cook for 5–10 minutes until the flavours are well combined. Add lemon juice to taste, then add the coriander leaves. Chill before serving.

1 Heat half the oil in a frying pan, add the aubergine chunks and fry until brown, adding more oil if necessary. When cooked, transfer the aubergine to a strainer, standing over a bowl, and leave to drain.

VARIATION
To make a Middle Eastern-style ratatouille, cut 2 courgettes (zucchini) and one red (bell) pepper into chunks. Add to the pan with the onions and garlic and continue as before.

MEGADARRA

THIS DISH OF RICE AND LENTILS IS A CLASSIC MEAL FOR BOTH JEWS AND ARABS, FROM EGYPT AND LIBYA TO GALILEE AND GREECE. IT IS OFTEN ENJOYED WITH A BOWL OF VEGETABLES, ANOTHER OF COOLING YOGURT, AND A PLATE OF CRISP SALAD.

SERVES SIX TO EIGHT

INGREDIENTS
  400g/14oz/1¾ cups large brown or
    green lentils
  45ml/3 tbsp olive oil
  3–4 onions, 1 chopped and
    2–3 thinly sliced
  5ml/1 tsp ground cumin
  2.5ml/½ tsp ground cinnamon
  3–5 cardamom pods
  300g/11oz/1½ cups long grain
    rice, rinsed
  about 250ml/8fl oz/1 cup
    vegetable stock
  salt and ground black pepper
  natural (plain) yogurt, to serve

1 Put the lentils in a pan with enough water to cover generously. Bring to the boil, then simmer for about 30 minutes, or until tender. Skim off any scum that forms on top.

2 Heat half the oil in a pan, add the chopped onion and fry for 5 minutes, or until golden brown. Stir in half the cumin and half the cinnamon.

3 Add the fried onion to the pan of lentils with the cardamom pods, rice and stock. Mix well, then bring to the boil. Reduce the heat, cover and simmer until the rice is tender and all the liquid has been absorbed. If the mixture appears a little too dry, add some extra water or stock. Season with salt and pepper to taste.

4 Meanwhile, heat the remaining oil in a pan, add the sliced onions and fry for about 10 minutes, until dark brown, caramelized and crisp. Sprinkle in the remaining cumin and cinnamon just before the end of cooking.

5 To serve, pile the rice and lentil mixture on to a serving dish, then top with the browned, caramelized onions. Serve the megadarra immediately, with natural yogurt.

NOODLES, KUGELS AND PANCAKES

Noodles were once the glory of the Ashkenazi kitchen; eaten in innumerable ways
or filled to make dumplings. Kugels are the classic savoury pudding of
noodles or vegetables, bound with egg and baked until firm and crispy,
while pancakes — whether filled blintzes or crispy latkes — are definitively Jewish.

ITALIAN COLD PASTA

THIS IS THE TRADITIONAL COLD PASTA DISH OF THE ITALIAN JEWISH COMMUNITY. THE EGG NOODLES ARE DRESSED WITH GARLIC, PARSLEY AND OLIVE OIL AND EATEN COLD FOR SHABBAT, THE ONE DAY OF THE WEEK WHEN NO COOKING IS ALLOWED. SERVE IT AS A FIRST COURSE OR AS AN ACCOMPANIMENT TO A MEAT, FISH OR DAIRY MEAL.

SERVES FOUR

INGREDIENTS
   250g/9oz dried egg noodles
   30–60ml/2–4 tbsp extra virgin
      olive oil
   3 garlic cloves, finely chopped
   60–90ml/4–6 tbsp/¼–⅓ cup roughly
      chopped fresh parsley
   25–30 pitted green olives, sliced or
      roughly chopped
   salt

COOK'S TIP
Because this dish is so simple, always
use the best quality ingredients.

1 Cook the noodles in salted boiling
water as directed on the packet, or until
just tender. Drain and rinse under cold
running water.

2 Tip the pasta into a bowl, then add
the olive oil, garlic, parsley and olives
and toss together. Chill overnight
before serving.

KASHA VARNISHKES

THIS COMBINATION OF BUCKWHEAT, MUSHROOMS AND BOW-SHAPED PASTA IS A CLASSIC ASHKENAZI DISH. TO PEOPLE WHO HAVE NOT BEEN RAISED ON BUCKWHEAT IT MAY TASTE GRAINY AND HEAVY BUT FOR OTHERS, WHO HAVE EATEN IT THROUGHOUT THEIR CHILDHOOD, IT IS CONSIDERED HEAVENLY.

SERVES FOUR TO SIX

INGREDIENTS
25g/1oz dried well-flavoured
   mushrooms, such as ceps
500ml/17fl oz/2¼ cups boiling stock
   or water
45ml/3 tbsp rendered chicken fat (for
   a meat meal), vegetable oil (for a
   pareve meal) or 40g/1½oz/3 tbsp
   butter (for a dairy meal)
3–4 onions, thinly sliced
250g/9oz mushrooms, sliced
300g/11oz/1½ cups whole, coarse,
   medium or fine buckwheat
200g/7oz pasta bows
salt and ground black pepper

3 In a large, heavy frying pan, toast the buckwheat over a high heat for 2–3 minutes, stirring. Reduce the heat.

4 Stir the remaining boiling stock or water and the reserved mushroom soaking liquid into the buckwheat, cover the pan, and cook for about 10 minutes until the buckwheat is just tender and the liquid has been absorbed.

5 Meanwhile, cook the pasta in a large pan of salted boiling water as directed on the packet, or until just tender, then drain.

6 When the kasha is cooked, toss in the onions and mushrooms, and the pasta. Season and serve hot.

1 Put the dried mushrooms in a bowl, pour over half the boiling stock or water and leave to stand for 20–30 minutes, until reconstituted. Remove the mushrooms from the liquid, then strain and reserve the liquid.

2 Heat the chicken fat, oil or butter in a frying pan, add the onions and fry for 5–10 minutes until softened and beginning to brown. Remove the onions to a plate, then add the sliced mushrooms to the pan and fry briefly. Add the soaked mushrooms and cook for 2–3 minutes. Return the onions to the pan and set aside.

VARIATION
To cook kasha without mushrooms, omit both kinds and simply add all of the boiling stock in step 4.

FARFEL

ALSO KNOWN AS EGG BARLEY BECAUSE OF THEIR SIZE AND SHAPE, FARFEL ARE LITTLE DUMPLINGS MADE OF GRATED NOODLE DOUGH. IN YIDDISH, FARFALLEN MEANS FALLEN AWAY, WHICH DESCRIBES THE DOUGH AS IT IS GRATED. FARFEL ARE EATEN ON ROSH HASHANAH BY ASHKENAZIM. THE MANY TINY DUMPLINGS REPRESENT FERTILITY, WHILE THEIR ROUND SHAPE SYMBOLIZES A WELL-ROUNDED YEAR.

SERVES FOUR AS AN ACCOMPANIMENT

INGREDIENTS
225g/8oz/2 cups plain
  (all-purpose) flour
2 eggs
salt
chopped parsley, to garnish (optional)

COOK'S TIPS
• The dough can be made a day ahead and stored in the refrigerator.
• Farfel are delicious tossed with browned mushrooms or braised wild mushrooms.
• They can also be stuffed into the cavity of a small chicken or poussin and roasted.

1 Put the flour, eggs and a pinch of salt in a bowl and mix together. Gradually add 15–30ml/1–2 tbsp water until the dough holds together.

2 Continue mixing or kneading the dough, until it forms a smooth, non-sticky ball. Add a little more flour if needed. Place in a covered bowl and leave to rest for at least 30 minutes.

3 On a lightly floured surface, roll the dough into a thick rope using your hands. Leave at room temperature for at least 1 hour, and up to 2 hours, in order to let it dry out a little.

4 Cut the dough into chunks, then grate into barley-sized pieces, using the largest holes of a grater. Lightly toss the dumplings in flour and spread on a baking sheet or greaseproof (waxed) paper to dry.

5 To cook the dumplings, bring a pan of salted water to the boil, tip in the dumplings and boil for about 6 minutes, until just tender. Drain well and serve hot, in a bowl of chicken soup or as an accompaniment to a main dish. Garnish with parsley, if you like.

PIEROGI

THESE POLISH DUMPLINGS OF SPICY MASHED POTATO, SERVED WITH MELTED BUTTER AND SOUR CREAM, ARE HEARTY ENOUGH TO WARD OFF THE RIGOURS OF A COLD WINTER. IN NEW YORK, THERE ARE MANY POLISH LUNCH BARS WHERE YOU CAN SIT AT THE COUNTER AND EAT A BOWL OF BORSCHT ACCOMPANIED BY THESE SAVOURY DUMPLINGS.

4 Place 15–30ml/1–2 tbsp of the potato filling in the centre of each square of dough or wrapper, then top with another sheet. Press the edges together and pinch with your fingers or use a fork to seal well. Set aside to allow the edges to dry out and seal firmly.

5 Bring a large pan of salted water to the boil, then lower the heat to a simmer. Carefully slip the dumplings into the water, keeping it simmering gently, and cook for about 2 minutes if using wonton wrappers and slightly longer for noodle dough until tender. (Do not overcrowd the pan.)

SERVES FOUR TO SIX

INGREDIENTS
675g/1½lb baking potatoes, peeled and cut into chunks
50–75g/2–3oz/4–5 tbsp unsalted (sweet) butter, plus extra melted butter to serve
3 onions, finely chopped
2 eggs, lightly beaten
1 quantity of kreplach noodle dough or 250g/9oz packet wonton wrappers
salt and ground black pepper
chopped parsley, to garnish
sour cream, to serve

1 Cook the potatoes in a large pan of salted boiling water until tender. Drain well. Meanwhile, melt the butter in a frying pan, add the onions and fry over a medium heat for about 10 minutes, or until browned.

2 Mash the potatoes, then stir in the fried onions and leave to cool. When cool, add the eggs and mix together. Season generously.

3 If using noodle dough, roll out and cut into 7.5cm/3in squares. Brush the edges of the dough or wonton wrappers with a little water.

6 Using a slotted spoon, remove the dumplings from the water and drain. Serve the dumplings on plates or in bowls. Drizzle with butter and sour cream and garnish with chopped parsley.

VARIATION
Add a sprinkling of chopped spring onions (scallions) to the topping.

KREPLACH

THESE TRIANGULAR STUFFED PASTA DUMPLINGS SYMBOLIZE THE THREE PATRIARCHS: ABRAHAM, ISAAC AND JACOB. IN WESTERN EUROPE THESE STUFFED PASTA DUMPLINGS WERE ORIGINALLY ONLY FILLED WITH MEAT, WHILE IN SLAVIC LANDS, AS EARLY AS THE TWELFTH CENTURY, THEY WERE FILLED WITH CHEESE. IT WAS LATER, AFTER A GREAT MEAT SHORTAGE IN WESTERN EUROPE, THAT FRUIT-FILLED KREPLACH, KNOWN AS VARENIKES, BECAME POPULAR.

SERVES FOUR

INGREDIENTS
  225g/8oz/2 cups plain
    (all-purpose) flour
  2 eggs
  rendered chicken fat or vegetable
    oil (optional)
  salt
  whole and chopped fresh chives,
    to garnish
For the meat filling
  90–120ml/6–8 tbsp rendered chicken
    fat or vegetable oil
  1 large or 2 small onions, chopped
  400g/14oz leftover, pot-roasted meat
  2–3 garlic cloves, chopped
  salt and ground black pepper

1 To make the meat filling, fry the onions in the chicken fat or oil for 5–10 minutes. Mince (grind) or finely chop the meat. Add to the onion with the garlic, salt and pepper and stir.

2 Put the flour, eggs and a pinch of salt in a bowl and combine. Gradually add 15–30ml/1–2 tbsp water until the dough holds together. Continue mixing until the dough forms a non-sticky ball. Add more flour if needed. Place in a covered bowl and leave for 30 minutes.

3 Break off walnut-size pieces of dough and, on a lightly floured surface, roll out as thinly as possible. Cut the dough into squares measuring about 7.5cm/3in.

4 Working one at a time, dampen the edges of each square, then place a spoonful of filling in the centre (do not overfill). Fold the edges of the dough to form a triangular shape and press the edges together to seal.

5 Toss the dumplings in a little flour, then pile on to a non-stick baking sheet. Leave to stand for about 30 minutes.

6 Cook the dumplings in a pan of salted boiling water for about 5 minutes until just tender, then drain. If you like, heat a little chicken fat or oil in a pan and fry the dumplings until just turning brown. Serve, garnished with chives.

COOK'S TIP
Kreplach are eaten at festive meals. The filling varies according to the holiday. For high days and holy days meat-filled kreplach are served in chicken soup; for Purim they are filled with dried fruit, and for Shavuot they are filled with cheese.

NOODLE KUGEL FLAVOURED WITH APPLE AND CINNAMON

THIS BLISSFULLY BUTTERY NOODLE KUGEL, WHICH IS FRAGRANT WITH CINNAMON AND APPLES AND OOZING OLD COUNTRY CHARM, WAS BROUGHT TO NORTH AMERICA FROM RUSSIA. USE FLAT EGG NOODLES THAT ARE AT LEAST 1CM / ½IN WIDE.

SERVES FOUR TO SIX

INGREDIENTS

350–500g/12oz–1¼lb egg noodles
130g/4½oz/generous ½ cup plus
   15ml/1 tbsp unsalted (sweet) butter
2 well-flavoured cooking apples
250g/9oz/generous 1 cup cottage
   cheese
3–4 eggs, lightly beaten
10ml/2 tsp ground cinnamon
250g/9oz/1¼ cups sugar
2–3 handfuls of raisins
2.5ml/½ tsp bicarbonate of soda
   (baking soda)
salt

1 Preheat the oven to 180°C/350°C/Gas 4. Cook the noodles in salted boiling water according to the directions on the packet, or until just tender, then drain.

2 Melt the butter, then toss it with the noodles. Coarsely grate the apples and add to the noodles, then stir in the cottage cheese, eggs, cinnamon, sugar, raisins, bicarbonate of soda and a tiny pinch of salt.

3 Tip the noodle mixture into a deep rectangular ovenproof dish, measuring about 38 × 20cm/15 × 8in and bake for 1–1¼ hours, until browned and crisp. Serve immediately.

COOK'S TIP

This kugel is also good served cold. Serve leftovers the next day, as a snack.

KUGEL YERUSHALAYIM

THIS TRADITIONAL KUGEL THAT BEARS JERUSALEM'S NAME IS SAID TO HAVE BEEN BROUGHT TO THE RELIGIOUS QUARTER OF MEA SHEARIM IN THE EIGHTEENTH CENTURY BY THE GAON OF VILNA AND HIS FOLLOWERS. IT IS EQUALLY GOOD CUT INTO SQUARES AND SERVED COLD FOR BREAKFAST OR TEA OR, MADE SWEETER BY INCREASING THE SUGAR CONTENT, FOR A HEARTY, SATISFYING DESSERT.

SERVES FOUR

INGREDIENTS
  200g/7oz very thin noodles, such as
    spaghettini or fine egg noodles
  60ml/4 tbsp olive oil
  130g/4½oz/⅔ cup sugar or
    demerara (raw) sugar
  2 eggs, lightly beaten
  5ml/1 tsp ground black pepper
  2.5–5ml/½–1 tsp ground cinnamon
  1–2 handfuls of raisins
  salt

1 Preheat the oven to 180°C/350°F/
Gas 4. Cook the pasta in salted boiling
water according to the directions on the
packet, or until just tender, then drain.

VARIATION
Add about 250g/9oz grated pumpkin to
the noodles when adding to the caramel.

2 Put the oil and half the sugar in a
large, heavy pan and cook over a
medium heat, stirring with a wooden
spoon, until the oil and sugar combine
and the mixture turns light brown.

3 Remove the pan from the heat (the
mixture will continue to cook and turn
brown), pour over the pasta and mix
well to combine.

4 Add the remaining sugar, the eggs,
pepper, ground cinnamon, raisins and
2–3 pinches of salt to the pasta and
mix well.

5 Turn the mixture into an ovenproof
dish, 33 × 25cm/13 × 10in; spread into
an even layer. Bake for about 1 hour, or
until set and the top is lightly browned.
Serve hot or warm.

POTATO KUGEL

*THIS TRADITIONAL POTATO ACCOMPANIMENT CAN BE PREPARED WITH BUTTER BUT THIS RECIPE USES
VEGETABLE OIL, WHICH GIVES A MUCH LIGHTER, HEALTHIER RESULT. THE USE OF OIL RATHER THAN
BUTTER ALSO MEANS THAT THIS TASTY KUGEL IS PAREVE AND CAN BE ENJOYED WITH MEAT DISHES,
FOR WHICH IT IS A PERFECT PARTNER.*

2 Place the grated potatoes in a large bowl and add the beaten eggs, matzo meal, salt and ground black pepper. Mix together until well combined. Stir in the grated onions, then add 90ml/ 6 tbsp of the vegetable oil.

3 Pour the remaining 30ml/2 tbsp vegetable oil into a baking tin (pan) that is large enough to spread the potato mixture out to a thickness of no more than 4–5cm/1½–2in. Heat the tin in the oven for about 5 minutes until the oil is very hot.

4 Carefully remove the baking tin from the oven. Spoon the potato mixture into the tin, letting the hot oil bubble up around the sides and on to the top a little. (The sizzling oil helps to crisp the kugel as it cooks.)

5 Bake the kugel for 45–60 minutes, or until tender and golden brown and crisp on top. Serve immediately, cut into wedges.

SERVES SIX TO EIGHT

INGREDIENTS
2kg/4½lb potatoes
2 eggs, lightly beaten
120–180ml/8–12 tbsp medium
  matzo meal
10ml/2 tsp salt
3–4 onions, grated
120ml/4fl oz/½ cup vegetable oil
ground black pepper

1 Preheat the oven to 200°C/400°F/ Gas 6. Peel the potatoes and grate finely.

COOK'S TIPS
• Don't be tempted to grate the onions in the food processor as the action of the knife creates a bitter flavour by breaking down the cells of the onions.
• For a dairy meal, this kugel can be made with any flavourful cheese such as Cheddar. Add about 350g/12oz/3 cups grated cheese to the grated potato and toss together, then continue as above.

MATZO AND ONION KUGEL

MANY JEWISH COOKS USE MATZO MEAL FOR A KUGEL BUT THIS RECIPE USES PIECES OF LIGHTLY TOASTED MATZOS. THIS VERSION INVOLVES A LITTLE EXTRA WORK BUT PRODUCES A LIGHTER KUGEL WITH A RICHER TASTE THAT IS WELL WORTH THE EFFORT.

2 Heat the oil or fat in a frying pan, add the chopped onions and fry for 10 minutes, or until softened and browned. Season with salt and pepper.

3 Put the toasted matzos, onions and stock in an ovenproof dish and mix together, then add the eggs and stir well. Season with salt and pepper.

4 Bake the kugel for 25–30 minutes until tender and the top is golden brown. Serve immediately.

SERVES SIX TO EIGHT

INGREDIENTS
  500g/1¼lb matzos
  60ml/4 tbsp vegetable oil or rendered chicken fat
  3–4 onions, chopped
  500ml/17fl oz/2¼ cups hot chicken or mushroom stock
  3 eggs, lightly beaten
  salt and ground black pepper

COOK'S TIP
This kugel is particularly good served alongside slowly roasted lamb.

1 Preheat the oven to 200°C/400°F/ Gas 6. Break the matzos into bitesize pieces and arrange on a baking sheet in a single layer. Bake for 5–10 minutes, turning frequently, until lightly toasted.

VARIATIONS
• To make a matzo and mushroom kugel, add 250g/8oz thinly sliced, browned mushrooms to the onions, along with a handful of flavoursome dried mushrooms such as porcini or Polish field mushrooms, then continue as above.
• Instead of baking the kugel mixture, use it as a stuffing for a roast chicken or turkey. This is great for Pesach as it is leaven- or hametz-free.

MATZO MEAL AND COTTAGE CHEESE LATKES

CHEESE LATKES WERE PROBABLY ONCE THE MOST REVERED FOODS IN RUSSIA, THOUGH FLOUR, BUCKWHEAT AND MATZO MEAL LATKES WERE MORE COMMON. THE COTTAGE CHEESE AND MATZO VERSION HERE WAS MADE BY RUSSIAN ÉMIGRÉS. THE COTTAGE CHEESE GIVES A TANGY, SLIGHTLY GOOEY CONSISTENCY TO THE PANCAKE.

MAKES ABOUT TWENTY

INGREDIENTS
275g/10oz/1¼ cups
   cottage cheese
3 eggs, separated
5ml/1 tsp salt
250g/9oz/2¼ cups matzo meal
1 onion, coarsely grated, or
   3–5 spring onions (scallions),
   thinly sliced
2.5ml/½ tsp sugar
30–45ml/2–3 tbsp natural (plain)
   yogurt or water
vegetable oil, for shallow frying
ground black pepper

1 In a bowl, mash the cottage cheese. Mix in the egg yolks, half the salt, the matzo meal, onion, sugar, yogurt or water, and pepper.

2 Whisk the egg whites with the remaining salt until stiff. Fold one-third of the whisked egg whites into the batter, then fold in the remaining egg whites.

3 Heat the oil in a heavy frying pan to a depth of about 1cm/½in, until a cube of bread added to the pan turns brown immediately. Drop tablespoonfuls of the batter into the pan; fry over a medium-high heat until the undersides are golden brown. Turn carefully and fry the second side.

4 When cooked, remove the latkes from the pan with a slotted spoon and drain on kitchen paper. Serve immediately or place on a baking sheet and keep warm in the oven.

VARIATIONS
To make sweet latkes, omit the onion and add 15–30ml/1–2 tbsp sugar, chopped nuts and some ground cinnamon. Serve topped with a spoonful of jam or honey.

POTATO LATKES

LATKES ARE AS MUCH A PART OF THE ASHKENAZI CHANUKKAH AS ARE THE CANDLES, THE DREIDELS, THE WHOLE CELEBRATION. EATING FOODS FRIED IN OIL IS THE TRADITION FOR CHANUKKAH — THE OIL A COMMEMORATION OF THE OIL THAT BURNED FOR EIGHT DAYS IN THE REDEDICATED TEMPLE. SERVE THEM WITH SOUR CREAM OR YOGURT FOR A DAIRY MEAL OR SIMPLY WITH A BOWL OF APPLE SAUCE.

SERVES ABOUT FOUR

INGREDIENTS
3 large baking potatoes, total weight
  about 675g/1½lb, peeled
2 onions, grated
60ml/4 tbsp matzo meal or 30ml/
  2 tbsp matzo meal and 30ml/2 tbsp
  plain (all-purpose) flour
5ml/1 tsp baking powder
2 eggs, lightly beaten
2.5ml/½ tsp sugar
5ml/1 tsp salt
1.5ml/¼ tsp ground black pepper
vegetable oil, for shallow frying
sour cream or natural (plain) yogurt,
  to serve (optional)
For the cranberry apple sauce
5 green cooking apples or a
  combination of cooking and
  eating apples
1 cinnamon stick
¼ lemon
about 90g/3½oz/½ cup sugar
225g/8oz/2 cups cranberries

1 To make the cranberry apple sauce, peel, core and roughly chop the apples and place them in a heavy pan with the cinnamon stick. Pare the rind from the lemon, then squeeze the lemon juice over the apples and add the lemon rind to the pan. Add the sugar, cover and cook over a low to medium heat for 15–20 minutes, until they are just tender but have not disintegrated. Stir occasionally so that the apples do not burn.

2 Add the cranberries to the pan, cover again and cook for 5–8 minutes more, or until the berries pop and are just cooked. Taste for sweetness and leave to cool.

3 To make the latkes, coarsely or finely (or a combination of both) grate the potatoes. Put in a sieve and push out as much of their starchy liquid as possible with your hands.

4 Transfer the grated potato to a bowl, add the onion, matzo meal or matzo meal and flour, the baking powder, eggs, sugar, salt and pepper, and mix together until well combined.

5 Heat the oil in a heavy frying pan to a depth of about 1cm/½in, until a small piece of the potato mixture sizzles when added to the pan. Drop spoonfuls of the batter (depending on the size you want the latkes) into the pan; fry over a medium heat for 3–4 minutes, until the undersides are brown and crisp. Turn and fry the second side.

6 When cooked, remove the latkes from the pan with a slotted spoon and drain on kitchen paper. Serve at once or keep warm on a baking sheet in the oven for up to 20 minutes. Serve with sour cream or yogurt, if you like, and the cranberry apple sauce.

BLINTZES

THESE THIN CRÊPE-LIKE PANCAKES ARE COOKED ON ONE SIDE, STUFFED, THEN ROLLED TO ENCLOSE THE FILLING AND PAN-FRIED UNTIL CRISP AND BROWN. UNLIKE A CRÊPE BATTER, BLINTZ BATTER IS USUALLY MADE WITH WATER SO YOU CAN FILL THEM WITH MEAT OR, IF THEY ARE FILLED WITH FRUIT, THEY CAN ACCOMPANY A MEAT MEAL. THIS VERSION CONTAINS A LUSCIOUSLY SWEET, LEMONY COTTAGE CHEESE AND SULTANA FILLING.

4 Heat a pancake pan, add a slick of oil, then ladle a little batter into the pan, swirling it to form a thin pancake.

5 When the batter has set and the edges of the pancake begin to lift, gently loosen the edges and flip the pancake on to a plate. Continue with the remaining batter to make about 8–12 pancakes, stacking the pancakes as you cook them. (They won't stick.)

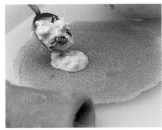

SERVES FOUR

INGREDIENTS
4 eggs
350ml/12fl oz/1½ cups water
pinch of salt
45ml/3 tbsp vegetable oil,
  plus extra, for frying
350g/12oz/3 cups plain
  (all-purpose) flour
For the filling
500g/1¼lb/2¼ cups cottage cheese
1 egg, lightly beaten
grated rind of ½–1 lemon
15–30ml/1–2 tbsp sugar
15–30ml/1–2 tbsp sour cream
30–45ml/2–3 tbsp sultanas
  (golden raisins) (optional)

1 To make the filling, put the cottage cheese in a sieve and leave for about 20 minutes to drain.

2 Put the cheese in a bowl and mash lightly with a fork. Add the beaten egg, lemon rind, sugar, sour cream and sultanas to the cheese and mix together.

3 To make the blintzes, whisk the eggs in a bowl, then add the water, salt and oil. Whisk in the flour and continue beating to form a smooth batter.

VARIATION
To make Lithuanian blintzes, omit the sugar and season with plenty of salt and ground black pepper.

6 Place 15–30ml/1–2 tbsp of the filling on the cooked side of a pancake and spread it out, leaving a border at the top and bottom. Fold in the top and bottom over the filling, then fold over one side and roll the pancake up carefully to enclose the filling completely.

7 To finish the blintzes, heat the pan, add a little oil, then place the pancakes in the pan and fry until the underside is golden brown. Turn the blintz over and fry the second side. Serve hot.

SALADS

The Ashkenazi lands, which shivered in the cold for so much of the year, did not give rise to a wealth of fresh salads. However, once Ashkenazim migrated to lands where fresh vegetables were plentiful, salads became an intrinsic part of every meal — even if it was only a plate of raw spring onions, a few green (bell) peppers or a cucumber cut into chunks. The Sephardi kitchen, on the other hand, has had a tradition of a variety of savoury vegetable salads, often cooked with fragrant spices and golden, healthful olive oil.

ARTICHOKES <u>WITH</u> GARLIC, LEMON <u>AND</u> OLIVE OIL

THIS CLASSIC DISH OF FLORENCE IS SAID TO BE OF JEWISH ORIGIN. IT IS NOT ONLY DELICIOUS AS A SALAD, BUT CAN ALSO BE ADDED TO ROASTED FISH, CHICKEN OR LAMB DURING COOKING.

SERVES FOUR

INGREDIENTS

4 globe artichokes
juice of 1–2 lemons, plus extra to acidulate water
60ml/4 tbsp extra virgin olive oil
1 onion, chopped
5–8 garlic cloves, roughly chopped or thinly sliced
30ml/2 tbsp chopped fresh parsley
120ml/4fl oz/½ cup dry white wine
120ml/4fl oz/½ cup vegetable stock or water
salt and ground black pepper

COOK'S TIP
Placing trimmed artichokes in a bowl of acidulated water prevents them discolouring.

1 Prepare the artichokes. Pull back and snap off the tough leaves. Peel the tender part of the stems and cut into bitesize pieces, then put in a bowl of acidulated water. Cut the artichokes into quarters and cut out the inside thistle heart. Add them to the bowl.

2 Heat the oil in a pan, add the onion and garlic and fry for 5 minutes until softened. Stir in the parsley and cook for a few seconds. Add the wine, stock and drained artichokes. Season with half the lemon juice, salt and pepper.

3 Bring the mixture to the boil, then lower the heat, cover and simmer for 10–15 minutes until the artichokes are tender. Lift the artichokes out with a slotted spoon and transfer to a serving dish.

4 Bring the cooking liquid to the boil and boil until reduced to about half its volume. Pour the mixture over the artichokes and drizzle over the remaining lemon juice. Taste for seasoning and cool before serving.

BEETROOT <u>WITH</u> FRESH MINT

THIS DEEP RED VEGETABLE IS OFTEN CONSIDERED TO BE QUINTESSENTIALLY JEWISH, ESPECIALLY IN ASHKENAZI COMMUNITIES, BUT ALSO IN MANY SEPHARDI ONES TOO. SERVE THIS SIMPLE AND DECORATIVE SALAD AS PART OF A SELECTION OF SALADS.

SERVES FOUR

INGREDIENTS

4–6 cooked beetroot (beets)
5–10ml/1–2 tsp sugar
15–30ml/1–2 tbsp balsamic vinegar
juice of ½ lemon
30ml/2 tbsp extra virgin olive oil
1 bunch fresh mint, leaves stripped
 and thinly sliced
salt

VARIATIONS
• To make Tunisian beetroot, add harissa to taste and substitute fresh coriander (cilantro) for the mint.
• To make Ashkenazi beetroot, add a chopped onion and some dill.

1 Slice the beetroot or cut into even-size dice with a sharp knife. Put the beetroot in a bowl. Add the sugar, balsamic vinegar, lemon juice, olive oil and a pinch of salt and toss together to combine.

2 Add half the thinly sliced fresh mint to the salad and toss lightly until well combined. Place the salad in the refrigerator and chill for about 1 hour. Serve garnished with the remaining thinly sliced mint leaves.

SALAD <u>WITH</u> WATERMELON <u>AND</u> FETA CHEESE

THE COMBINATION OF SWEET AND JUICY WATERMELON WITH SALTY FETA CHEESE IS AN ISRAELI ORIGINAL AND WAS INSPIRED BY THE TURKISH TRADITION OF EATING WATERMELON WITH SALTY WHITE CHEESE IN THE HOT SUMMER MONTHS.

SERVES FOUR

INGREDIENTS
30–45ml/2–3 tbsp extra virgin
  olive oil
juice of ½ lemon
5ml/1 tsp vinegar of choice,
  or to taste
sprinkling of fresh thyme
pinch of ground cumin
4 large slices of watermelon, chilled
1 frisée lettuce, core removed
130g/4½oz feta cheese,
  preferably sheep's milk feta,
  cut into bitesize pieces
handful of lightly toasted
  pumpkin seeds
handful of sunflower seeds
10–15 black olives

1 Pour the extra virgin olive oil, lemon juice and vinegar into a bowl or jug (pitcher). Add the fresh thyme and ground cumin, and whisk until well combined. Set the dressing aside until you are ready to serve the salad.

2 Cut the rind off the watermelon and remove as many seeds as possible. Cut the flesh into triangular-shaped chunks.

3 Put the lettuce leaves in a bowl, pour over the dressing and toss together. Arrange the leaves on a serving dish or individual plates and add the watermelon, feta cheese, pumpkin and sunflower seeds and black olives. Serve the salad immediately.

COOK'S TIP
The best choice of olives for this recipe are plump black Mediterranean olives such as kalamata, other shiny, brined varieties or dry-cured black olives such as the Italian ones.

GALILEE SALAD OF WILD GREENS, RAW VEGETABLES AND OLIVES

WILD GREENS WERE GATHERED IN THE GALILEE BY NECESSITY DURING TIMES OF AUSTERITY; NOW THEY ARE EATEN FOR PLEASURE AND HEALTH. SERVE THIS SALAD WITH LABNEH OR YOGURT CHEESE.

SERVES FOUR

INGREDIENTS

- 1 large bunch wild rocket (arugula), about 115g/4oz
- 1 packet mixed salad leaves
- ¼ white cabbage, thinly sliced
- 1 cucumber, sliced
- 1 small red onion, chopped
- 2–3 garlic cloves, chopped
- 3–5 tomatoes, cut into wedges
- 1 green (bell) pepper, seeded and sliced
- 2–3 mint sprigs, sliced or torn
- 15–30ml/1–2 tbsp chopped fresh parsley and/or tarragon or dill
- pinch of dried oregano or thyme
- 45ml/3 tbsp extra virgin olive oil
- juice of ½ lemon
- 15ml/1 tbsp red wine vinegar
- 15–20 black olives
- salt and ground black pepper

1 In a large salad bowl, put the rocket, mixed salad leaves, white cabbage, cucumber, onion and garlic. Toss gently with your fingers to combine the leaves and vegetables.

COOK'S TIP
Try to find mixed salad leaves that include varieties such as lamb's lettuce, purslane and mizuna.

2 Arrange the tomatoes, pepper, mint, fresh and dried herbs, salt and pepper on top of the greens and vegetables. Drizzle over the oil, lemon juice and vinegar, stud with the olives and serve.

VARIATION
Instead of making yogurt cheese, mash a little feta into natural (plain) yogurt and serve this instead.

ISRAELI CHOPPED VEGETABLE SALAD

THIS CLASSIC SUMMER SALAD LENDS ITSELF TO ENDLESS VARIETY: ADD OLIVES, DICED BEETROOT OR POTATOES, OMIT THE CHILLI, VARY THE HERBS, USE LIME OR LEMON IN PLACE OF THE VINEGAR OR ADD A GOOD PINCH OF GROUND CUMIN. IT IS ALWAYS WONDERFUL.

SERVES FOUR TO SIX

INGREDIENTS

1 each red, green and yellow (bell)
  pepper, seeded
1 carrot
1 cucumber
6 tomatoes
3 garlic cloves, finely chopped
3 spring onions (scallions),
  thinly sliced
30ml/2 tbsp chopped fresh coriander
  (cilantro) leaves
30ml/2 tbsp each chopped fresh dill,
  parsley and mint leaves
½–1 hot fresh chilli,
  chopped (optional)
45–60ml/3–4 tbsp extra virgin
  olive oil
juice of 1–1½ lemons
salt and ground black pepper

1 Using a sharp knife, finely dice the red, green and yellow peppers, carrot, cucumber and tomatoes and place them in a large mixing bowl.

2 Add the garlic, spring onions, coriander, dill, parsley, mint and chilli, if using, to the chopped vegetables and toss together to combine.

3 Pour the olive oil and lemon juice over the vegetables, season with salt and pepper to taste and toss together. Chill before serving.

COOK'S TIP
This classic chopped salad is the most commonly eaten dish of the land. It is particularly refreshing eaten for breakfast.

MOROCCAN VEGETABLE SALAD

IN ISRAEL THERE ARE MANY JEWS OF MOROCCAN ORIGIN WHO HAVE ADAPTED THEIR TRADITIONAL NATIVE DISHES TO SUIT THE FARE OF ISRAEL. THEIR SALADS ARE FRESH AND INVIGORATING.

SERVES FOUR

INGREDIENTS

1 large cucumber, thinly sliced
2 cold, boiled potatoes, sliced
1 each red, yellow and green (bell)
  pepper, seeded and thinly sliced
300g/11oz/2⅔ cups pitted olives
½–1 hot fresh chilli, chopped or
  2–3 shakes of cayenne pepper
3–5 garlic cloves, chopped
3 spring onions (scallions), sliced
  or 1 red onion, finely chopped
60–90ml/4–6 tbsp extra virgin olive oil
15–30ml/1–2 tbsp white wine vinegar
juice of ½ lemon, or to taste
15–30ml/1–2 tbsp chopped fresh
  mint leaves
15–30ml/1–2 tbsp chopped fresh
  coriander (cilantro) leaves
salt (optional)

1 Arrange the cucumber, potato and pepper slices and the pitted olives on a serving plate or in a dish.

2 Sprinkle the chopped fresh chilli or cayenne pepper over the salad and season with salt, if you like. (Olives tend to be very salty so you may not wish to add any extra salt.)

3 Sprinkle the garlic, onions, olive oil, vinegar and lemon juice over the salad. Chill before serving, sprinkled with the chopped mint leaves and coriander leaves.

VARIATION
Serve the salad garnished with sliced or diced cooked beetroot (beet).

TURNIP SALAD IN SOUR CREAM

THIS ASHKENAZI SALAD MAKES A DELICIOUS ACCOMPANIMENT FOR A DAIRY MEAL OR PART OF A SELECTION OF SALADS. TRADITIONALLY, IF TURNIPS WERE NOT AVAILABLE, LARGE RADISHES WOULD BE USED INSTEAD.

SERVES FOUR

INGREDIENTS

2–4 young, tender turnips, peeled
¼–½ onion, finely chopped
2–3 drops white wine vinegar,
  or to taste
60–90ml/4–6 tbsp sour cream
salt and ground black pepper
chopped fresh parsley or paprika,
  to garnish

VARIATION
Crème fraîche can be used instead of the sour cream, if you like.

1 Thinly slice or coarsely grate the turnips. Alternatively, thinly slice half the turnips and grate the remaining half. Put in a bowl.

2 Add the onion, vinegar, salt and pepper, toss together then stir in the sour cream. Serve chilled, garnished with a sprinkling of parsley or paprika.

CURRIED RED CABBAGE SLAW

CABBAGE HAS LONG BEEN A FAVOURITE JEWISH VEGETABLE AND, AT ONE TIME, IT WAS ALMOST THE ONLY VEGETABLE OF THE ASHKENAZIM. SPICY SLAWS ARE FAVOURED THROUGHOUT ISRAEL, WHERE THEY HAVE TAKEN UP THE SPICING TRADITIONS OF THE MIDDLE EAST.

SERVES FOUR TO SIX

INGREDIENTS

½ red cabbage, thinly sliced
1 red (bell) pepper, chopped
  or very thinly sliced
½ red onion, chopped
60ml/4 tbsp red, white wine
  vinegar or cider vinegar
60ml/4 tbsp sugar, or to taste
120ml/4fl oz/½ cup Greek
  (US strained plain) yogurt or
  natural (plain) yogurt
120ml/4fl oz/½ cup mayonnaise,
  preferably home-made
1.5ml/¼ tsp curry powder
2–3 handfuls of raisins
salt and ground black pepper

1 Put the cabbage, peppers and red onions in a bowl and toss to combine. In a small pan, heat the vinegar and sugar until the sugar has dissolved, then pour over the vegetables. Leave to cool slightly.

2 Combine the yogurt and mayonnaise, then mix into the cabbage mixture. Season to taste with curry powder, salt and ground black pepper, then mix in the raisins.

3 Chill the salad for at least 2 hours before serving. Just before serving, drain off any excess liquid and briefly stir the slaw again.

VARIATIONS

• To make a pareve slaw, suitable for serving with a meat meal, omit the yogurt and mayonnaise and add a little more vinegar.
• If you prefer, ready-made low-fat mayonnaise can be used.

MOROCCAN CARROT SALAD

GRATED RAW CARROT SALADS CAN BE FOUND ALL OVER ISRAEL AND ARE OFTEN EASTERN EUROPEAN IN ORIGIN. IN THIS INTRIGUING VARIATION FROM NORTH AFRICA, THE CARROTS ARE LIGHTLY COOKED BEFORE BEING TOSSED IN A CUMIN AND CORIANDER VINAIGRETTE. IT IS A PERFECT ACCOMPANIMENT FOR A FESTIVE OR EVERYDAY MEAL.

SERVES FOUR TO SIX

INGREDIENTS
   3–4 carrots, thinly sliced
   pinch of sugar
   3–4 garlic cloves, chopped
   1.5ml/¼ tsp ground cumin,
      or to taste
   juice of ½ lemon
   30–45ml/2–3 tbsp extra virgin
      olive oil
   15–30ml/1–2 tbsp red wine vinegar
      or fruit vinegar, such as raspberry
   30ml/2 tbsp chopped fresh coriander
      (cilantro) leaves or a mixture of
      coriander and parsley
   salt and ground black pepper

1 Cook the carrots by either steaming or boiling in lightly salted water until they are just tender but not soft. Drain, leave for a few moments to dry, then put in a bowl.

2 Add the sugar, garlic, cumin, lemon juice, olive oil and vinegar to the carrots and toss together. Add the herbs and season. Serve or chill before serving.

TUNISIENNE POTATO AND OLIVE SALAD

THIS DELICIOUS SALAD IS FAVOURED IN NORTH AFRICA. ITS SIMPLICITY AND ZESTY SPICING IS ONE OF ITS CHARMS. SERVE FOR LUNCH AS AN ACCOMPANIMENT OR AS AN APPETIZER.

SERVES FOUR

INGREDIENTS

8 large new potatoes
large pinch of salt
large pinch of sugar
3 garlic cloves, chopped
15ml/1 tbsp vinegar of your choice,
 such as a fruit variety
large pinch of ground cumin or whole
 cumin seeds
pinch of cayenne pepper or hot
 paprika, to taste
30–45ml/2–3 tbsp extra virgin
 olive oil
30–45ml/2–3 tbsp chopped fresh
 coriander (cilantro) leaves
10–15 dry-fleshed black
 Mediterranean olives

1 Chop the new potatoes into chunks. Put them in a pan, pour in water to cover and add the salt and sugar. Bring to the boil, then reduce the heat and boil gently for about 10 minutes, or until the potatoes are just tender. Drain well and leave in a colander to cool.

2 When cool enough to handle, slice the potatoes and put in a bowl.

3 Sprinkle the garlic, vinegar, cumin and cayenne or paprika over the salad. Drizzle with olive oil and sprinkle over coriander and olives. Chill before serving.

WHITE BEANS WITH GREEN PEPPERS IN SPICY DRESSING

TENDER WHITE BEANS ARE DELICIOUS IN THIS SPICY SAUCE WITH THE BITE OF FRESH, CRUNCHY GREEN PEPPER. THE DISH WAS BROUGHT TO ISRAEL BY THE JEWS OF BALKAN LANDS, SUCH AS TURKEY, BULGARIA AND GREECE. IT IS PERFECT FOR PREPARING AHEAD OF TIME.

SERVES FOUR

INGREDIENTS

750g/1⅔lb tomatoes, diced
1 onion, finely chopped
½–1 mild fresh chilli, finely chopped
1 green (bell) pepper, seeded
  and chopped
pinch of sugar
4 garlic cloves, chopped
400g/14oz can cannellini beans, drained
45–60ml/3–4 tbsp olive oil
grated rind and juice of 1 lemon
15ml/1 tbsp cider vinegar or
  wine vinegar
salt and ground black pepper
chopped fresh parsley, to garnish

1 Put the tomatoes, onion, chilli, green pepper, sugar, garlic, cannellini beans, salt and plenty of ground black pepper in a large bowl and toss together until well combined.

2 Add the olive oil, grated lemon rind, lemon juice and vinegar to the salad and toss lightly to combine. Chill before serving, garnished with chopped parsley.

TABBOULEH

THIS IS A WONDERFULLY REFRESHING, TANGY SALAD OF SOAKED BULGUR WHEAT AND MASSES OF FRESH MINT, PARSLEY AND SPRING ONIONS. FEEL FREE TO INCREASE THE AMOUNT OF HERBS FOR A GREENER SALAD. IT CAN BE SERVED AS AN APPETIZER OR AS AN ACCOMPANIMENT TO A MAIN COURSE.

SERVES FOUR TO SIX

INGREDIENTS
  250g/9oz/1½ cups bulgur wheat
  1 large bunch spring onions
    (scallions), thinly sliced
  1 cucumber, finely chopped or diced
  3 tomatoes, chopped
  1.5–2.5ml/¼–½ tsp ground cumin
  1 large bunch fresh parsley, chopped
  1 large bunch fresh mint, chopped
  juice of 2 lemons, or to taste
  60ml/4 tbsp extra virgin olive oil
  salt
  olives, lemon wedges, tomato wedges,
    cucumber slices and mint sprigs,
    to garnish (optional)
  cos or romaine lettuce and natural
    (plain) yogurt, to serve (optional)

1 Pick over the bulgur wheat to remove any dirt. Place it in a bowl, cover with cold water and leave to soak for about 30 minutes. Tip the bulgur wheat into a sieve and drain well, shaking to remove any excess water, then return it to the bowl.

2 Add the spring onions to the bulgur wheat, then mix and squeeze together with your hands to combine.

3 Add the cucumber, tomatoes, cumin, parsley, mint, lemon juice, oil and salt to the bulgur wheat and toss to combine.

4 Heap the tabbouleh on to a bed of lettuce and garnish with olives, lemon wedges, tomato, cucumber and mint sprigs, if you like. Serve with a bowl of natural yogurt, if you like.

VARIATION
Use couscous soaked in boiling water in place of the bulgur wheat and use chopped fresh coriander (cilantro) instead of parsley.

VEGETABLE DISHES

*The vegetables of the Old Country did not lend themselves to lightness but
in the spring young vegetables such as squash and new potatoes would be
cooked and served with sour cream and fresh herbs. Leafy greens such
as spinach, chard and leeks were made into pancakes and, often,
whatever vegetables were available would be shredded and baked
into a kugel. The Sephardi kitchen, on the other hand, was
abundant with vegetables such as okra, aubergine (eggplant) and
pumpkin, which were often stewed with olive oil, tomatoes and spices.*

SUMMER SQUASH <u>AND</u> BABY NEW POTATOES <u>IN</u> WARM DILL SOUR CREAM

THIS IS AN ISRAELI DISH OF FRESH VEGETABLES AND FRAGRANT DILL THAT ARE TOSSED IN A RICH, BUTTERY SOUR CREAM SAUCE.

SERVES FOUR

INGREDIENTS
400g/14oz mixed squash, such as
  yellow and green courgettes
  (zucchini), and pale green patty pan
400g/14oz tiny, baby new potatoes
pinch of sugar
40–75g/1½–3oz/3–5 tbsp butter
2 bunches spring onions (scallions),
  thinly sliced
1 large bunch fresh dill, finely chopped
300ml/½ pint/1¼ cups sour cream
  or Greek (US strained plain) yogurt
salt and ground black pepper

COOK'S TIP
Choose small specimens of squash with bright skins that are free of blemishes and bruises.

1 Cut the squash into pieces about the same size as the potatoes. Put the potatoes in a pan and add water to cover, with the sugar and salt. Bring to the boil, then simmer for about 10 minutes, until almost tender. Add the squash and continue to cook until the vegetables are just tender, then drain.

2 Melt the butter in a large pan; fry the spring onions until just wilted, then gently stir in the dill and vegetables.

3 Remove the pan from the heat and stir in the sour cream or yogurt. Return to the heat and heat gently until warm. Season with salt and pepper and serve.

BAKED WINTER SQUASH IN TOMATO SAUCE

THIS DISH IS ITALIAN JEWISH IN ORIGIN AND A FAVOURITE OF THE JEWS OF NORTHERN ITALY, FROM AROUND MANTUA, WHERE THE MOST MAGNIFICENT SQUASH GROW.

SERVES FOUR TO SIX

INGREDIENTS
45–75ml/3–5 tbsp olive oil
1kg/2½lb pumpkin or orange winter
  squash, peeled and sliced
1 onion, chopped
3–5 garlic cloves, chopped
2 × 400g/14oz cans chopped tomatoes
pinch of sugar
2–3 sprigs of fresh rosemary, stems
  removed and leaves chopped
salt and ground black pepper

VARIATION
Acorn, butternut or Hubbard squash
can all be used in this recipe.

1 Preheat the oven to 160°C/325°F/
Gas 3. Heat 45ml/3 tbsp of the oil in
a pan and fry the pumpkin slices in
batches until golden brown, removing
them from the pan as they are cooked.

2 In the same pan, add the onion, with
more oil if necessary, and fry for about
5 minutes until softened.

3 Add the garlic to the pan and cook
for 1 minute, then add the tomatoes
and sugar and cook over a medium-
high heat until the mixture is of a sauce
consistency. Stir in the rosemary and
season with salt and pepper to taste.

4 Layer the pumpkin slices and tomato
sauce in an ovenproof dish, ending
with some sauce. Bake for 35 minutes,
or until the top is lightly glazed and
beginning to brown, and the pumpkin
is tender. Serve immediately.

CAULIFLOWER WITH GARLIC CRUMBS

THIS ASHKENAZI DISH IS SO SIMPLE AND, BEING PAREVE, MAKES A GREAT ACCOMPANIMENT TO ANY MEAT OR DAIRY MEAL. IN JERUSALEM IT IS OFTEN EATEN WITH MEAT OR FISH WRAPPED IN FILO PASTRY AS THE TEXTURES AND FLAVOURS COMPLEMENT EACH OTHER PERFECTLY.

2 Heat 60–75ml/4–5 tbsp of the olive or vegetable oil in a pan, add the breadcrumbs and cook over a medium heat, tossing and turning, until browned and crisp. Add the garlic, turn once or twice, then remove from the pan and set aside.

3 Heat the remaining oil in the pan, then add the cauliflower, mashing and breaking it up a little as it lightly browns in the oil. (Do not overcook but just cook lightly in the oil.)

SERVES FOUR TO SIX

INGREDIENTS
  1 large cauliflower, cut into
    bitesize florets
  pinch of sugar
  90–120ml/6–8 tbsp olive or
    vegetable oil
  130g/4½oz/2¼ cups dry white or
    wholemeal (whole-wheat)
    breadcrumbs
  3–5 garlic cloves, thinly sliced
    or chopped
  salt and ground black pepper

1 Steam or boil the cauliflower in a pan of water, to which you have added the sugar and a pinch of salt, until just tender. Drain and leave to cool.

4 Add the garlic breadcrumbs to the pan and cook, stirring, until well combined and some of the cauliflower is still holding its shape. Season with salt and pepper and serve hot or warm.

COOK'S TIPS
• Serve, as they do in Italy, with cooked pasta such as spaghetti or rigatoni.
• To serve with a dairy meal, sprinkle the browned cauliflower with grated Cheddar cheese and place it under a hot grill (broiler) until golden and sizzling.

DEEP-FRIED ARTICHOKES

CARCIOFI ALLA GIUDIA ARE A GREAT SPECIALITY OF THE JEWS OF ROME, NAMED AFTER THE ROMAN GHETTO GIUDIA. THE ARTICHOKES ARE PRESSED TO OPEN THEM, THEN PLUNGED INTO HOT OIL WHERE THEIR LEAVES TWIST AND BROWN, TURNING THE ARTICHOKES INTO CRISPY FLOWERS.

SERVES FOUR

INGREDIENTS
2–3 lemons, halved
4–8 small globe artichokes
olive or vegetable oil, for deep-frying
salt

1 Fill a large bowl with cold water and stir in the juice of one or two of the lemons. Trim and discard the stems of the artichokes, then trim off their tough end and remove all the tough outer leaves until you reach the pale pointed centre.

2 Carefully open the leaves of one of the artichokes by pressing it against the table or poking them open. Trim the tops if they are sharp. (Take care not to knock off the remaining leaves.)

3 If there is any choke inside the artichoke, remove it with a melon baller or small pointed spoon. Put the artichoke in the acidulated water and prepare the remaining artichokes in the same way.

4 Put the artichokes in a large pan and pour over water to cover. Bring to the boil and cook over a medium-high heat for 15 minutes, or until the artichokes are partly cooked. If the artichokes are small, cook them for only 10 minutes.

COOK'S TIPS
If you like, prepare and boil the artichokes ahead and deep-fry just before serving.

5 Remove the artichokes from the pan, place upside down on a baking sheet and leave to cool. When they are cool enough to handle, press them open gently but firmly, being careful not to break them apart.

6 Fill a wok or pan with oil to a depth of 5–7.5cm/2–3in and heat until hot.

7 Add one or two artichokes to the oil, with the leaves uppermost, and press down with a slotted spoon to open up the leaves, being careful not to splash the hot oil. Fry for 5–8 minutes, turning, until golden and crisp. Remove from the pan, and drain on kitchen paper. Serve immediately or place on a baking sheet and keep warm in the oven.

SPINACH WITH RAISINS AND PINE NUTS

LIGHTLY COOKED SPINACH WITH A LITTLE ONION, OLIVE OIL, RAISINS AND PINE NUTS, IS A TYPICAL JEWISH ITALIAN DISH, WHICH ECHOES THE SWEET-NUT COMBINATION THAT IS SO POPULAR ON THE ARAB-INFLUENCED SICILIAN TABLE. IT IS UNIVERSAL THROUGHOUT THE JEWISH COMMUNITIES OF ITALY AND ALSO IN OTHER SEPHARDI COMMUNITIES, FOR EXAMPLE IN GREECE, TURKEY AND SPAIN.

2 Steam or cook the spinach in a pan over a medium-high heat, with only the water that clings to the leaves after washing, for 1–2 minutes until the leaves are bright green and wilted. Remove from the heat and drain well. Leave to cool.

3 When the spinach has cooled, chop roughly with a sharp knife.

4 Heat the oil in a frying pan over a medium-low heat, then lower the heat further and add the spring onions or onions. Fry for about 5 minutes, or until soft, then add the spinach, raisins and pine nuts. Raise the heat and cook for 2–3 minutes to warm through. Season with salt and ground black pepper to taste and serve hot or warm.

SERVES FOUR

INGREDIENTS
  60ml/4 tbsp raisins
  1kg/2¼lb fresh spinach
    leaves, washed
  45ml/3 tbsp olive oil
  6–8 spring onions (scallions), thinly
    sliced or 1–2 small yellow or white
    onions, finely chopped
  60ml/4 tbsp pine nuts
  salt and ground black pepper

COOK'S TIP
Pine nuts can turn rancid quickly, so always buy them in small quantities.

1 Put the raisins in a small bowl and pour over boiling water to cover. Leave to stand for about 10 minutes until plumped up, then drain.

VARIATION
For a deeper flavour, add a finely chopped garlic cloves. Fry with the spring onions or onions.

SEPHARDI SPICY CABBAGE WITH TOMATOES, TURMERIC AND PEPPERS

THIS DISH OF HUMBLE CABBAGE IS FAR MORE EXCITING THAN YOU COULD IMAGINE AND NOT ONE TO PASS BY. THE LEAVES BECOME SILKY, FROM BEING THINLY SLICED AND PAR-BOILED, AND SPICY AND COMPLEX WHEN COOKED WITH YEMENITE-INSPIRED SPICING.

SERVES FOUR TO SIX

INGREDIENTS

  1 green or white cabbage,
    thinly sliced
  30–60ml/2–4 tbsp olive oil
  2 onions, chopped
  5–8 garlic cloves, chopped
  1/2 green (bell) pepper, chopped
  2.5ml/1/2 tsp curry powder
  2.5ml/1/2 tsp ground cumin
  2.5ml/1/2 tsp ground turmeric,
    or more to taste
  seeds from 3–5 cardamom pods
  1 mild fresh chilli, chopped, or
    2–3 pinches of dried chilli flakes
  400g/14oz can tomatoes
  pinch of sugar
  juice of 1/2–1 lemon
  45–60ml/3–4 tbsp chopped fresh
    coriander (cilantro) leaves

1 Cook the cabbage in a pan of boiling water for 5–8 minutes, or until tender. Drain well and set aside.

2 Meanwhile, heat the oil in a pan, add the onions and fry until softened, then add half the garlic and the green pepper and cook for 3–4 minutes, or until the pepper softens but the garlic does not turn brown.

VARIATION
Pan-fry meatballs until browned all over, then add them to the cabbage with the tomatoes and cook as above.

3 Sprinkle all the spices into the pan, stir and cook for 1–2 minutes to bring out their flavour. Add the reserved cabbage, the tomatoes and sugar, cover the pan and cook over a low heat for 15–30 minutes, or until the sauce is thick and flavoursome. If necessary, remove the lid and cook off any excess liquid.

4 Add the lemon juice and remaining garlic to the cabbage and cook for about 10 minutes. Stir in the chopped coriander and serve immediately. If you prefer, leave the cabbage to cool slightly before serving the dish warm. Alternatively, cool completely, then chill and serve as a cold salad.

TZIMMES

THIS IS A BAKED DISH OF VEGETABLES AND DRIED FRUIT, ALTHOUGH SOMETIMES FRESH APPLES AND PEARS ARE ADDED. SOME TZIMMES ALSO CONTAIN MEAT AND CAN BE SERVED AS A MAIN DISH RATHER THAN AS AN ACCOMPANIMENT. THE YIDDISH EXPRESSION GANTZE TZIMMES, MEANING A "BIG DEAL", IS INSPIRED BY THIS DISH, WHICH IS FULL OF RICH, SWEET AND SPICY FLAVOURS.

SERVES SIX

INGREDIENTS
  250g/9oz carrots, peeled and sliced
  1 sweet potato, peeled and cut
    into chunks
  1 potato, peeled and cut into chunks
  pinch of sugar
  25g/1oz/2 tbsp butter or 30ml/2 tbsp
    rendered chicken fat or vegetable oil
  1 onion, chopped
  10 pitted prunes, halved
    or quartered
  30–45ml/2–3 tbsp currants
  5 dried apricots, roughly chopped, or
    30ml/2 tbsp sultanas (golden raisins)
  30ml/2 tbsp honey
  5–10ml/1–2 tsp chopped fresh
    root ginger
  1 cinnamon stick or 2–3 shakes of
    ground cinnamon
  juice of ½ lemon
  salt

1 Preheat the oven to 160°C/325°F/ Gas 3. Put the carrots, sweet potato and potato into a pan of sugared and salted boiling water and cook until they are almost tender. Drain, reserving the cooking liquid, and set aside.

VARIATION
To make a meat tzimmes, braise about 500g/1¼ lb beef, cut into chunks, for 1–1½ hours until tender. In step 2 use oil, rather than butter, and add the meat to the pan with the vegetables.

2 Heat the butter or oil in a flameproof casserole, add the onion and fry until softened. Add the cooked vegetables and enough of the cooking liquid to cover the vegetables completely, then add the remaining ingredients.

3 Cover the casserole with a lid and cook in the oven for about 40 minutes. Towards the end of cooking time, check the amount of liquid in the casserole. If there is too much liquid, remove the lid for the last 10–15 minutes.

STEWED OKRA WITH TOMATOES AND ONIONS

THIS IS A FAVOURITE WAY FOR MIDDLE EASTERN JEWS TO PREPARE OKRA. INDIAN JEWS OFTEN MAKE A SIMILAR VERSION USING THEIR OWN TRADITIONAL SPICE MIXTURES.

SERVES FOUR TO SIX

INGREDIENTS
90–120ml/6–8 tbsp olive oil
2 onions, thinly sliced
5–8 garlic cloves, roughly chopped
90ml/6 tbsp chopped fresh coriander
  (cilantro) leaves
800g/1¾lb okra
1kg/2¼lb fresh tomatoes, diced
  or 400g/14oz can tomatoes plus
  30–60ml/2–4 tbsp tomato
  purée (paste)
1.5–2.5ml/¼–½ tsp ground cumin
pinch of ground cinnamon
pinch of ground cloves
5ml/1 tsp sugar, or to taste
cayenne pepper
salt and ground black pepper
1 lemon, to serve

3 Add the tomatoes, cumin, cinnamon and cloves to the pan, then season to taste with the sugar, cayenne pepper, salt and pepper, and cook until the liquid boils. Reduce the heat to low, then simmer for 20–30 minutes until the okra is tender, stirring occasionally.

4 Taste for spicing and seasoning, and adjust if necessary, then stir in the remaining olive oil and coriander. If serving hot or warm, squeeze in the lemon juice and add to the okra or, if serving cold, cut the lemon into wedges and serve with the okra.

1 Heat about half the oil in a pan. Add the onions, garlic and half the coriander and fry for about 10 minutes until the onions are softened and turning brown.

2 Add the okra to the onions and stir-fry for 2–3 minutes.

COOK'S TIPS
• Trimming the okra and leaving them whole means that they will be succulent and not slimy.
• Choose medium-size okra instead of large ones.
• For an Indian-inspired flavour, fry 7.5ml/1½ tsp curry powder, 5ml/1 tsp ground turmeric and 2.5ml/½ tsp ground ginger with the onion and garlic.

LEEK FRITTERS

THESE CRISPY FRIED MORSELS FEATURE PROMINENTLY IN THE SEPHARDI KITCHEN. LEGEND HAS IT THAT THESE WERE WHAT THE FLEEING ISRAELITES WERE MISSING AND MOANING FOR WHEN THEY WERE IN THE DESERT. THEY ARE BEST SERVED AT ROOM TEMPERATURE WITH A GOOD SQUEEZE OF LEMON JUICE AND A SPRINKLING OF SALT.

SERVES FOUR

INGREDIENTS

4 large leeks, total weight about
  1kg/2¼lb, thickly sliced
120–175ml/4–6fl oz/½–¾ cup
  coarse matzo meal
2 eggs, lightly beaten
large pinch of dried thyme
  or basil
freshly grated nutmeg
olive or vegetable oil, for
  shallow frying
salt and ground black pepper
lemon wedges, to serve

1 Cook the leeks in salted boiling water for 5 minutes, or until just tender and bright green. Drain and leave to cool.

2 Chop the leeks roughly. Put in a bowl and combine with the matzo meal, eggs, herbs, nutmeg and seasoning.

3 Heat 5mm/¼in oil in a frying pan. Using two tablespoons, carefully spoon the leek mixture into the hot oil. Cook over a medium-high heat until golden brown on the underside, then turn and cook the second side. Drain on kitchen paper. Cook the rest of the mixture, adding oil if needed. Serve with lemon wedges and salt.

VARIATIONS
To make spinach or chard fritters, replace the leeks with 400–500g/ 14oz–1¼lb fresh spinach or chard leaves and 1 finely chopped onion. Cook the spinach or chard leaves, in only the water that clings to their leaves after washing, until wilted. Leave to cool, reserving the cooking liquid. Roughly chop the greens and continue as in the recipe above, adding enough of the cooking liquid to make a thick batter.

LEEK, SPINACH AND COURGETTE KUGEL

FRESH DILL, SPRING ONIONS AND GARLIC GIVE THEIR FLAVOURS TO THE SPRINGTIME GREENS OF LEEKS, SPINACH AND COURGETTES IN THIS CRISP SEPHARDI KUGEL. BOTH PERSIAN AND TURKISH JEWS FAVOUR LEEKS AT PESACH. SERVE WITH ROAST CHICKEN OR, AS A DAIRY DISH, ACCOMPANIED BY YOGURT.

SERVES SIX TO EIGHT

INGREDIENTS

    90ml/6 tbsp olive oil
    2 large leeks, thinly sliced
    500g/1¼ lb spinach, washed
    1 courgette (zucchini),
      coarsely grated
    1 baking potato
    3 garlic cloves, chopped
    3 spring onions (scallions), chopped
      or thinly sliced
    1–2 pinches of ground turmeric
    about 45ml/3 tbsp medium
      matzo meal
    15–30ml/1–2 tbsp chopped fresh
      dill, plus extra to garnish
    3 eggs, lightly beaten
    salt and ground black pepper
    lemons wedges, to serve

1 Preheat the oven to 200°C/400°F/Gas 6. Heat half the oil in a pan, add the leeks and fry until just tender. Remove from the heat.

2 Cook the spinach in only the water that clings to it after washing until just tender. Drain and, when cool enough to handle, roughly chop. Add the spinach and courgette to the leeks, and stir to combine.

3 Peel and coarsely grate the potato, then squeeze in your hands to remove its excess starch and liquid. Add to the leeks with the garlic, spring onions, turmeric and plenty of salt and ground black pepper.

4 Add enough matzo meal to the vegetable mixture to form a thick dough consistency. Stir the dill into the eggs, then add to the vegetable mixture.

5 Pour the remaining oil into a baking tin (pan) and heat in the oven for about 5 minutes. When the oil is hot, spoon the vegetable mixture evenly into the tin, letting the hot oil bubble up around the sides and on to the top.

6 Bake the kugel for about 15 minutes, then reduce the oven temperature to 180°C/350°F/Gas 4 and bake for a further 15–20 minutes, until the kugel is firm to the touch and the top is golden brown and puffy. Sprinkle with chopped dill to garnish and serve hot or warm with the lemon wedges for squeezing over.

BREADS

At the Jewish table a meal begins with a blessing over the bread. It is one of the most basic foods in the Jewish diet. The variety of breads is staggering, from sweet and tender challah eaten on Shabbat, to hefty sourdough ryes of the Ukraine, flat breads of the Middle East, and crisp unleavened matzos that Jews all over the world eat ritually for Pesach. These breads are usually made without milk or butter so that they may be eaten with either meat or dairy meals.

CHALLAH

Sweet, shiny challah is the traditional braided Ashkenazi bread served at celebrations.
Each Shabbat, it is challah that ushers in the observances, along with wine and candles.
It is said that the shape resembles the hair of a Polish maiden for whom a baker had an
unrequited passion – it was the most beautiful shape that he could think of for his bread.

MAKES TWO LOAVES

INGREDIENTS

15ml/1 tbsp dried active yeast
15ml/1 tbsp sugar
250ml/8fl oz/1 cup lukewarm water
500g/1¼lb/4½ cups strong white
  bread flour, plus extra if needed
30ml/2 tbsp vegetable oil
2 eggs, lightly beaten, plus 1 extra
  for glazing
pinch of sugar
salt
poppy or sesame seeds,
  for sprinkling

1 In a mixer, food processor or large bowl, mix together the yeast, sugar and 120ml/4fl oz/½ cup water. Sprinkle the mixture with a little flour, cover and leave for about 10–12 minutes until bubbles appear on the surface.

2 Beat 5ml/1 tsp salt, the oil and eggs into the mixture until well mixed, then add the flour, slowly at first until completely absorbed, then more quickly. Knead for 5–10 minutes until the mixture forms a dough that leaves the sides of the bowl. If the dough is still sticky, add a little more flour and knead again.

3 Place the dough in a lightly oiled bowl. Cover with a clean dishtowel and leave in a warm place for 1½–2 hours, or until doubled in size.

4 Turn the dough on to a lightly floured surface and knead gently, then return to the bowl. Cover and place in the refrigerator overnight to rise.

5 Turn the dough on to a lightly floured surface, punch down and knead until shiny and pliable. Divide the dough into two equal pieces, then divide each piece into three. Roll each into a long sausage shape.

6 Pinch the ends of three pieces together, then braid into a loaf. Repeat with the remaining dough and place the loaves on a non-stick baking sheet. Cover with a dishtowel and leave to rise for 1 hour, or until doubled in size.

7 Preheat the oven to 190°C/375°F/ Gas 5. In a bowl, combine the remaining egg, the sugar and salt, and brush over the loaves, then sprinkle with the poppy or sesame seeds. Bake for 40 minutes, or until well browned. Leave to cool on a wire rack.

VARIATION
To make challah for Rosh Hashanah, knead 200g/7oz/scant 1 cup glacé (candied) fruit or sultanas (golden raisins) into the dough before braiding. Sprinkle with hundreds and thousands before baking.

MOUNA

THIS IS THE TRADITIONAL EGG BREAD OF THE ALGERIAN JEWISH COMMUNITY, MUCH AS CHALLAH IS OF THE ASHKENAZIM. IT IS DELICATE AND SWEET AND SOMETIMES, AS IN THIS RECIPE, CONTAINS A BIG SPOONFUL OF JAM IN THE CENTRE. IT IS PERFECT FOR A SHABBAT BREAKFAST.

MAKES TWO LOAVES

INGREDIENTS

500g/1¼lb/4½ cups unbleached
  plain (all-purpose) flour
130g/4½oz/scant ⅔ cup sugar
7g packet easy-blend (rapid-rise)
  dried yeast
45ml/3 tbsp lukewarm water
105ml/7 tbsp lukewarm milk
4 eggs
130g/4½oz/generous ½ cup butter
grated rind of 1 orange
oil, for greasing
90–120ml/6–8 tbsp jam
15ml/1 tbsp cold water
icing (confectioners') sugar,
  for dusting (optional)

1 Combine half the flour, half the sugar and the yeast in a large bowl. Stir the water and milk into the dry ingredients and mix until thoroughly combined. Cover and leave in a warm place for about 1 hour until doubled in size.

2 Whisk together half the remaining sugar and three of the eggs. Mix in the butter and orange rind. Gradually add the remaining flour and knead until smooth. Set aside until risen.

3 Knead the yeast mixture into the egg mixture for about 10 minutes until smooth and elastic. With oiled hands, shape the dough into a ball. Place the dough in a bowl, cover and leave in a warm place for about 1 hour, or until doubled in size.

4 Turn the dough on to a lightly floured surface and punch down with your fists. Knead for 3–4 minutes, then divide the dough in half and shape each piece into a round loaf. Make a large indentation in each loaf and spoon in the jam. Close up and pinch the dough together.

5 Lightly oil two baking sheets and then sprinkle with flour, or use non-stick baking sheets. Place the loaves on the prepared baking sheets and cut slits around the sides of the loaves, taking care not to let any jam leak out.

6 Cover the loaves with a clean dishtowel and leave to rise for 45–60 minutes, or until doubled in size.

7 Preheat the oven to 190°C/375°F/ Gas 5. In a small bowl, beat the remaining egg with the cold water. Brush the glaze on to the loaves, then sprinkle over the remaining sugar. Bake the loaves for about 20 minutes, or until golden brown. Dust with icing sugar, if you like.

NEW YORK SEEDED CORN RYE SOURDOUGH

FORTUNATELY YOU DO NOT HAVE TO BE JEWISH TO LOVE THIS EASTERN EUROPEAN JEWISH BREAD. IT IS SURPRISINGLY EASY TO MAKE, ALTHOUGH YOU NEED TO PREPARE THE BREAD WELL IN ADVANCE AS THE STARTER TAKES A FEW DAYS TO FERMENT.

MAKES TWO LOAVES

INGREDIENTS
  1.6kg/3½lb/14 cups unbleached
    strong white bread flour
  7g packet easy-blend (rapid-rise)
    dried yeast
  250ml/8fl oz/1 cup lukewarm water
  60ml/4 tbsp caraway or dill seeds
  15ml/1 tbsp salt
  corn meal, for sprinkling
For the sourdough starter
  250g/9oz/2¼ cups unbleached strong
    white bread flour or a mixture of
    ¾ strong white bread flour and
    ¼ wholemeal (whole-wheat) flour
  7g easy-blend (rapid-rise) dried yeast
  250ml/8fl oz/1 cup lukewarm water
For the sponge
  200g/7oz/1¾ cups rye flour
  250ml/8fl oz/1 cup lukewarm water

1 To make the sourdough starter, put the flour into a large bowl and stir in the yeast. Make a central well, stir in the water and mix together. Cover tightly. Leave at room temperature for 2 days or in the refrigerator for 1 week.

2 To make the sponge, put the rye flour into a large bowl, mix in the sourdough starter and water. Cover tightly. Leave at room temperature for 8 hours or in the refrigerator for up to 2 days.

3 Put the flour into a large bowl and add the sponge mixture, yeast, water, caraway or dill seeds and salt and mix to form a soft, slightly sticky dough.

4 Turn the dough into a large, clean bowl, sprinkle the top with flour, cover with a clean dishtowel and leave to rise in a warm place for about 2 hours, or until doubled in size.

5 Turn the dough on to a lightly floured surface and punch down with your fists. Knead for 3–4 minutes until smooth and elastic. Divide the dough in half, then shape each piece into a round loaf.

6 Sprinkle two baking sheets with corn meal. Place the loaves on the top and score each one with a sharp knife.

7 Cover each loaf loosely with a clean dishtowel and leave in a warm place to rise for about 45 minutes, or until doubled in size.

8 Preheat the oven to 220°C/425°F/ Gas 7. Fill a roasting pan with boiling water and place in the bottom of the oven. Alternatively, if you have a tile or pizza stone place this in the oven – it will help to create a thick, crunchy crust. Bake the loaves for about 35 minutes until lightly browned and hollow-sounding when tapped on the bottom. Cool on a wire rack.

PUMPERNICKEL

Dark bread was the mainstay of most meals during the centuries of Jewish life in Poland, Russia and the Baltic states and might be spread with butter, chicken fat or sour cream, or simply rubbed with onion or garlic.

MAKES TWO LOAVES

INGREDIENTS

65g/2½oz plain (semi-sweet) chocolate or cocoa powder (unsweetened)
7g packet easy-blend (rapid-rise) dried yeast
200g/7oz/1¾ cups rye flour
300–400g/11–14oz/2¾–3½ cups strong white bread flour
5ml/1 tsp salt
2.5ml/½ tsp sugar
15ml/1 tbsp instant coffee powder
15ml/1 tbsp caraway seeds (optional)
105ml/7 tbsp warm dark beer
15ml/1 tbsp vegetable oil
90ml/6 tbsp treacle (molasses)
corn meal, for sprinkling

3 Make a well in the flour mixture, then pour in the chocolate or cocoa, 175ml/6fl oz/¾ cup water, the beer, oil and treacle. Mix well to form a dough.

4 Turn the dough out on to a lightly floured surface and knead for about 10 minutes, or until smooth.

5 Place the dough in a lightly oiled bowl and turn the dough to coat in oil. Cover with a dishtowel and leave to rise for 1½ hours, or until doubled in size.

6 Oil a baking sheet and sprinkle with corn meal. Turn the dough on to a lightly floured surface and punch down. Knead for 3–4 minutes, then divide the dough and shape into two round or oval loaves. Place the loaves on the baking sheet, cover with a clean dishtowel and leave to rise in a warm place for 45 minutes, or until doubled in size.

7 Preheat the oven to 185°C/360°F/Gas 4½. Bake the loaves for about 40 minutes, or until they sound hollow when tapped on the base. Leave to cool on a wire rack.

1 Place a bowl over a pan of water and heat the chocolate or cocoa with 50ml/2fl oz/¼ cup water. Stir to combine, then set aside.

2 Combine the yeast, flours, salt, sugar, coffee and caraway seeds, if using.

BAGELS

THESE RING-SHAPED ROLLS ARE ONE OF THE EASTERN EUROPEAN JEWS' BEST CONTRIBUTIONS TO THE GASTRONOMY OF THE WORLD. THE DOUGH IS FIRST BOILED TO GIVE IT A CHEWY TEXTURE AND THEN BAKED. THE BAGELS CAN BE TOPPED WITH ALMOST ANYTHING: SCHMEARS, FLAVOURED CREAM CHEESE, LOX OR FRESH, CHOPPED VEGETABLES ARE JUST A FEW EXAMPLES.

MAKES TEN TO TWELVE

INGREDIENTS
7g packet easy-blend (rapid-rise)
 dried yeast
25ml/1½ tbsp salt
500g/1¼lb/4½ cups strong
 white bread flour
250ml/8fl oz/1 cup lukewarm
 water
oil, for greasing
30ml/2 tbsp sugar
corn meal, for sprinkling
1 egg yolk

1 In a bowl, combine the yeast, salt and flour. Pour the lukewarm water into a separate large bowl.

2 Gradually add half the flour to the lukewarm water, beating until it forms a smooth, soft batter.

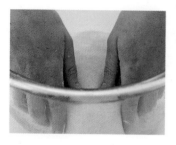

3 Knead the remaining flour into the batter until the mixture forms a fairly firm, smooth dough.

4 On a lightly floured surface knead the dough by hand for 10–20 minutes or, if using a bread machine, 5–8 minutes, until shiny and smooth. If the dough is sticky, add a little more flour. (The dough should be much firmer than ordinary bread dough.)

5 Lightly oil a bowl. Place the dough in it and turn to coat it completely in oil. Cover with a clean dishtowel and leave in a warm place for about 40 minutes, or until doubled in size.

6 Turn the dough on to a lightly floured surface and punch down with your fists. Knead for 3–4 minutes, or until smooth and elastic.

7 Divide the dough into 10–12 balls. Poke your thumb through each one then, working with your fingers, open the hole to form a bagel measuring 6–7.5cm/2½–3in in diameter. Place on a floured board and leave to rise for 20 minutes, or until doubled in size.

8 Preheat the oven to 200°C/400°F/ Gas 6. Bring 3–4 litres/5–7 pints/ 2½–3½ quarts water to the boil in a large pan and add the sugar. Lower the heat to a gentle boil. Lightly oil a baking sheet and sprinkle with corn meal. Beat the egg yolk with 15ml/1 tbsp water.

9 Add the bagels, one at a time, to the boiling water, until you have a single layer of bagels, and cook for 8 minutes, turning occasionally so that they cook evenly. Remove from the pan with a slotted spoon, drain and place on the prepared baking sheet.

10 Brush each bagel with the egg mixture. Bake for 25–30 minutes until well browned. Cool on a wire rack.

VARIATIONS
Add dried onions, garlic granules or poppy seeds to the bagel dough or top the bagels with poppy seeds, sesame seeds, caraway seeds, dried onion or garlic granules before baking.

ONION ROLLS

THESE SWEET-SMELLING, TENDER ROLLS ARE BASED ON THOSE FOUND IN THE UKRAINIAN BAKERIES OF McALLISTER STREET IN SAN FRANCISCO, WHICH USED TO BE LIKE A TINY SHTETL. SERVE THEM HOT, SPREAD WITH BUTTER, OR COLD, FILLED WITH SANDWICH INGREDIENTS, OR EAT WITH A BOWL OF WARMING SOUP FOR A SATISFYING LUNCH.

MAKES TWELVE TO FOURTEEN

INGREDIENTS
  15ml/1 tbsp dried active yeast
  15ml/1 tbsp sugar
  250ml/8fl oz/1 cup lukewarm
    water
  30ml/2 tbsp vegetable oil
  2 eggs, lightly beaten
  500g/1¼lb/4½ cups strong
    white bread flour
  3–4 onions, very, very
    finely chopped
  60ml/4 tbsp poppy seeds
  salt

1 In a mixer fitted with a dough hook, a food processor fitted with a dough blade, or a large bowl, mix together the yeast, sugar and water. Sprinkle the mixture with a little flour, cover and leave for 10–12 minutes until bubbles appear on the surface.

2 Beat 5ml/1 tsp salt, the oil and one of the eggs into the mixture until well mixed, then gradually add the flour and knead for 5–10 minutes until the dough leaves the sides of the bowl. If the dough is still slightly sticky, add a little more flour.

3 Lightly oil a bowl. Place the dough in it and turn to coat. Cover with a dishtowel. Leave to rise in a warm place for about 1½ hours, or until doubled in size.

4 Turn the dough on to a lightly floured surface, punch down with your fists, knead the dough for 3–4 minutes, then knead half the onions into the dough. Form the dough into egg-size balls, then press each ball into a round 1cm/½in thick. Place on a baking sheet.

5 Lightly beat the remaining egg with 30ml/2 tbsp water and a pinch of salt. Press an indentation on top of each round of dough and brush with the egg mixture. Sprinkle the remaining onions and the poppy seeds on to the rolls and leave to rise in a warm place for 45 minutes, or until doubled in size.

6 Preheat the oven to 190°C/375°F/ Gas 5. Bake the rolls for 20 minutes, or until pale golden brown. Serve hot from the oven or leave to cool.

PITTA BREAD

Throughout the Mediterranean, pitta is the most commonly found bread. There are many different types from very flat ones, to those with pockets, to a thicker cushiony one. The best pitta bread is always soft, tender and moist.

5 Heat a large, heavy frying pan over a medium-high heat. When smoking hot, gently lay one piece of flattened dough in the pan and cook for 15–20 seconds. Carefully turn it over and cook the second side for about 1 minute.

6 When large bubbles start to form on the bread, turn it over again. It should puff up. Using a clean dishtowel, gently press on the bread where the bubbles have formed. Cook for a total of 3 minutes, then remove the pitta from the pan. Repeat with the remaining dough until all the pittas have been cooked.

7 Wrap the pitta breads in a clean dishtowel, stacking them as each one is cooked. Serve the pittas hot while they are soft and moist.

MAKES TWELVE

INGREDIENTS
500g/1¼lb/4½ cups strong white bread flour, or half white and half wholemeal (whole-wheat)
7g packet easy-blend (rapid-rise) dried yeast
15ml/1 tbsp salt
15ml/1 tbsp olive oil
250ml/8fl oz/1 cup water

1 Combine the flour, yeast and salt. In a large bowl, mix together the oil and water, then stir in half of the flour mixture, stirring in the same direction, until the dough is stiff. Knead in the remaining flour.

2 Place the dough in a clean bowl, cover with a clean dishtowel and leave in a warm place for at least 30 minutes and up to 2 hours.

3 Knead the dough for 10 minutes, or until smooth. Lightly oil the bowl, place the dough in it, cover again and leave to rise in a warm place for about 1 hour, or until doubled in size.

4 Divide the dough into 12 equal-size pieces. With lightly floured hands, flatten each piece, then roll out into a round measuring about 20cm/8in and about 5mm–1cm/¼–½in thick. Keep the rolled breads covered with a clean dishtowel while you make the remaining pittas.

VARIATION
To cook the breads in the oven, preheat the oven to 220°C/425°F/Gas 7. Fill an unglazed or partially glazed dish with hot water and place in the bottom of the oven. Alternatively, arrange a handful of unglazed tiles in the bottom of the oven. Use either a non-stick baking sheet or a lightly oiled ordinary baking sheet and heat in the oven for a few minutes. Place two or three pieces of flattened dough on to the hot baking sheet and place in the hottest part of the oven. Bake for 2–3 minutes. They should puff up. Repeat with the remaining dough until all the pittas have been cooked.

CORIANDER AND CHEESE YEASTED FLAT BREADS

THESE FLAT BREADS ARE SALTY FROM THE HALLOUMI CHEESE AND ARE BEST EATEN WITH A LITTLE UNSALTED BUTTER, MIXED WITH CHOPPED RAW GARLIC, OR WITH A BOWL OF YOGURT SPRINKLED WITH GARLIC, AND WITH SPRING ONIONS, COS OR ROMAINE LETTUCE AND CUCUMBER SLICES.

2 Knead the dough for 5–10 minutes until smooth. Lightly oil a bowl, place the dough in it, cover with a clean dishtowel and leave to rise in a warm place for about 1 hour, or until doubled in size.

3 Turn the dough on to a lightly floured surface and punch down with your fists. Knead in the cheese, then knead for a further 3–4 minutes.

4 Preheat the oven to 220°C/425°F/ Gas 7. Divide the dough into 10 pieces and shape each piece into a flat round about 1cm/½in thick. Place the dough rounds on non-stick baking sheets and leave to rise for about 10 minutes, or until doubled in size.

5 Bake the flat breads for about 15 minutes until they are risen and golden brown. Eat immediately.

VARIATION
For a less salty result, use finely diced Cheddar in place of the halloumi.

MAKES TEN

INGREDIENTS
500g/1¼lb/4½ cups strong white
  bread flour
2 × 7g packets easy-blend
  (rapid-rise) dried yeast
5ml/1 tsp sugar
1 bunch fresh chives, chopped
60–90ml/4–6 tbsp chopped fresh
  coriander (cilantro)
45–75ml/3–5 tbsp dried onion flakes
200ml/7fl oz/scant 1 cup water
60ml/4 tbsp natural (plain) yogurt
45ml/3 tbsp olive oil
250g/9oz halloumi cheese, finely diced

1 Mix the flour, yeast, sugar, chives, coriander and onion flakes in a bowl, mixer or food processor. Add the water, yogurt and oil and mix to form a dough.

YEMENI SPONGE FLAT BREADS

THESE FLAT BREADS, KNOWN AS LAHUHS AND MADE FROM A BATTER, ARE BUBBLY AND SOFT AND SIMILAR TO A THIN CRUMPET. THEY ARE EATEN WITH SOUPS BUT ARE ALSO GOOD DIPPED INTO THE ISRAELI HOT SAUCE ZCHUG OR SERVED WITH ROASTED TOMATOES AND GOAT'S CHEESE.

SERVES FOUR

INGREDIENTS
15ml/1 tbsp dried active yeast
15ml/1 tbsp sugar
500ml/17fl oz/2¼ cups lukewarm
  water
350g/12oz/3 cups plain
  (all-purpose) flour
5ml/1 tsp salt
50g/2oz/¼ cup butter, melted, or
  60ml/4 tbsp vegetable oil

COOK'S TIP
Use two or three frying pans at the same time so that the flat breads are ready together and so can be eaten piping hot.

1 In a bowl, dissolve the dried yeast and a pinch of the sugar in about 75ml/2½fl oz/⅓ cup of the water. Leave in a warm place for about 10 minutes, or until frothy.

2 Stir the remaining water and sugar, the flour, salt and melted butter or vegetable oil into the yeast mixture and mix until it forms a smooth batter. Cover with a clean dishtowel, then leave in a warm place for about 1 hour, until doubled in size.

3 Stir the thick, frothy batter and, if it seems too thick to ladle out, add a little extra water. Cover and leave in a warm place for about 1 hour.

4 Cook the flat breads in a non-stick frying pan. Ladle 45–60ml/3–4 tbsp of batter (or less for smaller breads) into the pan and cook over a low heat until the top is bubbling and the colour has changed. (Traditionally these breads are only cooked on one side but they can be turned over and the second side cooked for just a moment if you wish.)

5 Remove the cooked flat bread from the pan and keep warm in a clean dishtowel. Repeat until you have used up all the remaining batter.

DESSERTS, CAKES AND SWEETMEATS

*No Bar or Bat Mitzvah kiddush would be complete without a
table of sweetmeats — from the cookies of the Ashkenazim to the
syrupy exotic cakes of the Sephardim. Many cakes are made
without flour, just with nut meal or matzo meal, risen with
beaten egg whites, to eat during the festival of Pesach
when leavened foods are not allowed but festive meals
are the order of the day.*

TROPICAL SCENTED RED AND ORANGE FRUIT SALAD

THIS FRESH FRUIT SALAD, WITH ITS SPECIAL COLOUR AND EXOTIC FLAVOUR, IS PERFECT AFTER A RICH, HEAVY MEAL. IT IS A GREAT DISH TO SERVE AT PESACH, WHICH FALLS AT THE END OF THE ORANGE SEASON AND THE BEGINNING OF THE STRAWBERRY SEASON.

SERVES FOUR TO SIX

INGREDIENTS
   350–400g/12–14oz/3–3½ cups
     strawberries, hulled and halved
   3 oranges, peeled and segmented
   3 small blood oranges, peeled
     and segmented
   1–2 passion fruit
   120ml/4fl oz/½ cup dry white wine
   sugar, to taste

VARIATION
Other fruit that can be added include
pear, kiwi fruit and banana.

1 Put the strawberries and oranges into a serving bowl. Halve the passion fruit and spoon the flesh into the fruit.

2 Pour the wine over the fruit and add sugar to taste. Toss gently and then chill until ready to serve.

DRIED FRUIT COMPÔTE

FRUIT COMPÔTES ARE A TRADITIONAL JEWISH DESSERT AS THEY ARE LIGHT, HEALTHY AND REFRESHING AFTER A HEAVY FESTIVE MEAL. DRIED FRUIT COMPÔTES ARE JUST AS WONDERFUL AS THOSE MADE WITH FRESH FRUITS, ESPECIALLY IN THE MIDDLE OF WINTER WHEN FRESH FRUIT IS SCARCE.

SERVES FOUR

INGREDIENTS
225g/8oz/1⅓ cups mixed
  dried fruit
75g/3oz/⅔ cup dried cherries
75g/3oz/⅔ cup sultanas
  (golden raisins)
10 dried prunes
10 dried apricots
hot, freshly brewed fragrant tea,
  such as Earl Grey or jasmine,
  to cover
15–30ml/1–2 tbsp sugar
¼ lemon, sliced
60ml/4 tbsp brandy

1 Put the dried fruits in a bowl and pour over the hot tea. Add sugar to taste and the lemon slices. Cover with a plate, set aside and leave to cool to room temperature.

2 When the fruits have cooled sufficiently, chill in the refrigerator for at least 2 hours and preferably overnight. Just before serving, pour in the brandy and stir well.

BUTTERED CHALLAH PUDDING WITH PEARS, CHERRIES AND ALMONDS

LEFTOVER CHALLAH MAKES SUPER BREAD PUDDING, AS ANYONE WHO HAS EATEN IT WILL AGREE. IF YOU PLAN TO SERVE IT AFTER A MEAT MEAL, USE FRUIT JUICE, SUCH AS PEAR JUICE, IN PLACE OF THE MILK.

SERVES SIX TO EIGHT

INGREDIENTS
75–115g/3–4oz/6–8 tbsp butter or
    pareve margarine, softened, plus
    extra for greasing
750ml/1¼ pints/3 cups milk
4 eggs, lightly beaten
2.5ml/½ tsp vanilla essence (extract)
2.5ml/½ tsp almond essence (extract)
1.5ml/¼ tsp salt
500g/1¼lb leftover, slightly
    dry challah, thickly sliced and
    lightly toasted
130g/4½oz/1 cup dried cherries
3 firm, ripe pears
200–250g/7–9oz/1–1¼ cups
    demerara (raw) sugar
130g/4½oz/generous 1 cup flaked
    (sliced) almonds
cream, to serve (optional)

1 Preheat the oven to 190°C/375°F/
Gas 5. Butter a 25cm/10in square or
oval baking dish. Mix together the milk,
eggs, vanilla, almond essence and salt.

3 Add the buttered challah and dried
cherries to the milk mixture and fold in
gently so that all of the bread is coated
with the liquid.

4 Core and dice the pears but do not
peel. Layer the bread, sugar, almonds
and pears in the dish, ending with a
layer of sugar. Dot with butter. Bake for
40–50 minutes, or until caramelized.
Serve with cream, if you like.

2 Spread the challah toast with butter,
reserving 40g/1½oz/3 tbsp, then cut
the challah into bitesize chunks.

VARIATION
To make an apple version, replace the
almond essence with more vanilla
essence and add 15ml/1 tbsp ground
cinnamon to the milk. Use raisins or
sultanas (golden raisins) instead of dried
cherries, broken walnuts in place of the
almonds, and apples instead of pears.

CLASSIC AMERICAN CREAMY CHEESECAKE

*THERE ARE A MILLION CHEESECAKE RECIPES, INCLUDING ONES THAT ARE TOPPED WITH FRUIT OR
SCENTED WITH LEMON, BUT THIS CLASSIC VERSION IS THE MOST TEMPTING. IT MAKES THE PERFECT
DESSERT FOR A BAR OR BAT MITZVAH OR FAMILY MEAL, OR KEEP IT AS A STANDBY IN THE FREEZER.*

SERVES SIX TO EIGHT

INGREDIENTS

130g/4½oz/generous ½ cup butter,
  melted, plus extra for greasing
350g/12oz digestive biscuits
  (graham crackers), finely crushed
350–400g/12–14oz/1¾–2 cups
  caster (superfine) sugar
350g/12oz/1½ cups full-fat
  soft white (farmer's) cheese
3 eggs, lightly beaten
15ml/1 tbsp vanilla essence (extract)
350g/12oz/1½ cups sour cream
strawberries, blueberries, raspberries
  and icing (confectioners') sugar,
  to serve (optional)

1 Butter a deep 23cm/9in springform
tin (pan). Put the biscuit crumbs and
60ml/4 tbsp of the sugar in a bowl and
mix together, then add the melted
butter and mix well. Press the mixture
into the prepared tin to cover the base
and sides. Chill for about 30 minutes.

2 Preheat the oven to 190°C/375°F/
Gas 5. Using an electric mixer, food
processor or wooden spoon, beat the
cheese until soft. Beat in the eggs, then
250g/9oz/1½ cups of the sugar and
10ml/2 tsp of the vanilla essence.

3 Pour the mixture over the crumb
base and bake for 45 minutes, or until
a cocktail stick (toothpick), inserted in
the centre, comes out clean. Leave to
cool slightly for about 10 minutes. (Do
not turn the oven off.)

4 Meanwhile, combine the sour cream
and remaining sugar, to taste. Stir in the
remaining vanilla essence. When the
cheesecake has cooled, pour over
the topping, spreading it out evenly.
Return to the oven and bake for a
further 5 minutes to glaze.

5 Leave the cheesecake to cool to
room temperature, then chill. Serve with
a few fresh strawberries, blueberries
and raspberries, dusted with icing
sugar, if you like.

VARIATIONS
• To make a strawberry cheesecake, in
place of the sour cream, mix together
130g/4½oz/generous 1 cup fresh
strawberries, sliced, with 30–45ml/
2–3 tbsp melted redcurrant jelly.
Spread the mixture over the top of the
cheesecake and return to the oven until
warmed through. Leave to cool, then
chill before serving.
• For a lemon cheesecake, instead of the
vanilla essence, flavour the cheesecake
with the grated rind and juice of 1 lemon.

CHEESE-FILLED JERUSALEM KODAFA DRENCHED WITH SYRUP

IN JERUSALEM AND THROUGHOUT THE MIDDLE EAST, KODAFA ARE MADE IN HUGE METAL TRAYS. YOU CAN SEE THEM BEING CARRIED THROUGH THE STREETS ON SELLER'S HEADS. THIS SWEET PASTRY IS USUALLY MADE WITH KADAIF, A SHREDDED WHEAT-LIKE PASTRY THAT CAN BE BOUGHT READY-MADE. THE VERSION HERE USES COUSCOUS, WHICH GIVES AN EQUALLY DELICIOUS RESULT.

SERVES SIX

INGREDIENTS
200–250g/7–9oz/1–1½ cups
   couscous
500ml/17fl oz/2¼ cups
   boiling water
130–200g/4½–7oz/½–scant 1 cup
   butter, cut into small pieces
1 egg, lightly beaten
pinch of salt
400g/14oz/1¾ cups ricotta cheese
175–200g/6–7oz cheese, such as
   mozzarella, Taleggio or Monterey
   Jack, grated or finely chopped
350ml/12fl oz/1½ cups
   clear honey
2–3 pinches of saffron threads
   or ground cinnamon
120ml/4fl oz/½ cup water
5ml/1 tsp orange flower water or
   lemon juice
90ml/6 tbsp roughly chopped shelled
   pistachio nuts

1 Put the couscous in a large bowl and pour over the boiling water. Stir together with a fork, then leave to soak for about 30 minutes until the water has been completely absorbed.

2 When the couscous is cool enough to handle, break up all the lumps with your fingers.

3 Stir the butter into the couscous, then stir in the beaten egg and salt.

4 Preheat the oven to 200°C/400°F/ Gas 6. Spread half the couscous into a 25–30cm/10–12in round cake tin (pan).

5 In a bowl, combine the cheeses and 30ml/2 tbsp of the honey. Spread on top of the couscous, then top with the remaining couscous. Press down gently and bake for 10–15 minutes.

6 Meanwhile, put the remaining honey, the saffron threads or cinnamon, and the water in a pan. Bring to the boil, then boil for 5–7 minutes, or until the liquid forms a syrup. Remove from the heat and stir in the orange flower water or lemon juice.

7 When the kodafa is cooked, place under the grill (broiler) and cook until it is lightly browned on top and a golden crust is formed.

8 Sprinkle the pistachio nuts on top of the kodafa. Serve warm, cut into wedges, with the syrup.

VARIATIONS
• Other versions of this pastry are made with biscuit (cookie) crumbs and broken pistachio nuts.
• If you like, warm this kodafa through in the microwave before serving with strong coffee or mint tea.

TUSCAN CITRUS SPONGE

THIS PESACH CAKE COMES FROM THE LITTLE TUSCAN TOWN OF PITIGLIANO, WHOSE RICH JEWISH TRADITION DATES BACK TO THE THIRTEENTH CENTURY. MADE WITH MATZO AND POTATO FLOUR, IT IS KOSHER FOR THE FESTIVAL BUT RICH AND SPECIAL ENOUGH FOR ANY FESTIVITY.

SERVES SIX TO EIGHT

INGREDIENTS
 12 eggs, separated
 300g/11oz/1½ cups caster
   (superfine) sugar
 120ml/4fl oz/½ cup fresh
   orange juice
 grated rind of 1 orange
 grated rind of 1 lemon
 50g/2oz/½ cup potato flour, sifted
 90g/3½oz/¾ cup fine matzo meal
   or matzo meal flour, sifted
 large pinch of salt
 icing (confectioners') sugar, for
   dusting (optional)

1 Preheat the oven to 160°C/325°F/ Gas 3. Whisk the egg yolks until pale and frothy, then whisk in the sugar, orange juice, orange rind and lemon rind.

2 Fold the sifted flours into the egg mixture. In a clean bowl, whisk the egg whites with the salt until stiff, then fold into the egg yolk mixture.

3 Pour the cake mixture into a deep, ungreased 25cm/10in cake tin (pan) and bake for about 1 hour, or until a cocktail stick (toothpick), inserted in the centre, comes out clean. Leave to cool in the tin.

4 When cold, turn out the cake and invert it on to a serving plate. Dust the top with a little icing sugar before serving, if you wish.

COOK'S TIPS
• When testing to see if the cake is cooked, if you don't have a cocktail stick to hand, use a strand of raw dried spaghetti instead – it will work just as well.
• This light and tangy sponge makes a wonderful dessert for Pesach, especially when served with a refreshing fruit salad.

PESACH ALMOND CAKES

THIS FIRM BISCUIT-LIKE CAKE HAS THE FLAVOUR OF MACAROONS AND MARZIPAN. IT IS EASY TO MAKE AND TASTES DELICIOUS SERVED WITH A CUP OF TEA OR COFFEE. IF YOU CAN WAIT, THE TEXTURE AND FLAVOUR OF THE CAKE ARE IMPROVED BY A FEW DAYS OF STORAGE.

3 Put the oil, sugars, egg yolks, almond essence, vanilla essence, orange juice and half the brandy in a separate bowl. Stir, then add the almond mixture to form a thick batter. (It may be slightly lumpy.)

4 Whisk the egg whites until stiff. Fold one-third of the egg whites into the mixture to lighten it, then fold in the rest. Pour the mixture into the prepared tin and bake for 25–30 minutes.

5 Meanwhile, mix the remaining brandy with the icing sugar. If necessary, add a little water to make an icing (frosting) with the consistency of single (light) cream. Remove the cake from the oven and prick the top all over with a skewer.

SERVES SIXTEEN

INGREDIENTS
350g/12oz/3 cups ground almonds
50g/2oz/½ cup matzo meal
1.5ml/¼ tsp salt
30ml/2 tbsp vegetable oil
250g/9oz/1¼ cups sugar
300g/11oz/1⅓ cups brown sugar
3 eggs, separated
7.5ml/1½ tsp almond essence (extract)
5ml/1 tsp vanilla essence (extract)
150ml/¼ pint/⅔ cup orange juice
150ml/¼ pint/⅔ cup brandy
200g/7oz/1¾ cups icing
    (confectioners') sugar
90g/3½oz/scant 1 cup flaked
    (sliced) almonds

1 Preheat the oven to 180°C/350°F/ Gas 4. Lightly grease a 30–38cm/ 12–15in square cake tin (pan).

2 Put the ground almonds, matzo meal and salt in a bowl and mix together.

6 Pour the icing evenly over the top of the cake, then return the cake to the oven for a further 10 minutes, or until the top is crusty.

7 Leave the cake to cool in the tin, then serve cut into squares.

POLISH APPLE CAKE

THIS CAKE IS FIRM AND MOIST, WITH PIECES OF APPLE PEEKING THROUGH THE TOP. IT IS BASED ON A RECIPE FROM AN OLD POLISH LADY IN A CALIFORNIAN LUBAVITCHER COMMUNITY WHO ALWAYS USED TO SERVE IT FOR SHABBAT.

2 Put the sliced apples in a bowl and mix with the cinnamon and 75ml/5 tbsp of the sugar.

3 In a separate bowl, beat together the eggs, remaining sugar, vegetable oil, orange juice and vanilla essence until well combined. Sift in the remaining flour and salt, then stir into the mixture.

4 Pour two-thirds of the cake mixture into the prepared tin, top with one-third of the apples, then pour over the remaining cake mixture and top with the remaining apple. Bake for about 1 hour, or until golden brown.

5 Leave the cake to cool in the tin to allow the juices to soak in. Serve while still warm, cut into squares.

SERVES SIX TO EIGHT

INGREDIENTS
375g/13oz/3¼ cups self-raising
  (self-rising) flour
3–4 large cooking apples, or
  cooking and eating apples
10ml/2 tsp ground cinnamon
500g/1¼lb/2½ cups caster
  (superfine) sugar
4 eggs, lightly beaten
250ml/8fl oz/1 cup vegetable oil
120ml/4fl oz/½ cup
  orange juice
10ml/2 tsp vanilla essence
  (extract)
2.5ml/½ tsp salt

1 Preheat the oven to 180°C/350°F/Gas 4. Grease a 30 × 38cm/12 × 15in square cake tin (pan) and dust with a little of the flour. Core and thinly slice the apples, but do not peel.

COOK'S TIP
This sturdy little cake is good to serve with tea on a Shabbat afternoon. Using orange juice instead of milk is typical of Jewish baking as it allows the cake to be eaten with both meat and dairy meals.

RUSSIAN POPPY SEED CAKE

THIS PLAIN AND SIMPLE CAKE IS STUDDED WITH TINY BLACK POPPY SEEDS THAT GIVE IT A NUTTY, DISTINCTIVE TASTE THAT IS UTTERLY DELICIOUS. TRADITIONALLY CALLED MOHN TORTE, *IT IS THE STAPLE OF RUSSIAN BAKERIES, WHERE IT IS SERVED WITH HOT TEA.*

SERVES ABOUT EIGHT

INGREDIENTS

130g/4½oz/generous 1 cup
  self-raising (self-rising) flour
5ml/1 tsp baking powder
2.5ml/½ tsp salt
2 eggs
225g/8oz/generous 1 cup caster
  (superfine) sugar
5–10ml/1–2 tsp vanilla
  essence (extract)
200g/7oz/scant 1½ cups poppy
  seeds, ground
15ml/1 tbsp grated lemon rind
120ml/4fl oz/½ cup milk
130g/4½oz/generous ½ cup
  unsalted (sweet) butter, melted
  and cooled
30ml/2 tbsp vegetable oil
icing (confectioners') sugar, sifted,
  for dusting

1 Preheat the oven to 180°C/350°F/Gas 4. Grease and base-line a 23cm/9in springform tin (pan). Sift together the flour, baking powder and salt.

2 Using an electric whisk, beat together the eggs, sugar and vanilla essence for 4–5 minutes until pale and fluffy. Stir in the poppy seeds and the lemon rind.

VARIATION
To make a poppy seed tart, pour the cake mixture into a par-cooked pastry crust, then bake for 30 minutes, or until the filling is firm and risen.

3 Gently fold the sifted ingredients into the egg and poppy seed mixture, working in three batches and alternating with the milk, then fold in the melted butter and vegetable oil.

4 Pour the mixture into the tin and bake for 40 minutes, or until firm. Cool in the tin for 15 minutes, then invert the cake on to a wire rack. Serve cold, dusted with icing sugar.

LEKACH

THIS CLASSIC HONEY CAKE IS RICHLY SPICED, REDOLENT OF GINGER, CINNAMON AND OTHER SWEET, AROMATIC SCENTS. FOR THIS REASON IT IS A FAVOURITE AT ROSH HASHANAH, WHEN SWEET FOODS, PARTICULARLY HONEY, ARE EATEN IN THE HOPE OF A SWEET NEW YEAR.

SERVES ABOUT EIGHT

INGREDIENTS

175g/6oz/1½ cups plain
   (all-purpose) flour
75g/3oz/⅓ cup caster
   (superfine) sugar
2.5ml/½ tsp ground ginger
2.5–5ml/½–1 tsp ground cinnamon
5ml/1 tsp mixed (apple pie) spice
5ml/1 tsp bicarbonate of soda
   (baking soda)
225g/8oz/1 cup clear honey
60ml/4 tbsp vegetable or olive oil
grated rind of 1 orange
2 eggs
75ml/5 tbsp orange juice
10ml/2 tsp chopped fresh root
   ginger, or to taste

1 Preheat the oven to 180°C/350°F/ Gas 4. Line a rectangular baking tin (pan), measuring 25 × 20 × 5cm/ 10 × 8 × 2in, with greaseproof (waxed) paper. In a large bowl, mix together the flour, sugar, ginger, cinnamon, mixed spice and bicarbonate of soda.

2 Make a well in the centre of the flour mixture and pour in the clear honey, vegetable or olive oil, orange rind and eggs. Using a wooden spoon or electric whisk, beat until smooth, then add the orange juice. Stir in the chopped ginger.

3 Pour the cake mixture into the prepared tin, then bake for about 50 minutes, or until firm to the touch.

4 Leave the cake to cool in the tin, then turn out and wrap tightly in foil. Store at room temperature for 2–3 days before serving to allow the flavours of the cake to mature.

COOK'S TIP
This honey cake keeps very well. It can be made in two loaf tins (pans), so that one cake can be eaten, while the other is wrapped in clear film (plastic wrap) and stored or frozen for a later date.

TUNISIAN ALMOND CIGARS

THESE PASTRIES ARE A GREAT FAVOURITE OF THE JEWS FROM NORTH AFRICA, ESPECIALLY TUNISIA.
SERVE THEM WITH A SMALL CUP OF FRAGRANT MINT TEA OR STRONG, DARK COFFEE.

MAKES EIGHT TO TWELVE

INGREDIENTS
250g/9oz almond paste
1 egg, lightly beaten
15ml/1 tbsp rose water or orange
  flower water
5ml/1 tsp ground cinnamon
1.5ml/¼ tsp almond essence
  (extract)
8–12 sheets filo pastry
melted butter, for brushing
icing (confectioners') sugar
  and ground cinnamon,
  for dusting
mint tea or black coffee, to serve

1 Knead the almond paste until soft,
then put in a bowl, and mix in the egg,
flower water, cinnamon and almond
essence. Chill for 1–2 hours.

2 Preheat the oven to 190°C/375°F/
Gas 5. Lightly grease a baking sheet.
Place a sheet of filo pastry on a piece of
greaseproof (waxed) paper, keeping the
remaining pastry covered with a damp
cloth, and brush with the melted butter.

3 Shape 30–45ml/2–3 tbsp of the
filling mixture into a cylinder and place
at one end of the pastry. Fold the pastry
over to enclose the ends of the filling,
then roll up to form a cigar shape.
Place on the baking sheet and make
7–11 more cigars in the same way.

4 Bake the pastries for about
15 minutes, or until golden. Leave
to cool, then serve, dusted with sugar
and cinnamon, and with tea or coffee.

VARIATION
Instead of dusting with sugar, drench the
pastries in syrup. In a pan, dissolve 250g/
9oz/1¼ cups sugar in 250ml/8fl oz/1 cup
water and boil until thickened. Stir in a
squeeze of lemon juice and a few drops
of rose water and pour over the pastries.
Allow the syrup to soak in before serving.

STRUDEL

THIS CRISP PASTRY ROLL, FILLED WITH FRUIT AND JAM, IS A CLASSIC ASHKENAZI SWEET TREAT TO ACCOMPANY TEA. NO ONE CAN RESIST A SLICE OF STRUDEL SERVED WITH A GLASS OF LEMON TEA.

MAKES THREE

INGREDIENTS
    250g/9oz/generous 1 cup butter,
        softened
    250g/9oz/generous 1 cup sour cream
    30ml/2 tbsp sugar
    5ml/1 tsp vanilla essence (extract)
    large pinch of salt
    250g/9oz/2¼ cups plain
        (all-purpose) flour
    icing (confectioners') sugar, sifted,
        for dusting
For the filling
    2–3 cooking apples
    45–60ml/3–4 tbsp sultanas (golden
        raisins) or raisins
    45ml/3 tbsp light muscovado
        (brown) sugar
    115g/4oz/1 cup walnuts,
        roughly chopped
    5–10ml/1–2 tsp ground cinnamon
    60ml/4 tbsp apricot jam or conserve

1 To make the pastry, beat the butter until light and fluffy, then add the sour cream, sugar, vanilla essence and salt, and beat together.

2 Stir the flour into the mixture, then put in a plastic bag and chill overnight or longer.

COOK'S TIPS
• Filo pastry dries out quickly, so always keep wrapped or covered when not using.
• To follow a meat meal, substitute the butter and sour cream with 120ml/ 4fl oz/½ cup sweet white wine and 120ml/4fl oz/½ cup vegetable oil.

3 Preheat the oven to 180°C/350°F/ Gas 4. To make the filling, core and finely chop the apples but do not peel. Put the apples in a bowl, add the sultanas or raisins, sugar, walnuts, cinnamon and apricot jam or conserve and mix together until well combined.

4 Divide the pastry into three equal pieces. Place one piece on a sheet of lightly floured greaseproof (waxed) paper and roll out to a rectangle measuring about 45 × 30cm/18 × 12in.

5 Spread one-third of the filling over the pastry, leaving a 1–2cm/½–¾in border. Roll up the pastry to enclose the filling and place, seam-side down, on a non-stick baking sheet. Repeat with the remaining pastry and filling. Bake the strudels for 25–30 minutes until golden brown all over.

6 Remove the strudels from the oven and leave for 5 minutes to become slightly firm, then cut into slices. Allow to cool, then dust with icing sugar.

RUGELACH

THESE CRISP, FLAKY COOKIES, ROLLED AROUND A SWEET FILLING, RESEMBLE A SNAKE OR CROISSANT. THEY ARE THOUGHT TO HAVE COME FROM POLAND WHERE THEY ARE A TRADITIONAL SWEET TREAT AT CHANUKKAH. CHOCOLATE CHIP RUGELACH ARE VERY POPULAR IN THE UNITED STATES.

MAKES FORTY-EIGHT TO SIXTY

INGREDIENTS
    115g/4oz/½ cup unsalted
      (sweet) butter
    115g/4oz/½ cup full-fat soft white
      (farmer's) cheese
    15ml/1 tbsp sugar
    1 egg
    2.5ml/½ tsp salt
    about 250g/9oz/2¼ cups plain
      (all-purpose) flour
    about 250g/9oz/generous 1 cup
      butter, melted
    250g/9oz/scant 2 cups sultanas
      (golden raisins)
    130g/4½oz/generous 1 cup chopped
      walnuts or walnut pieces
    about 225g/8oz/generous 1 cup
      caster (superfine) sugar
    10–15ml/1–2 tsp ground cinnamon

1 To make the pastry, put the butter and cheese in a bowl and beat with an electric mixer until creamy. Beat in the sugar, egg and salt.

4 Preheat the oven to 180°C/350°F/ Gas 4. Divide the dough into six equal pieces. On a lightly floured surface, roll out each piece into a round about 3mm/⅛in thick, then brush with a little of the melted butter and sprinkle over the sultanas, chopped walnuts, a little sugar and the cinnamon.

5 Cut the rounds into eight to ten wedges and carefully roll the large side of each wedge towards the tip. (Some of the filling will fall out.) Arrange the rugelach on baking sheets, brush with a little butter and sprinkle with the sugar. Bake for 15–30 minutes until lightly browned. Leave to cool before serving.

2 Fold the flour into the creamed mixture, a little at a time, until the dough can be worked with the hands. Continue adding the flour, kneading with the hands, until it is a consistency that can be rolled out. (Add only as much flour as needed.)

3 Shape the dough into a ball, then cover and chill for at least 2 hours or overnight. (The dough will be too soft if not chilled properly.)

HAMANTASHEN

THESE TRIANGULAR-SHAPED PASTRIES ARE EATEN AT PURIM, THE FESTIVAL CELEBRATING THE STORY OF ESTHER, MORDECAI AND HAMAN. THEIR SHAPE REPRESENTS THE HAT OF HAMAN, WHOSE PLOT TO EXTERMINATE ALL THE JEWS OF PERSIA WAS FOILED. THEY CAN BE MADE WITH A COOKIE DOUGH OR A YEAST DOUGH, AND VARIOUS SWEET FILLINGS.

MAKES ABOUT TWENTY-FOUR

INGREDIENTS
  115g/4oz/½ cup unsalted (sweet)
    butter, at room temperature
  250g/9oz/1¼ cups sugar
  30ml/2 tbsp milk
  1 egg, beaten
  5ml/1 tsp vanilla or almond
    essence (extract)
  pinch of salt
  200–250g/7–9oz/1½–2¼ cups plain
    (all-purpose) flour
  icing (confectioners') sugar, for
    dusting (optional)
For the apricot filling
  250g/9oz/generous 1 cup dried
    apricots
  1 cinnamon stick
  45ml/3 tbsp sugar
For the poppy seed filling
  130g/4½oz/1 cup poppy seeds,
    coarsely ground
  120ml/4fl oz/½ cup milk
  75g/3oz/½ cup sultanas (golden
    raisins), roughly chopped
  45–60ml/3–4 tbsp sugar
  30ml/2 tbsp golden (light corn) syrup
  5–10ml/1–2 tsp grated lemon rind
  5ml/1 tsp vanilla essence (extract)
For the prune filling
  250g/9oz/generous 1 cup pitted
    ready-to-eat prunes
  hot, freshly brewed tea or water,
    to cover
  60ml/4 tbsp plum jam

1 In a large bowl, cream the butter and sugar until pale and fluffy.

2 In a separate bowl mix together the milk, egg, vanilla or almond essence and salt. Sift the flour into a third bowl.

COOK'S TIP
Every Jewish family has its own favourite filling for this hefty little pastry-cake. Their size can also vary, from small and dainty to the size of a hand – it just depends on your traditions and preference.

3 Beat the creamed butter mixture with one-third of the flour, then gradually add the remaining flour, in three batches, alternating with the milk mixture. The dough should be the consistency of a loose shortbread dough. If it is too stiff, add a little extra milk. Cover and chill for at least 1 hour.

4 To make the apricot filling, put the dried apricots, cinnamon stick and sugar in a pan and add enough water to cover. Heat gently, then simmer for 15 minutes, or until the apricots are tender and most of the liquid has evaporated. Remove the cinnamon stick, then purée the apricots in a food processor or blender with a little of the cooking liquid until they form a consistency like thick jam.

5 To make the poppy seed filling, put all the ingredients, except the vanilla essence, in a pan and simmer for 5–10 minutes or until the mixture has thickened and most of the milk has been absorbed. Stir in the vanilla essence.

6 To make the prune filling, put the prunes in a bowl and add enough hot tea or water to cover. Cover the bowl, then set aside for about 30 minutes, or until the prunes have absorbed the liquid. Drain, then purée in a food processor or blender with the jam.

7 To make the hamantashen, preheat the oven to 180°C/350°F/Gas 4. On a lightly floured surface, roll out the dough to a thickness of about 3–5mm/ ⅛–¼in, then cut into rounds about 7.5cm/3in in diameter using a pastry (cookie) cutter.

8 Place 15–30ml/1–2 tbsp of filling in the centre of each round, then pinch the pastry together to form three corners, leaving a little of the filling showing in the middle of the pastry.

9 Place the pastries on a baking sheet and bake for about 15 minutes, or until pale golden. Serve warm or cold, dusted with icing sugar, if you like.

MANDELBROT

THESE CRISP, TWICE-BAKED BISCUITS, STUDDED WITH ALMONDS, ARE SIMILAR TO ITALIAN ALMOND BISCOTTI. THEY WERE PROBABLY BROUGHT TO ITALY BY THE JEWS OF SPAIN, WHO THEN TOOK THEM TO EASTERN EUROPE IN THE EXPULSION THAT FOLLOWED. SERVE THEM WITH COFFEE, TEA OR, LIKE THEIR ITALIAN COUNTERPARTS, WITH A GLASS OF SCHNAPPS (IN PLACE OF VIN SANTO).

MAKES TWENTY-FOUR TO THIRTY-SIX

INGREDIENTS
375g/13oz/3¼ cups plain
  (all-purpose) flour
115g/4oz/1 cup ground almonds
5ml/1 tsp bicarbonate of soda
  (baking powder)
1.5ml/¼ tsp salt
3 eggs
250g/9oz/1¼ cups caster
  (superfine) sugar
grated rind of 1 lemon
5ml/1 tsp almond essence (extract)
5ml/1 tsp vanilla essence (extract)
130g/4½oz/1 cup blanched almonds,
  roughly chopped

1 Preheat the oven to 180°C/350°F/
Gas 4. Lightly grease two baking sheets.
Sift together the plain flour, ground
almonds, bicarbonate of soda and salt.

2 Using an electric whisk or mixer, beat
together the eggs and sugar for about
5 minutes, or until light and fluffy, then
beat in the lemon rind and almond and
vanilla essences. Slowly add the flour
and ground almonds, a little at a time,
mixing until well blended. Add the
chopped almonds and mix well.

3 Turn the mixture on to a floured
surface and knead gently for about
5 minutes. Divide the dough into two
pieces and form each into a long, flat loaf.
Place on the baking sheets and bake for
35 minutes, or until golden brown.

4 Remove the loaves from the oven
and leave for about 15 minutes to cool
slightly. When cool, cut them into
1cm/½in diagonal slices, taking care
not to break or crush the soft insides
of the loaves.

5 Arrange the slices on clean baking
sheets (working in batches). Bake for
6–7 minutes until the undersides are
golden and flecked with brown. Turn the
slices over and bake for 6–7 minutes
more. Cool on a wire rack.

POMERANTZEN

THIS CANDIED CITRUS PEEL IS A SPECIALITY OF JEWS WHOSE ORIGINS LIE IN GERMANY. AT FESTIVALS
PEOPLE OFTEN OFFER A BOX OF POMERANTZEN AS A GIFT, USUALLY DIPPED IN DARK CHOCOLATE.
THEY ARE EASY TO MAKE, AND APPEAL TO THE FRUGAL AS THE PEEL WOULD USUALLY BE THROWN
AWAY, RATHER THAN BEING TRANSFORMED INTO SUCH A TREAT.

2 When the peels are cool enough to handle, gently scrape off as much of the white pith as possible. Cut the peel lengthways into narrow strips.

3 Put the sugar, water and golden syrup in a pan and bring to the boil. When clear, add the peels; simmer for 1 hour until translucent, taking care that they do not burn.

4 Stand a rack over a baking sheet. Remove the peels from the pan and arrange them on the rack. Leave to dry for 2–3 hours, then put in a plastic container or jar, cover and store in the refrigerator until required.

SERVES FOUR TO SIX

INGREDIENTS
  3 grapefruit and 5–6 oranges or
    6–8 lemons, unwaxed
  300g/11oz/1¾ cups sugar
  300ml/½ pint/1¼ cups water
  30ml/2 tbsp golden (light corn) syrup
  caster (superfine) sugar (optional)

5 If serving as a sweetmeat, cover a large flat plate with caster sugar and toss the drained peels in the sugar. Leave to dry for 1 hour. Sprinkle with sugar again and place in a covered container or jar. Store in a cool, dry place for up to 2 weeks or in the refrigerator for up to 2 months.

COOK'S TIP
If you find it too much trouble to remove the pith from the fruit, omit this step as once the pith has been simmered, its bitterness fades.

1 Score the fruit, to remove the peels neatly, then peel. Put the peels in a pan, fill with cold water and bring to the boil. Simmer for 20 minutes, then drain.

PICKLES AND CONDIMENTS

Kosher dill pickles, resplendent with garlic and dill, are a deli treat brought to America from Eastern Europe. But these are not the only pickles in the Jewish kitchen. There are a wide variety of pickles and condiments, from pink pickled turnips to the golden mixed vegetables of the Sephardi kitchen. Hot peppers, herbs and other aromatics make up a grand array of condiments too, from the green chutneys of Indian Jews to the spiced chilli sauces of Israel's Yemenite and North African Jews.

KOSHER DILL PICKLES

REDOLENT OF GARLIC, SALTY DILL PICKLES CAN BE SUPPLE AND SUCCULENT OR CRISP AND CRUNCHY.
EVERY PICKLE MAVEN (AFICIONADO) HAS HIS OR HER FAVOURITE TYPE.

MAKES ABOUT FOUR JARS

INGREDIENTS
  20 small, ridged or knobbly
    pickling cucumbers
  2 litres/4 pints/2 quarts water
  175g/6oz/generous ¾ cup kosher salt
    or coarse sea salt
  15–20 garlic cloves, unpeeled
  2 bunches fresh dill
  15ml/1 tbsp dill seeds
  30ml/2 tbsp mixed
    pickling spice
  ½ hot chilli, quartered

1 Scrub the cucumbers and rinse well in a bowl of cold water. Leave to dry.

2 Put the measured water and kosher or sea salt in a large pan and bring to the boil. Turn off the heat and leave to cool to room temperature.

3 Using the flat blade of a knife or a wooden mallet, lightly crush each garlic clove, breaking the papery skin.

4 Pack the cucumbers tightly into four 1.2 litre/2 pint wide-necked, sterilized jars, layering them with the garlic, fresh dill, dill seeds and mixed pickling spice. Add one piece of chilli to each jar. Pour over the cooled brine, making sure that the cucumbers are completely covered.

5 Cover the jars and leave to stand at room temperature for 4–7 days before serving. Store in the refrigerator.

COOK'S TIPS
• If you cannot find ridged or knobbly pickling cucumbers, use any kind of small cucumbers instead.
• If you have a dishwasher, prepare the jars by running them through on the highest heat setting.

PRESERVED LEMONS

THESE ARE WIDELY USED IN MIDDLE EASTERN COOKING. THE INTERESTING THING ABOUT PRESERVED LEMONS IS THAT YOU ACTUALLY ONLY EAT THE PEEL, WHICH CONTAINS THE ESSENTIAL FLAVOUR OF THE LEMON. TRADITIONALLY WHOLE LEMONS ARE PRESERVED BUT THIS RECIPE USES LEMON WEDGES THAT CAN BE PACKED EASILY INTO JARS.

MAKES ABOUT TWO JARS

INGREDIENTS
10 unwaxed lemons
about 200ml/7fl oz/scant 1 cup fresh
    lemon juice or a combination
    of fresh and preserved
boiling water
sea salt

1 Wash the lemons well and cut each into six to eight wedges. Press a generous amount of salt into the cut surfaces, pushing it into every crevice.

2 Pack the salted lemon wedges into two 1.2 litre/2 pint sterilized jars. To each jar, add 30–45ml/2–3 tbsp salt and 90ml/6 tbsp lemon juice, then top up with boiling water, to cover the lemons. (If using larger jars, use more lemon juice and less boiling water.)

3 Cover the jars and leave to stand for 2–4 weeks before serving.

4 To serve, rinse the preserved lemons well to remove some of the salty flavour, then pull off the flesh and discard. Cut the lemon peel into strips or leave in chunks and use as desired.

COOK'S TIP
The salty, well-flavoured juice that is used to preserve the lemons can be added to salads or hot sauces, such as zchug, horef and harissa.

TORSHI

THIS MIDDLE EASTERN SPECIALITY OF PICKLED TURNIPS IS PREPARED BY THE JEWS OF PERSIA, ISRAEL AND THE ARAB LANDS. THE TURNIPS, RICH RED IN THEIR BEETROOT-SPIKED BRINE, NOT ONLY LOOK GORGEOUS IN THEIR JARS BUT ALSO MAKE A DELICIOUS PICKLE TO ADD TO FALAFEL OR AS PART OF AN ASSORTMENT OF APPETIZERS.

MAKES ABOUT FOUR JARS

INGREDIENTS
  1kg/2¼lb young turnips
  3–4 raw beetroot (beets)
  about 45ml/3 tbsp kosher salt or
    coarse sea salt
  about 1.5 litres/2½ pints/
    6¼ cups water
  juice of 1 lemon

1 Wash the turnips and beetroot, but do not peel them, then cut into slices about 5mm/¼in thick. Put the salt and water into a bowl, stir and leave until the salt has completely dissolved.

2 Sprinkle the beetroot with lemon juice and place in the bases of four 1.2 litre/2 pint sterilized jars. Top with turnip, packing them in very tightly. Pour over the brine, making sure that the vegetables are covered.

3 Seal the jars and leave in a cool place for 7 days before serving.

CHRAIN

THIS ASHKENAZI HORSERADISH AND BEETROOT SAUCE IS OFTEN EATEN AT PESACH, FOR WHICH HORSERADISH IS ONE OF THE TRADITIONAL BITTER FLAVOURS. HOWEVER, IT IS A DELICIOUS ACCOMPANIMENT TO GEFILTE FISH, FRIED FISH PATTIES OR ROASTED MEAT AT ANY TIME OF THE YEAR.

SERVES ABOUT EIGHT

INGREDIENTS
    150g/5oz grated fresh horseradish
    2 cooked beetroot (beets), grated
    about 15ml/1 tbsp sugar
    15–30ml/1–2 tbsp red wine vinegar
    salt

1 Put the horseradish and beetroot in a bowl and mix together, then season with sugar, vinegar and salt to taste.

2 Spoon the sauce into a sterilized jar, packing it down firmly, and seal. Store in the refrigerator where it will keep for up to 2 weeks.

COOK'S TIPS
• Fresh horseradish is very potent so, when grating the fresh root, protect yourself well. Horseradish may also be purchased ready-grated.
• You can use either fresh cooked beetroot or beetroot pickled in vinegar for this recipe.

TURKISH GREEN OLIVE AND TOMATO RELISH

THIS RELISH OF GREEN OLIVES IN A SAUCE OF TOMATOES AND SWEET PEPPERS IS WONDERFUL SERVED AT A BUFFET OR PICNIC WITH A SELECTION OF OTHER SALADS, OR ALONGSIDE A CRUSTY SANDWICH.

SERVES ABOUT TEN

INGREDIENTS
45ml/3 tbsp extra virgin olive oil
1 green (bell) pepper, chopped
    or sliced
1 red (bell) pepper, chopped
    or sliced
1 onion, chopped
2–3 mild, large red and green
    chillies, thinly sliced
1–2 hot, small chillies, chopped or
    thinly sliced (optional)
5–7 garlic cloves, roughly chopped or
    thinly sliced
5–7 tomatoes, quartered or diced
5ml/1 tsp curry powder or hawaij
1.5ml/¼ tsp ground cumin
1.5ml/¼ tsp turmeric
large pinch of ground ginger
15ml/1 tbsp tomato purée (paste)
juice of ¼ lemon, or to taste
200g/7oz/1¾ cups pitted or
    pimiento-stuffed green olives

1 Heat the extra virgin olive oil in a pan, add the chopped or sliced peppers, the onion and chillies, and fry for 5–10 minutes, or until the vegetables have softened.

COOK'S TIP
This relish is extremely popular in Israel and is particularly good with chunks of tuna fish as a cooling lunch on a hot afternoon. It is also good with cold pasta or a diced potato salad.

2 Add the garlic and tomatoes to the pan and fry for a further 2–3 minutes, until the tomatoes have become the consistency of a sauce, then add the curry powder or hawaij, the cumin, turmeric, ginger and tomato purée, then remove from the heat.

3 Stir the lemon juice into the mixture, then add the olives. Leave to cool, then chill in the refrigerator, preferably overnight, before serving.

CHOPPED VEGETABLE SALAD RELISH

THESE SALADS ARE BELOVED IN ISRAEL. THEY COMBINE THE FRESHNESS AND CRUNCHINESS OF THE SALADS ENJOYED BY THE ARABS WITH THE CHOPPED SALADS ADORED BY THE EASTERN EUROPEANS. IN SPAIN, TOO, CHOPPED SALADS ARE SERVED AS TAPAS, ESPECIALLY IN ANDALUCIA WHERE THE JEWISH AND MOORISH IMPRINTS ARE DISTINCT.

SERVES ABOUT FOUR

INGREDIENTS
2–3 ripe tomatoes, finely chopped
½ cucumber, finely chopped
½ green (bell) pepper,
    finely chopped
1–2 garlic cloves, chopped
2 spring onions (scallions), sliced
30ml/2 tbsp finely chopped
    fresh mint, dill or coriander
    (cilantro) leaves
30ml/2 tbsp finely chopped
    fresh parsley
grated rind and juice of 1 lemon
⅛ red cabbage, chopped (optional)
salt

1 Put the tomatoes, cucumber, pepper, garlic, spring onions, herbs and lemon rind and juice in a bowl. Mix together well, then chill in the refrigerator until ready to serve.

2 If using red cabbage, add to the relish just before serving, as its colour will run and spoil the fresh and vibrant colours of the other vegetables. Add a little salt to taste and stir to mix.

INSTANT SEPHARDI PICKLE OF MIXED VEGETABLES

YOU WILL FIND THIS PICKLE ON FALAFEL STANDS THROUGHOUT ISRAEL AND ON SEPHARDI TABLES THROUGHOUT THE WORLD. IT IS SPICED WITH DIFFERENT FLAVOURS BUT ALWAYS CRISP AND TANGY.

SERVES TWELVE

INGREDIENTS
½ cauliflower head, cut into florets
2 carrots, sliced
2 celery sticks, thinly sliced
¼–½ cabbage, thinly sliced
115g/4oz/1 cup runner (green)
  beans, cut into bitesize pieces
6 garlic cloves, sliced
1–4 fresh chillies, whole or sliced
30–45ml/2–3 tbsp sliced fresh
  root ginger
1 red (bell) pepper, sliced
2.5ml/½ tsp turmeric
105ml/7 tbsp white wine vinegar
15–30ml/1–2 tbsp sugar
60–90ml/4–6 tbsp olive oil
juice of 2 lemons
salt

1 Toss the cauliflower, carrots, celery, cabbage, beans, garlic, chillies, ginger and pepper with salt and leave to stand in a colander for 4 hours.

COOK'S TIP
This spicy pickle can be stored in the refrigerator for up to 2 weeks.

2 Transfer the salted vegetables to a bowl and add the turmeric, vinegar, sugar to taste, the oil and lemon juice. Toss to combine, then add enough water to balance the flavours.

3 Cover and chill for at least 1 hour, or until ready to serve.

TAHINI SAUCE

MADE OF GROUND SESAME SEEDS AND SPICED WITH GARLIC AND LEMON JUICE, THIS IS ISRAEL'S MOST FAMOUS SAUCE. IT MAKES A DELICIOUS DIP, SERVED WITH PITTA BREAD AND, WHEN THINNED WITH WATER, CAN BE SPOONED OVER FALAFEL.

SERVES FOUR TO SIX

INGREDIENTS
150–175g/5–6oz/²⁄₃–³⁄₄ cup tahini
3 garlic cloves, finely chopped
juice of 1 lemon
1.5ml/¹⁄₄ tsp ground cumin
small pinch of ground coriander
small pinch of curry powder
50–120ml/2–4fl oz/¹⁄₄–¹⁄₂ cup water
cayenne pepper
salt
For the garnish
15–30ml/1–2 tbsp extra virgin
olive oil
chopped fresh coriander (cilantro)
leaves or parsley
handful of olives and/or
pickled vegetables
a few chillies or a hot
pepper sauce

1 Put the tahini and garlic in a food processor or bowl and mix together well. Stir in the lemon juice, cumin, ground coriander and curry powder.

COOK'S TIP
Tahini sauce forms the basis of many of the salads and dips found in Israel and the Middle East.

2 Slowly add the water to the tahini, beating all the time. The mixture will thicken, then become thin. Season with cayenne pepper and salt.

3 To serve, spread the mixture on to a serving plate, individual plates or into a shallow bowl. Drizzle over the oil and sprinkle with the other garnishes.

HOREF

THE WORD HOREF *IS ROUGHLY TRANSLATED FROM HEBREW AS HOT PEPPER AND HERE, IN THIS SEPHARDI RELISH FROM ISRAEL, THE PEPPERS ARE SIMMERED WITH MILD ONES, AS WELL AS TOMATOES AND FRAGRANT SPICES. THE RELISH IS EQUALLY DELICIOUS SERVED WITH RICE, BREAD, SALAD, ROASTED MEATS AND CHICKEN. IT IS ALSO GOOD SERVED WITH TOASTED CHEESE, SCRAMBLED EGGS, FALAFEL, BARBECUED MEAT, FISH AND POULTRY OR AS AN APPETIZER TO PRECEDE COUSCOUS.*

SERVES FOUR TO SIX

INGREDIENTS
45ml/3 tbsp olive oil
1 green (bell) pepper, chopped
  or sliced
2–3 mild, large chillies,
  thinly sliced
1–2 hot, small chillies, chopped
  or thinly sliced (optional)
5–7 garlic cloves, roughly chopped
  or thinly sliced
5–7 tomatoes, quartered or diced
5ml/1 tsp curry powder or hawaij
seeds from 3–5 cardamom pods
large pinch of ground ginger
15ml/1 tbsp tomato purée (paste)
juice of ¼ lemon
salt

1 Heat the olive oil in a large, heavy pan, add the chopped or sliced green pepper, large and small chillies and garlic. Fry over a medium-high heat, stirring, for about 10 minutes, or until the peppers are softened. (Be careful not to let the garlic brown.)

2 Add the tomatoes, curry powder or hawaij, cardamom seeds and ginger to the pan, and cook until the tomatoes have softened to a sauce. Stir the tomato purée and lemon juice into the mixture, season with salt and leave to cool. Chill until ready to serve.

HARISSA

THIS RECIPE IS A QUICKLY MADE VERSION OF HARISSA, THE NORTH AFRICAN CHILLI SAUCE THAT'S TERRIFIC TO ADD TO COUSCOUS, DRIZZLE ON SOUPS OR ACCOMPANY BRIKS. IF SERVING WITH COUSCOUS, USE STOCK OR LIQUID FROM THE COUSCOUS STEW.

SERVES FOUR TO SIX

INGREDIENTS
45ml/3 tbsp paprika
2.5–5ml/½–1 tsp cayenne pepper
1.5ml/¼ tsp ground cumin
250ml/8fl oz/1 cup water or stock
juice of ¼–½ lemon
2–3 pinches of caraway
  seeds (optional)
salt
15ml/1 tbsp chopped coriander
  (cilantro) leaves, to serve

VARIATION
For a long-keeping harissa, soak about 3 dried red chillies, then process with a little water to make a purée. Continue as above, using only 5ml/1 tsp paprika.

1 Put the paprika, cayenne pepper, ground cumin, water or stock in a large, heavy pan and season with salt to taste.

2 Bring the spice mixture to the boil, then immediately remove the pan from the heat.

3 Stir the lemon juice and caraway seeds, if using, into the hot spice mixture and leave to cool.

4 Just before serving, pour the sauce into a serving dish and sprinkle with the chopped coriander leaves.

ZCHUG

This is the Yemenite chilli sauce that has become Israel's national seasoning. It is hot with chillies, pungent with garlic, and fragrant with exotic cardamom. Eat it with rice, couscous, soup, chicken or other meats. It can be stored in the refrigerator for up to 2 weeks.

MAKES ABOUT 475ML/16FL OZ/2 CUPS

INGREDIENTS

5–8 garlic cloves, chopped
2–3 medium-hot chillies, such
   as jalapeño
5 fresh or canned tomatoes, diced
1 small bunch coriander (cilantro),
   roughly chopped
1 small bunch parsley, chopped
30ml/2 tbsp extra virgin olive oil
10ml/2 tsp ground cumin
2.5ml/½ tsp turmeric
2.5ml/½ tsp curry powder
seeds from 3–5 cardamom pods
juice of ½ lemon
pinch of sugar, if necessary
salt

1 Put all the ingredients except the sugar and salt in a food processor or blender. Process until well combined, then season with sugar and salt.

2 Pour the sauce into a serving bowl, cover and chill in the refrigerator until ready to serve.

VARIATIONS
• To make a spicy yemenite dip, put 400g/14oz chopped fresh tomatoes, or a combination of chopped fresh and canned tomatoes in a bowl. Stir in 120ml/4fl oz/½ cup zchug, or to taste, and season with salt, if necessary. Spread the dip on to wedges of flat breads or serve in a bowl with strips of raw vegetables for dipping.

• To make hilbeh, a spicy tomato relish, soak 30ml/2 tbsp fenugreek seeds in cold water for at least 2 hours and preferably overnight. Drain, then grind the seeds in a spice grinder or pound them in a mortar with a pestle until they form a smooth paste. In a bowl, combine the paste with 15ml/1 tbsp zchug and 2 diced tomatoes. Season with salt and black pepper to taste.

CORIANDER, COCONUT AND TAMARIND CHUTNEY

COOLING FRAGRANT CHUTNEYS MADE OF FRESH CORIANDER AND MINT ARE BELOVED OF THE INDIAN JEWISH COMMUNITY. THIS DELICIOUS BLEND OF CORIANDER, MINT AND COCONUT, WITH A HINT OF CHILLI, A TANG OF TAMARIND AND THE SWEET FLAVOUR OF DATES, IS A TRADITIONAL CONDIMENT FOR THE BENE ISRAEL, ONE OF THE THREE MAJOR GROUPS OF INDIAN JEWS.

MAKES ABOUT 450G/1LB/2 CUPS

INGREDIENTS
  30ml/2 tbsp tamarind paste
  30ml/2 tbsp boiling water
  1 large bunch fresh coriander
    (cilantro), roughly chopped
  1 bunch fresh mint,
    roughly chopped
  8–10 pitted dates, roughly chopped
  75g/3oz dried coconut or
    50g/2oz creamed coconut,
    coarsely grated
  2.5cm/1in piece fresh root
    ginger, chopped
  3–5 garlic cloves, chopped
  2–3 fresh chillies, chopped
  juice of 2 limes or lemons
  about 5ml/1 tsp sugar
  salt
  30–45ml/2–3 tbsp water
    (for a meat meal) or natural
    (plain) yogurt (for a dairy meal),
    to serve

1 Place the tamarind paste in a jug (pitcher) or bowl and pour over the boiling water. Stir thoroughly until the paste is completely dissolved and set aside.

2 Place the fresh coriander, mint and pitted dates in a food processor and process briefly until finely chopped. Alternatively, chop finely by hand using a sharp knife. Place in a bowl.

3 Add the coconut, ginger, garlic and chillies to the chopped herbs and dates and stir in the tamarind. Season with citrus juice, sugar and salt. Spoon into sterilized jars, seal and chill.

4 To serve, thin the chutney with the water, if serving with a meat meal, or with yogurt for a dairy meal.

COOK'S TIPS
• This chutney can be stored in the refrigerator for up to 2 weeks.
• Serve with any vegetable dish or simple boiled rice. It is also good spooned over a spicy couscous salad.
• Make this chutney as mild or as fiery as you like by adjusting the amount of ginger, garlic and chillies.

FRAGRANT PERSIAN HALEK

THIS HALEK IS FRAGRANT WITH ROSE WATER AND THE SWEET FLAVOURS OF DRIED FRUITS AND NUTS, WHICH ARE SO BELOVED BY PERSIAN JEWS.

SERVES ABOUT TEN

INGREDIENTS

60ml/4 tbsp blanched almonds
60ml/4 tbsp unsalted pistachio nuts
60ml/4 tbsp walnuts
15–30ml/1–2 tbsp skinned hazelnuts
30ml/2 tbsp unsalted shelled
    pumpkin seeds
90ml/6 tbsp raisins, chopped
90ml/6 tbsp pitted prunes, diced
90ml/6 tbsp dried apricots, diced
60ml/4 tbsp dried cherries
sugar or honey, to taste
juice of ½ lemon
30ml/2 tbsp rose water
seeds from 4–5 cardamon pods
pinch of ground cloves
pinch of freshly grated nutmeg
1.5ml/¼ tsp ground cinnamon
fruit juice of choice, if necessary

1 Roughly chop the almonds, pistachio nuts, walnuts, hazelnuts and pumpkin seeds and put in a bowl.

2 Add the chopped raisins, prunes, apricots and cherries to the nuts and seeds and toss to combine. Stir in sugar or honey to taste and mix well until thoroughly combined.

3 Add the lemon juice, rose water, cardamom seeds, cloves, nutmeg and cinnamon to the fruit and nut mixture and mix until thoroughly combined.

4 If the halek is too thick, add a little fruit juice to thin the mixture. Pour into a serving bowl, cover and chill in the refrigerator until ready to serve.

ASHKENAZI CHAROSSET

A CHAROSSET IS A PASTE OF FRUIT THAT IS HELD TOGETHER WITH SWEET WINE. IT IS EATEN IN EVERY JEWISH HOUSEHOLD DURING THE PASSOVER FESTIVAL. THIS RECIPE IS THE CLASSIC COMBINATION OF APPLE, WALNUT AND SWEET WINE THAT IS FAVOURED BY ASHKENAZI JEWS.

SERVES SIX TO EIGHT

INGREDIENTS
3 apples
75–115g/3–4oz/¾–1 cup
  walnut pieces
7.5ml/1½ tsp ground cinnamon
75–90ml/5–6 tbsp sweet Pesach
  red wine
sugar or honey, to taste

COOK'S TIP
This will keep in the refrigerator for the duration of the Passover festival. It can be eaten as a snack or part of a meal, usually spread on matzos.

1 Quarter the apples and remove their cores but do not peel them. Grate them by hand or chop the fruit very finely using a sharp knife.

2 Put the apples and all the remaining ingredients in a bowl and mix together. Tip into a serving bowl, cover and chill in the refrigerator until ready to serve.

GLOSSARY OF TERMS AND FOODS

Adeni spice mixtures Adeni Jews have many different spice mixtures. The one for cooking is made of coriander, cumin, cardamom and pepper; the one for tea is made of cinnamon, cloves and cardamom; and the one for strong black coffee is made of ginger, cardamom, cloves and cinnamon.

Afikomen The piece of matzo, broken from the middle of the three matzos used at the Pesach Seder, that is wrapped and put aside to be searched for as part of the ceremony.

Ashkenazim Central and Eastern European Jews, including Yiddish-speaking Jews and their descendants.

Bagels Bread rolls with a hole in the middle, symbolizing the endless circle of life. They are boiled before being baked.

Baklava A crisp pastry of filo and nuts soaked in a honey syrup, which is often flavoured with rose or orange flower water or sweet spices.

Bar/Bat Mitzvah The coming of age ceremony for a boy (bar) or girl (bat) in which they assume the religious duties and responsibilities of an adult. A boy reaches this age at 13 years old, a girl at 12 years old.

Berbere The mixture of chillies and fragrant spices such as cardamom, black cardamom and ginger that forms the main flavouring of the Ethiopian cuisine. It is also the name of a certain type of chilli.

Besan See gram flour.

Betza/beitzah/baitzah Hebrew for egg. Betza is eaten by all Jewish communities and are considered pareve; they play an important role in the ritual plate for the Pesach Seder.

Betzel A Jewish North African cheese cracker, light and crisp, usually enjoyed for tea.

Bishak A Sephardi Bukharan pastry filled with pumpkin.

Blintz A thin pancake rolled around a savoury or sweet filling. They are often fried.

Borekas The flaky savoury pastries beloved by Turkish Jews. Borekas are usually half-moon shaped and have many different fillings. They may be made with filo dough, but a true boreka is made with a home-made dough.

Borscht Soup of Ashkenazi origins made from beetroot (beet) and sometimes other vegetables; it is eaten hot or cold.

Botarga Sephardi salted or smoked dried fish roe such as sea bass and grey mullet. It can be purchased or home-made; if purchased it should have certification to show that it is from a kosher fish.

Brik A deep-fried Moroccan-Tunisian pastry made from warka dough.Tuna and egg is a very popular filling.

Buricche Little Sephardi savoury pies of Italian/Turkish/Mediterranean origin. Fillings include chicken liver, tuna, pumpkin and chickpeas.

Challah The braided Ashkenazi Shabbat and holiday bread.

Chanukkah The festival of lights commemorating the Maccabean victory over the Seleucians in 165BCE (BC). Also known as Hanukkah.

Charosses/Charosset The paste of nuts, spices, wine and fruit eaten at Pesach to symbolize the mortar used by the Jews to build the pyramids. Also known as Harosset.

Chassidim A movement of very Observant Jews originating in Poland, the Ukraine and Galicia.

Chellou Persian rice, cooked with butter and allowed to form a crisp bottom crust. Vegetables, herbs, fruits and nuts may be added.

Chermoula A Moroccan spice and herb paste, often used with fish.

Chickpea flour See gram flour.

Cholent Ashkenazi, long-simmered stew of meat and beans. Adafina, dafina, hamim, cocido and skhena, are Sephardi equivalents.

Chrain Horseradish and beetroot condiment of Ashkenazi origin.

Chremslach Ashkenazi matzo meal pancakes, often eaten at Pesach. They may be savoury or eaten with sweet spices.

Dafina A long-baked Shabbat stew, made of beef (often with a cow's foot), potato, beans and hard-boiled eggs. It is a speciality of Moroccan Jews.

Dairy Refers to a meal made with milk products.

Desayuno Sephardi Shabbat breakfast.

Einbren flour Flour browned with fat. Traditionally, it is used to thicken soup in the German Ashkenazi kitchen.

Eingemachts A sweet preserve made from beetroot (beets), radishes, carrots, cherries, lemons or walnuts, eaten with a spoon along with tea. It is favoured at Pesach.

Etrog Large yellow citron used to celebrate Sukkot.

Falafel Deep-fried chickpea or broad (fava) bean croquettes, adopted from the Arabs. They are eaten with salads, tucked into pitta bread.

Farfel Pellet-shaped dumplings made from grated noodle dough or crumbled matzo.

Fassoulia White beans, often stewed with meats and vegetables, eaten as an appetizer or stew, popular with the Jews of Greece.

Fleyshig Yiddish for meals or products made of or prepared with meat.

Forspeizen Yiddish for a tasty appetizer.

Gefilte fish Ashkenazi balls of minced (ground) fish, eaten cold, poached and jellied or fried. *Gefilte* means stuffed, and originally the fish was stuffed back into its skin.

Glatt A particularly stringent form of Kashrut, favoured by Chassidic Jews.

Gram flour Also known as chickpea flour and besan. It is made from ground chickpeas and is used in Indian pakoras, spicy pastries, and falafel. It is also used in Mediterranean cooking: in Nice it is made into a pancake called socca and in Provence into cakes known as panisses.

Haimishe Yiddish for traditional home-made food.

Halek Date syrup, eaten for Pesach by the Jews of Iraq, India and Yemen, in addition to or in place of Charosses. In the Bible, "halek" is thought to refer to honey.

Halva A sweetmeat made from sesame paste and sugar or honey, and flavourings, then pressed into blocks and dried. Chocolate, pistachio nuts or almonds may also be added. Halva is popular with Jews from Middle Eastern and Balkan lands.

Hamantashen .Triangular-shaped, Ashkenazi cookies with various fillings such as prunes, poppy seeds, apricots or nuts; eaten at Purim.

Hamim See Cholent.

Hanukkah See Chanukkah.

Harissa North African fiery paste of red chillies and spices, often served with mild foods such as couscous.

Harosset/Harosseth See Charosses/Charosset.

Havdalah The ceremony that marks the end of Shabbat and the start of the new week. Prayers are said over wine, special spices are smelled, and a braided candle is lit.

Hawaij A Yemeni spice mixture that includes cardamom, saffron and turmeric; used in most Yemenite cooking.

Helzel Yiddish for a stuffed chicken, turkey, goose or duck neck, filled with kishke stuffing and roasted so that the skin becomes crisp.

Hilbeh A pungent spice paste of soaked ground fenugreek seeds, often served with spicy zchug. Hilbeh is slighly bitter and has a unique aroma, almost like brown sugar. Yemenite in origin, it is eaten in Sephardi restaurants in Israel.

Holishkes Ashkenazi stuffed cabbage, often simmered or baked in a sweet-and-sour tomato sauce.

Horef Hebrew for hot pepper or spicy. Used in Israel to describe the spicy sauce or peppers eaten with falafel.

Huevos Haminados Sephardi long-cooked eggs; often placed in meat stews.

Injeera Ethiopian flat bread made from teff flour, a grain specific to Ethiopia. It is made from a fermented batter, which gives it a slightly sour flavour, formed into a huge pancake. It is used as a plate and pieces are used to pick up food.

Kaddaif Shredded dough used in Middle Eastern pastries to wrap around nuts, then baked and soaked in syrup.

Kaes The Yiddish word for cheese. Any dish that has kaes attached to its name has cheese as a component.

Kama A Moroccan spice mixture of pepper, turmeric, ginger, cumin and nutmeg, used for stews and soups.

Kapparot The symbolic ritual that takes place on the eve of Yom Kippur whereby a chicken is swung over the head and offered as ransom in atonement for a person's sins. Nowadays, a coin is often used instead of a chicken.

Karpas The parsley, lettuce or herbs placed on the Seder plate and dipped in salt water.

Kasha Toasted buckwheat.

Kashrut Jewish dietary laws dictating what may be eaten.

Katchapuri Flaky pastries filled with goat's cheese or feta cheese; brought to Israel from Georgian Russia.

Khoresht The sweet and sour Persian stew that is ladled over rice and features in the everyday diet of Persian Jews.

Kibbeh Dumplings of Middle Eastern origin made from minced (ground) lamb and soaked bulgur wheat eaten either raw, formed into patties and baked or fried, or layered with vegetables and baked.

Kichelach Light, crisp, slightly sweet cookies of Lithuanian Ashkenazi origin. They are traditional in areas where there is a large Ashkenazi population such as South Africa and the USA.

Kiddush Sanctifying blessing over the wine and challah.

Kindli Another name for Ashkenazi poppy-seed cake or mohn torte.

Kishke Stuffed intestine filled with matzo, chicken fat, onion and paprika. It is served roasted or poached.

Klops Meatloaf or meatballs of Ashkenazi German origin.

Knaidlach/Knaidl Matzo meal dumplings.

Knish Savoury pastry filled with meat, cheese, potato or kasha.

Kosher Term used to describe any food deemed fit to eat by the laws of Kashrut.

Kosher salt Large grains of salt for sprinkling on to meat, to drain out blood, as stipulated in the laws of Kashrut.

Kreplach Small meat-filled dumplings made of noodle dough, often served in chicken soup. At Shavuot they are filled with cheese and eaten with fruit and sour cream.

Krupnik Ashkenazi mushroom and barley soup. It is a traditional dish in Eastern European, particularly Poland, Lithuania and the Ukraine.

Kubaneh A Sephardi Shabbat breakfast dish cooked for a long time, often overnight.

Kubbeh Meat dumplings favoured by Iraqi Jews as well as those who emigrated to India and Israel. Kubbeh are eaten in soups and stews, and may also be steamed or fried.

Kuchen An Ashkenazi yeast raised cake that is slightly sweet and often stuffed with fruit. It is eaten with coffee or tea for morning or afternoon breaks, or as dessert for festivals or holiday meals.

Kugel Baked dish of noodles, vegetables, potatoes or bread; it may be sweet or savoury.

Lag b'Omer Holiday falling on the 33rd day of the counting of the Omer, the days between Pesach and Shavuot.

Lahuhua A Yemenite flat bread cooked in a frying pan. It has a crumpet-like texture and is eaten with soups and stews, often spread with zchug.

Latkes Fried potato pancakes eaten by Ashkenazi Jews at Chanukkah. Latkes can also be made with other vegetables or matzo meal.

Lekakh Traditional honey cake.

Lokshen Yiddish for noodles.

Lox Yiddish for smoked salmon.

Lubia Black-eyed beans (peas), popular in Sephardi cooking, especially in Israel where they are added to spicy soups and stews.

Lulav The palm branch carried and waved as part of the Sukkot observance.

Mamaliga A creamy porridge-like mixture of corn meal, similar to polenta, eaten as the starchy staple by Romanians. It can be eaten hot or cold.

Mandelbrot Amond cookies resembling Italian biscotti. They are double-baked, giving a crisp, hard texture.

Mandlen The Yiddish word for almonds, which are favoured in Ashkenazi cooking (most famously in mandelbrot). Also the name of the crisp, baked or fried soup garnishes made from noodle dough.

Maror Bitter herbs eaten at Pesach/Passover.

Matjes herring See Salt herring.

Matzo/Matzah The unleavened, thin brittle bread ritually eaten during Pesach/Passover.

Matzo cake meal A fine flour made from crushed matzo, used to make cakes, cookies and other baked goods. Matzo cake meal may be used for Pesach, as long as it is labelled as matzo for Pesach.

Matzo meal A meal made from crushed matzo, used to coat fish and other foods for frying, bind together patties of meat, fish or vegetables and as the main ingredient for knaidlach. Matzo meal is available in medium or fine grade.

Megillah Scroll of the Book of Esther, read aloud at Purim as part of the observance.

Melawah Crisp North African pancakes made from pastry brushed with butter and rolled up thinly, similar to a Chinese spring roll pancake. When rolled out and baked, the layers puff up and become rich and flaky.

Menorah Also known as Chanukkia, the candelabra used at Chanukkah. It has spaces for eight candles, plus an extra in the middle, which is used for lighting the others.

Milshig Yiddish for milk or dairy, as opposed to meat.

Minhag Yiddish for different families' or communities' traditions and customs.

Mohn torte The Russian poppy-seed cake. *Mohn* means poppy seeds in Yiddish. See Kindli.

Mouna North African yeasted sweet tea bread, often stuffed with jam, served for Shabbat or a festival breakfast.

Muhammara A Middle Eastern paste of red (bell) pepper and bulgur wheat, particularly popular among Turks.

Nosh Yiddish, meaning to eat; can be a noun, meaning something to eat.

Oy Yiddish exclamation for any occasion: "Oy yoy yoy" and "oy vay s'mear" are variations.

Pareve Yiddish, describing the neutral foods that are neither dairy nor meat.

Pastrami A cured dried beef that is considered a speciality of the USA, though some say it was adapted from pastirma of Turkey, Romania and the Balkans. Traditional American pastrami is cured in salt, spices, pepper and garlic, then smoked and steamed.

Pesach/Passover The festival that celebrates the Israelites' exodus from Egypt.

Petcha Calf's foot jelly, a very traditional Ashkenazi dish that has now fallen out of fashion.

Pierogi Little pasta dumplings, of Polish origin, filled with fillings such as cabbage, mashed potatoes, onions, cheese and kasha and served with sour cream. The sweet, dessert version are varenikes.

Piroshki Ashkenazi savoury pastries of Russian origin made with a yeast dough and filled with cabbage, meat and hard-boiled egg, spinach and cheese, or kasha. They may be tiny, one-bite appetizers or large pastries, and either baked or fried.

Pitta bread Known as *khubz* in Arabic, pitta is a round flat bread that is cooked on a flat pan and puffs up as it cooks. The bread may be slashed open and its hollow inside filled like a sandwich. In addition to the pitta that we know in the West, there are many other pittas, for *pitta* simply means bread.

Plaetschen Ashkenazi term for little squares of pasta, which are eaten in soup.

Plava Very simple Ashkenazi sponge cake. It was once the favourite British Jewish cake and every bakery in London's East End had its own version.

Plotz Yiddish, meaning to faint, as in: "Oy, so delicious I could plotz!"

Pomerantzen Candied citrus peel, a classic sweet treat of the Ashkenazi Jews of Eastern Europe, especially Germany. Sometimes it may be dipped in chocolate.

Porge To ritually remove the blood and fat from meat.

Potato flour Used as a light and translucent thickening agent for sauces and cakes. It is popular during Pesach when grain flours are forbidden.

Preserved lemons A North African speciality, lemons are salted and layered in jars, which imparts a tangy flavour. They are often added to dishes such as tagines and salads.

Purim Festival celebrating the rescue of the Jewish people from Haman, as described in the Book of Esther.

Ras al hanout A Moroccan spice mixture that literally means head of the shop. Ras al hanout can contain myriad ingredients, and each spice shop guards its own secret recipe. For this reason, Kashrut is a consideration; many ras al hanout mixtures contain spices derived from insects or other ingredients that are not kosher. Check for a kashrut certification insignia.

Rosh Hashanah The Jewish New Year, literally meaning head of the year.

Rugelach Crisp, Ashkenazi cinnamon-and-sugar layered biscuits (cookies).

Rye bread A typical bread from Eastern Europe, especially the Ukraine, where it is made with sourdough studded with caraway seeds. It is often baked on a corn meal-coated baking sheet and is, therefore, sometimes known as corn rye.

Salt herring Herring preserved in wooden barrels in layers of salt. Ashkenazi salt herring need to be soaked in cold water before being eating.

Sambousak Crisp half-moon pastries, of Sephardi Middle Eastern origin, often filled with cheese and hard-boiled egg, and coated in sesame seeds. They are popular in Israel and may be eaten hot or cold, dipped into zahtar.

Sauerkraut Fermented, pickled cabbage, made by salting shredded cabbage. It is a staple of the people of Eastern and parts of Western Europe.

Schav A refreshing, sour green soup made from sorrel and eaten cold. It is a traditional Ashkenazi soup and can be bought in bottles in American delis. It is sometimes referred to as green borscht.

Schmaltz Yiddish for fat, usually referring to rendered chicken fat.

Schmaltz herring See Salt herring.

Schnitzel Tender escalopes (scallops) of meat or poultry, coated in crumbs and fried. They originate from Vienna.

Seder The ceremonial dinner eaten on the eve of Pesach, commemorating the flight of the Jews from Egypt.

Sephardim Jews who settled in Iberia (Spain and Portugal), after the destruction of the Second Temple. This group, and their descendants, later spread to Greece, Turkey, the Middle East, England, the Netherlands and the Americas.

Shabbat The religious day of rest, which falls on a Saturday.

Shalach manot Food given at Purim. Shalach manot is often given to friends and family and people who are less well off.

Shalet Baked Ashkenazi dessert of apple and eggs, favoured by the Jews of Alsace. Other ingredients such as matzo, challah, dried fruit and spices may be added.

Shavuot Feast of the weeks, commemorating the revelation of the Ten Commandments.

Shochet The ritual butcher, licensed to slaughter and prepare meat according to the laws of Kashrut.

Shtetl Yiddish for the Jewish villages of Eastern Europe.

Shulchan Arukh A code of Jewish law.

Simchat Torah The festival of the Torah, celebrated by parading the Torah through the synagogue.

Sour salt Citric acid, a souring agent used in Russia and in traditional Jewish cooking. It is available in crystals or grains.

Spaetzel Tiny dumplings made of noodle dough batter, dripped into boiling water. Also known as farfel, spaetzel.

Strudel Eastern European speciality of crisp, layered pastry filled with fruit, sprinkled with sugar and served as a mid-afternoon treat with tea. Strudel can be savoury, filled with vegetables, meat and sometimes fish.

Sufganiot Israeli jam-filled doughnuts, eaten to celebrate Chanukkah.

Sukkot The autumn harvest festival, the celebration of which includes eating meals in gaily decorated three walled huts known as sukkah.

Sumac/Sumak A sour-tasting, red spice made from ground berries of the sumac plant. Israelis, and some Sephardim, sprinkle the spice over salads, breads and rice.

Tahina/Tahini A Middle Eastern paste of toasted hulled sesame seeds, mixed with lemon juice, garlic and spices, and thinned with water. It is eaten as a sauce, dip, or ingredient in dishes such as hummus.

Tapadas Big Sephardi pies of Turkish origin, filled with a similar filling to that of Borekas. They are served cut into individual-sized pieces.

Teiglach Ashkenazi cookies that have been cooked in honey. They are a Lithuanian speciality, which are popular in communities that celebrate their Lithuanian origins, such as South Africa. They are favoured at Rosh Hashanah when sweet foods are eaten in hope of a sweet new year..

Tisha b'Av A mourning and fast day in commemoration of the destruction of the First and Second Temples in Jerusalem. It is observed on the 9th of the month of Av.

Torah The scroll used in the synagogue, consisting of the first five books of the Bible, which include the Ten Commandments. The Torah was given to the Jews by God on Mount Sinai.

Torshi Pickled vegetables, eaten throughout the Middle East, especially Persia. All kinds of vegetables are made into torshi, particularly turnips, which are pickled in a tangy vinegar and salt brine, with the addition of beetroot (beets) to give the pale-coloured turnips a bright pink hue.

Treyf Meaning not kosher. Also known as tref and trefah.

Tu b'Shevat Festival known as the birthday of the trees.

Tzimmes A sweet dish of carrots, vegetables, dried fruit and sweetening agent such as honey or sugar. Spices, and sometimes meat, are added.

Varenikes Ashkenazi fruit-filled pasta dumplings. They may be filled with apricots, cherries or prunes.

Varnishkes Noodles shaped like bow ties or butterflies, often served with Kasha.

Warka Very thin, transparent pastry from Morocco.

Wats/Wots Spicy Ethiopian stews, enjoyed by the Bene Israel (Ethiopian Jews). They are often eaten for Shabbat.

Yom Kippur The Day of Atonement, a solemn holy day upon which fasting is strictly observed.

Zahtar/Za'atar This is both the name of the wild thyme/hyssop that grows in the hillsides of Israel and the Middle East, and the name of the spice mixture made with it, which includes zahtar, ground cumin, toasted sesame seeds, coriander seeds and sometimes a little sumac and/or crushed toasted hazelnuts. Zahtar is eaten for breakfast, as a dip with fresh pitta bread, a drizzle of olive oil and fresh goat's cheese.

Zchug/Zhug/Zhoug This Yemenite seasoning paste is one of Israel's most popular spice mixtures. It may be red, based on chillies, garlic, spices, coriander (cilantro) and parsley, or it may be green, with more herbs and less or no tomatoes. Zchug is eaten as a dip with bread or as a relish or sauce.

Zeroa A lamb's bone, often a shank, roasted and placed on the ritual plate for Pesach. It represents the sacrificial lambs eaten on the eve of the flight of the Jews from Eygpt.

SHOPPING FOR JEWISH FOODS

Australia
Dainty Foods (Kravsz)
62 Glen Eira Road
Ripponlea
Melbourne VIC
Tel: (613) 9531 5032

Gefen Liquor Store
144 Chapel Street
Balaclava
Melbourne VIC
Tel: (613) 9531 5032

Grandma Moses Deli
511 Old South Head Road
Rose Bay
Sydney NSW
Tel: 371 0874

Kosher Imports
c/o Hebrew Congregation
13 Flemington Street
Glenside
Adelaide SA
Tel: (618) 9532 9994

Tempo Kosher Supermarket
391 Inkerman Street
St Kilda
Melbourne VIC
Tel: (613) 9527 5021

Canada
Avika's Kosher Food Market
3858 Bathurst Street
Toronto ON
Tel: (416) 635 0470

Bathurst Street Market
1570 Main Street
Winnipeg MB
Tel: (204) 338 4911

Capital United Kosher
    Market
5785 Victoria
Montreal PQ
Tel: (514) 735 1744

Glatt Kosher Self Service
215A St Louis
Montreal PQ
Tel: (514) 747 6531

Omnitsky Kosher
5866 Cambie Street
Vancouver BC
Tel: (604) 321 1818

South Africa
One Stop Superliner
217 Bronkhorst Street
Baileys Muckleneuck
Pretoria
Tel: (2712) 463 211

Saveways Supermarket
Fairmount Shopping Centre
cnr. Livingston
Johannesburg
Tel: (2711) 640 6592

United Kingdom
Amazing Grapes
94 Brent Street
London NW4
020 8202 2631

The Beigel Bake
159 Brick Lane
London E1
Tel: 020 7729 0616

Brownstein's Deli
24A Woodford Avenue
Ilford IG2
Tel: 020 8550 3900

Cantor's of Hove
20 Richardson Road
Brighton BN3
Tel: 01273 596 500

Carmelli Bakeries
128 Golder's Green Road
London NW11
Tel: 020 8455 3063

J. A. Corney Limited
9 Hallswelle Parade
Finchley Road
London NW11
Tel: 020 8455 9588

Country Market Limited
136 Golder's Green Road
London NW11
Tel: 020 8455 3289

Cousin's Bakery
Golder's Green Road
London NW11
Tel: 020 8201 9694

Daniel's Bagel Bakery
13 Hallswelle Parade
Finchley Road
London NW11
Tel: 020 8455 5826

E & M Kosher Foods
24 Moresby Road
London E5
Tel: 020 8806 2726

A. Gee Deli
75 Pershore Road
Birmingham B5
Tel: 0121 440 2160

Greenfelds Kosher Foods
Greenfeld House
10–20 Windus Road
London N16
Tel: 020 8806 3978

Helen's Salt Beef Bar
43 Norwood Road
London SE27
Tel: 020 8670 8790

Kelmans Kosher Products
20 Stadium Business Centre
North End Road
Wembly HA9
Tel: 020 8795 0300

Kosher Paradise
10 Ashborne Parade
Finchley Road
London NW11
Tel: 020 8455 2454

L & D Foods Limited
17 Lyttleton Road
London N2
Tel: 020 8455 8397

Panzer Delicatessen Limited
15 Circus Road
London NW8
Tel: 020 7722 8162

J. Rogg
137 Cannon Street Road
London E1
Tel: 020 7488 3368

Sam Stoller and Son
28 Temple Fortune Parade
London NW11
Tel: 020 8458 1429

United Kosher Ltd
5 Croxdale Road
Boreham Wood WD6
Tel: 020 8953 5935

United States
The Challah Connection
19 Sunset Hill Drive
Monroe CT06468
Tel: (877) 426 8694

Empress Kosher
Delicatessen
2210 86th Street
Brooklyn NY11214
Tel: (718) 265 8002

Kohn's Kosher Market
10405 Old Olive
    Street Road
St Louis MO63141
Tel: (341) 569 0727

Rubin's Kosher
    Delicatessen
500 Harvard Street
Brookline MA02446-2434
Tel: (617) 731 8787

World of Chantilly Inc.
4302 Farraght Road
Brooklyn NY11203
Tel: (718) 859 1110

BIBLIOGRAPHY

Avnon, Naf and Sella, Uri. *So Eat, My Darling; A Guide to the Yiddish Kitchen* (Massada Ltd, Israel, 1977)

Berenbaum, Rose Levy. *Rose's Melting Pot* (William Morros and Co, New York, 1993)

Bernadin, Tom. *The Ellis Island Immigrant Cookbook* (Tom Bernadin Pub, New York, 1994)

Cohen, Elizabeth Wolf. *New Jewish Cooking* (Apple Publishing, London, 1997)

Congregation B'nai Emuna. *The Kosher Gourmet* (self-published, San Francisco, undated)

De Silva, Cara (editor). *In Memory's Kitchen* (Jason Aronson, New Jersey and London, 1996)

Ehrlich, Elizabeth. *Miriam's Kitchen* (Penguin Books, New York, 1998)

Eley, John and Blue, Lionel. *Simply Divine* (British Broadcasting Corporation, London, 1986)

Fischer, Leah Loeb. *Mama Leah's Jewish Kitchen* (Macmillan, New York, 1990)

Fox, Rabbi Karen L, and

Miller, Phyllis Zimbler. *Seasons for Celebration* (Perigree Books, New York, 1992)

Friedland, Susan R. *The Passover Table* (Harper Perennial, 1994)

Freidman, Rose. *Jewish Vegetarian Cooking* (Thorsons Publishing, London, 1984)

Ganor, Avi and Ron Maiberg. *Taste of Israel* (Galahad Books, New York, 1993)

Ginor, Michael. *Foie Gras: a Passion* (John Wiley and Sons, New York, 1999)

Goldstein, Joyce. *Cucina Ebraica* (Chronicle Books, San Francisco, 1998)

Greenbaum, Florence Kreisler. *Jewish Cook Book* (Bloch Publishing, New York, 1926)

Greenberg, Florence. *Jewish Cookery* (Penguin Books, London, 1963)

Jackson, Judy. *Jewish: Traditional Recipes From a Rich Culinary Heritage* (Lorenz Books, London, 1998)

Jewish Fellowship of Davis. *99 Things You Always Wanted to Know About Jewish Cooking But Were*

Afraid to Ask (self-published booklet, Davis, California, 1974)

Kasden, Sara. *Love and Knishes* (Fawcett Crest Books, Connecticut, 1969)

Krietzman, Sue. *Deli* (Harmony Books, New York, 1977)

Lebewohl, Sharon and Bulkin, Rena. *The 2nd Ave Deli Cookbook* (Villard, New York, 1999)

Leonard, Leah. *Jewish Cookery* (Crown Publishers, New York, 1949)

Levy, Faye. *Faye Levy's International Jewish Cookbook* (Ebury Press, London, 1992)

Machlin, Edda Servi. *The Classic Cuisine of the Italian Jews* (Dodd Mead and Co, New York, 1982)

Marks, Copeland. *The Great Book of Couscous* (Donald I Fine Books, New York, 1994)

Marks, Copeland. *Sephardic Cooking* (Donald I Fine Books, New York, 1994)

Marks, Gil. *The World of Jewish Cooking* (Simon and Schuster, New York, 1996)

Nathan, Joan. *The Jewish*

Holiday Kitchen (Schocken Books, New York, 1988)

Roden, Claudia. *The Book of Jewish Food* (Viking Books, London, 1997)

Rose, Evelyn. *The Complete International Jewish Cookbook* (Pan Books, London and Sydney, 1976)

Rose, Evelyn. *The New Complete International Jewish Cookbook* (Robson Books, London, 1999)

Rose, Evelyn. *The Essential Jewish Festival Cookbook* (Robson Books, London, 2000)

Wolfert, Paula. *Couscous and Other Good Things from Morocco* (Harper Trade, 1987)

Author's Acknowledgements

Thanks to Alan "Kishke" McLaughlan, Dr Leah Spieler and Rev Jon Harford, Gretchen Spieler, Paula, Jojo and India Aspin, Dr Esther Novak and Rev John Chendo, Etty and Bruce Blackman, Jerome Freeman and the late Sheila Hannon, Paul Richardson, Nigel Patrick and Graham Ketteringham, Sue Kreitzman, Rabbi Mona Alfi, the late Rabbi Jason Gaber, so sadly missed, Katia Davies, Sandy Waks, Kamala Friedman, John and Mary Whiting, Fred and Mary Barclay, Amanda and Tim Hamilton Hemmeter, Gayle Merksamer, Antonietta Stefanic and her lovely girls Charlotte

and Caroline, Faye Levy, Joan Nathan, Evelyn Rose, Josephine Bacon and Emi Kazuko who has now taken her first bite of Jewish food and fed me sushi in return; Susie Morgenstern and her sister Effie who took me to eat hummus in Jaffa and sent me to the best Romanian restaurants in Tel Aviv; my sister-in-law MaTao and my late brother Bryan Smith who preferred Chinese food to Jewish food, though he loved Kosher dill pickles.

My thanks to agent Borra Garson, associate Martine Carter and Michelle Waddsley who keeps the administration running smoothly; Miriam Morgen, Michael Bauer and

Fran Irwin of the *San Francisco Chronicle* for letting me write about so many wonderful subjects, and *Saveur Magazine*, who sent me to Israel to write about falafel.

To my own Jewish family: parents Caroline and Izzy Smith (the famous baseball player, really!), aunt and uncle Sy and Estelle Opper, aunties Ella Smith and Sarah Rackusin who can rustle up latkes and cheesecake at the drop of a hat, and to my many cousins and nieces who are all good little eaters and good cooks too. As always, to Bachi for her love of good food, especially chicken soup, but this time she is sadly not here to enjoy it with me.

Publisher's Acknowledgements

All photographs are by William Lingwood except the following: pp10, 12 bottom, 21 bottom right, 24, 28 bottom, 29 top, 33 top AKG; pp20, 29 bottom The Art Archive; pp11, 21 bottom left The Bridgeman Art Library; p19 David Harris, Jerusalem/ photo courtesy of the Beth Hatefutsoth Photo Archive; pp25 top, 32 bottom Beth Hatefutsoth Photo Archive; pp12 top, 13, 15, 16, 18 top and bottom, 23 left, 26 bottom, 27 top, 30 bottom, 34, 35 top and bottom Hulton Getty Images; pp14, 17 The Jewish Museum, London.

INDEX

NOTES

NOTES

NOTES

NOTES

NOTES

NOTES

NOTES

NOTES